CREDO SERIES

God's Word Revealed in Sacred Scripture

Based on the Curriculum Framework
Course I: The Revelation of Jesus Christ in Scripture

WRITERS
Mícheál de Barra, BD, MA
Joseph F. McCann, MEd, PhD

GENERAL EDITOR
Thomas H. Groome, EdD

Professor Theology and Religious Education
Boston College

VERITAS

USA Office: Frisco, Texas

www.veritasreligion.com

The Subcommittee on the Catechism, United States Conference of Catholic Bishops, has found that this catechetical high school text, copyright 2013, is in conformity with the *Catechism of the Catholic Church* and that it fulfills the requirements of Core Course I of the *Doctrinal Elements of a Curriculum Framework for the Development of Catechetical Materials for Young People of High School Age.*

CREDO SERIES CONSULTANT: Maura Hyland
PUBLISHER, USA AND THEOLOGICAL EDITOR:
Ed DeStefano
TEXT CONSULTANTS:
Annette Honan
Ailís Travers
Hosffman Ospino
COPY EDITOR: Elaine Campion
DESIGN: Lir Mac Cárthaigh

INTERNET RESOURCES
There are internet resources available to support this text. Log on to www.credoseries.com

NIHIL OBSTAT
Rev. Msgr. Robert M. Coerver, S.T.L.
Censor Librorum

IMPRIMATUR
† Most Reverend Kevin J. Farrell
Bishop of Dallas
May 30, 2013

The *Nihil Obstat* and *Imprimatur* are official declarations that the work contains nothing contrary to Faith and Morals. It is not implied thereby that those granting the *Nihil Obstat* and *Imprimatur* agree with the contents, statements or opinions expressed.

SEND ALL INQUIRIES TO:
Veritas, Customer Service
P.O. Box 789
Westerville, OH 43086
Tel. 866-844-0582
info@veritasreligion.com
www.veritasreligion.com

ISBN 978 1 84730 491 9 (Student Edition)
ISBN 978 1 84730 288 5 (Teacher Resource Edition)
ISBN 978 1 84730 502 2 (E-book: Student Edition)

Printed in the United States of America
1 2 3 4 5 6 7 / 16 15 14 13

CONTENTS

BEFORE YOU BEGIN

LOOKING UP A BIBLICAL REFERENCE

Before you can begin to study the Bible, you need to be able to look up a Bible reference and know where to find the different books.

Each of the books in the Bible is made up of chapters and verses. The division into chapter and verse dates from the thirteenth century and was intended simply to facilitate easy navigation around the various texts. These divisions mean nothing in themselves.

Let's take a typical example of a biblical reference: **Genesis 15:18**. There are three elements here:

Genesis: The name of the first book in the Old Testament. This is sometimes abbreviated to *Gen*.

15: The number of the chapter.

18: The number of the verse.

Sometimes we are instructed to read more than one verse, for example 'Gen 1:1–5'. This means Genesis chapter 1, verses 1 to 5. And sometimes we are instructed to read more than one chapter, for example 'Gen 2:1–9; 3:1–7'. This means Genesis chapter 2, verses 1 to 9, and chapter 3, verses 1 to 7.

If you want to look up a Bible story or quotation but do not have the reference, you use a biblical Concordance. This is a book containing an alphabetical index of the principal words in the Bible. It lists references to where passages or quotations containing these words may be found in the Bible. For example, when you look up 'Samaritan',

you find the reference for, among others, Luke 10:33; around this verse you will find the parable of the Good Samaritan (Luke 10:25–37). Since the *Credo* series uses the New Revised Standard Version (NRSV), a Catholic edition of the Bible, it would be best to use the NRSV Concordance (Unabridged).

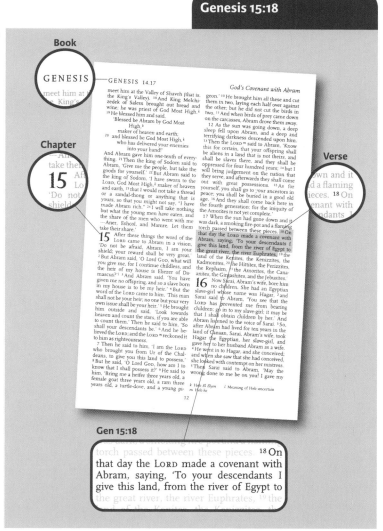

Genesis 15:18

Book — GENESIS

Chapter — 15

Verse

Gen 15:18

torch passed between these pieces. **18 On** that day the LORD made a covenant with Abram, saying, 'To your descendants I give this land, from the river of Egypt to the great river, the river Euphrates, [19] the

OLD TESTAMENT

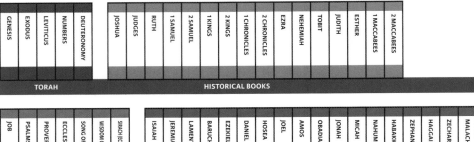

TORAH

GENESIS | EXODUS | LEVITICUS | NUMBERS | DEUTERONOMY

HISTORICAL BOOKS

JOSHUA | JUDGES | RUTH | 1 SAMUEL | 2 SAMUEL | 1 KINGS | 2 KINGS | 1 CHRONICLES | 2 CHRONICLES | EZRA | NEHEMIAH | TOBIT | JUDITH | ESTHER | 1 MACCABEES | 2 MACCABEES

WISDOM BOOKS

JOB | PSALMS | PROVERBS | ECCLESIASTES | SONG OF SOLOMON | WISDOM OF SOLOMON | SIRACH (ECCLESIASTICUS)

PROPHETIC BOOKS

ISAIAH | JEREMIAH | LAMENTATIONS | BARUCH | EZEKIEL | DANIEL | HOSEA | JOEL | AMOS | OBADIAH | JONAH | MICAH | NAHUM | HABAKKUK | ZEPHANIAH | HAGGAI | ZECHARIAH | MALACHI

NEW TESTAMENT

MATTHEW | MARK | LUKE | JOHN | ACTS OF THE APOSTLES | ROMANS | 1 CORINTHIANS | 2 CORINTHIANS | GALATIANS | EPHESIANS | PHILIPPIANS | COLOSSIANS | 1 THESSALONIANS | 2 THESSALONIANS | 1 TIMOTHY | 2 TIMOTHY | TITUS | PHILEMON | HEBREWS | JAMES | 1 PETER | 2 PETER | 1 JOHN | 2 JOHN | 3 JOHN | JUDE | REVELATION

THE BOOKS OF THE OLD TESTAMENT

The Old Testament is the first main part of the Bible. The Catholic Old Testament contains forty-six books, which are divided into four sections: the Torah (also known as the Law or the Pentateuch), the Historical Books, the Wisdom Books and the Prophetic Books.

The **Torah** is made up of the first five books of the Old Testament: Genesis, Exodus, Leviticus, Numbers and Deuteronomy.

⊙ Genesis: tells the stories of Creation and the Fall; the establishment of the Covenant; the choice of the Israelites (also known as Hebrews) as the Chosen People of God; the Patriarchs and Joseph.

⊙ Exodus: recounts the slavery and then the escape of the Israelites from Egypt; their settlement in the land that God promised them (Canaan, or Palestine); the establishment of their kingdom, and the Law of God (summarized in the Ten Commandments) that the people were expected to follow.

⊙ Leviticus: details the rites and ceremonies of the Israelite people.

⊙ Numbers: describes the years the Israelite people spent in the desert.

⊙ Deuteronomy: recounts the story of the Covenant and the death of Moses.

The **Historical Books** trace the history of Israel from the time of Moses to the exile of the Israelite people in Babylon. They cover the conquest under Joshua, the Judges, the Kings, especially the first three, Saul, David and Solomon, and the first Temple under Solomon

THE DEUTERONOMIC HISTORY

⊙ Joshua
⊙ Judges
⊙ Ruth
⊙ 1 Samuel and 2 Samuel
⊙ 1 Kings and 2 Kings

THE CHRONICLER'S HISTORY OR LATER HISTORIES

- ⊙ 1 and 2 Chronicles
- ⊙ Ezra
- ⊙ Nehemiah
- ⊙ Judith
- ⊙ Tobit
- ⊙ Esther
- ⊙ 1 Maccabees and 2 Maccabees

The **Wisdom Books** reflect the great spiritual wisdom and practical guidance that God revealed to the Israelites through wise and holy people over the generations. They offer good advice for life and praise of God. The Book of Psalms, which is a favorite Bible book for many people, and the Song of Songs, one of the most beautiful love poems ever written, are included among the seven Wisdom books.

Prophets carried God's message to the people at times of crisis. (The word 'prophet' means 'speak for'.) The eighteen **Prophetic Books** are the teachings of the people called by God who, through the ages, reminded the Israelites of the Law of God, especially when they were failing to keep the Covenant, and called them to repent of their sins. In these books especially, we hear how living as the People of God demands works of justice, care for the poor and making peace.

THE BOOKS OF THE NEW TESTAMENT

The Catholic New Testament contains twenty-seven books, further divided into four sections: the Gospels, the Acts of the Apostles, the Letters and the Book of Revelation.

The four **Gospels**—Matthew, Mark, Luke and John—tell the story of the life, teaching, Death, Resurrection and Ascension of Jesus, God's own Son. They reveal to us the Good News (Gospel) that he preached, the way of life that he modeled and how he made it possible for us to live as disciples by the events of his Paschal Mystery, his Death and Resurrection and Ascension.

The Gospels according to Matthew, Mark and Luke, though directed to different community audiences, share the same perspective and so are called the Synoptic (same view) Gospels. The Fourth Gospel, that according to St. John, provides a more developed theological view. It is obvious from reading St. John's account of the Gospel that the author had knowledge of the Synoptic Gospels.

The **Acts of the Apostles**, a single book, is a sequel to St. Luke's Gospel and takes up the story of the early Church, notably the ministry of Peter and Paul as they spread the Good News under the inspiration and guidance of the Holy Spirit. It ends with the apostle Paul reaching Rome as a prisoner.

The **Letters**, also called **Epistles**, are a collection of writings from the first Apostles and St. Paul the Apostle to the early Church. There are thirteen Epistles ascribed to St. Paul. The rest are by various authors: the Letter to the Hebrews, the two Letters of St. Peter, the three Letters of St. John and the Letters of St. Jude and St. James.

The last book in the Bible, the **Book of Revelation,** or **Apocalypse** (a Greek word meaning 'uncovering' or 'revealing'), is a dream prophecy attributed to St. John the Apostle, authored in his old age. It provided a wonderful visionary message of hope at a time when the early Church was suffering persecution.

CHAPTER 1

God's Desire for Us
Our Desire for God

HUMAN LIFE IS SPECIAL

THE DESIRE FOR GOD IS WRITTEN IN THE HUMAN HEART

CREATION ACCOUNTS IN THE BOOK OF GENESIS

GOD'S LOVE IS ALL AROUND US

HUMAN BEINGS SHARE IN GOD'S DIVINE LIFE

WE ARE MADE IN THE IMAGE AND LIKENESS OF GOD

THIS CHAPTER WILL HELP YOU TO FOCUS ON WHAT it is that you desire for yourself in life and to wonder about what God desires for you. Through exploring God's Word, divine Revelation in Sacred Scripture and in the teaching of the Church, it is hoped that you will begin to recognize God's purpose for your life and to trust in his love for you.

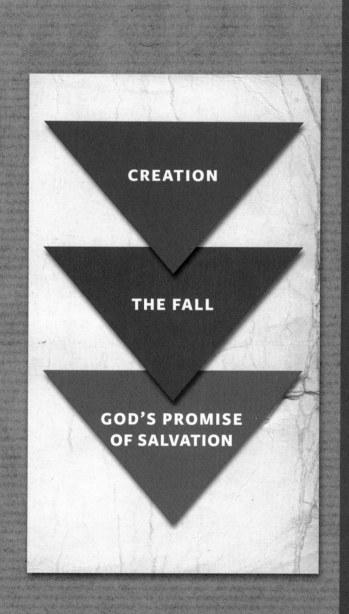

CREATION

THE FALL

GOD'S PROMISE OF SALVATION

Faith Focus: These teachings of the Catholic Church are the primary focus of the doctrinal content presented in this chapter:
- ⊙ Human beings are by nature searchers and seekers.
- ⊙ The human search for meaning is ultimately the search for God.
- ⊙ God is the Creator and the source of all life.
- ⊙ Human life is the high point of God's Creation.
- ⊙ God created human beings out of love and to love.
- ⊙ Man and woman are created equal in dignity.

Discipleship Formation: As a result of studying this chapter and discovering the meaning of the faith of the Catholic Church for your life, you should be better able to:
- ⊙ recognize your own restlessness and searching for meaning in your life as part of what it is to be human;
- ⊙ have a clearer understanding of God as Creator and of human beings as the high point of God's Creation;
- ⊙ value yourself as an image of God, whom he created to share in his life and love;
- ⊙ believe that God loves you;
- ⊙ appreciate how your Catholic faith can help you in your search for true happiness and fulfillment;
- ⊙ see your relationship with God as the foundation for making decisions about what is and is not important in your life.

Scripture References: These Scripture references are quoted or referred to in this chapter:
OLD TESTAMENT: Genesis 1:1—2:4a, 2:7, 16, 18–25; **Psalms** 42
NEW TESTAMENT: Matthew 18:20; **Ephesians** 2:10; **1 John** 4:7–8, 10

Faith Glossary: Familiarize yourself with the meaning of these key faith terms. Definitions are found in the Glossary: **Bible, Creation, Creator, evil, faith, Fall (the), Holy Spirit, Holy Trinity, human person, intellect/reason, Lord's Day, New Covenant, Original Sin, prayer, Sabbath, salvation, sin, Son of God, soul**

Faith Word: faith
Learn by Heart: Genesis 1:28
Learn by Example: St. Augustine of Hippo

Where do we find meaning in life?

All of us have wants and desires. Often we find ourselves dissatisfied with things as they are and we spend a lot of our time looking for something more. However, many of our wants and desires are of a very superficial nature and do not represent things that really matter.

OPENING ACTIVITY/CONVERSATION

⊙ Begin by thinking about your current wants and desires. Make a list of these.

⊙ When you have done this, join up with a partner and compare your lists.

⊙ Discuss: Which wants or desires do you share in common and which are different? What or who influences your wants and desires?

⊙ Now take a moment to revisit your list and mark the things that you think are *really* important.

⊙ If we take the time to think more deeply about our lives, we may find that our true desires are for things and values that are more lasting and more central in our lives. Share your thoughts about this.

GROUP EXERCISE/DISCUSSION

⊙ Imagine you are going to live on a desert island for a very long time. In groups of three or four, try to agree on six things you would bring with you in order to live a long and happy life. Discuss why each item would be important.

WANTS, NEEDS AND DESIRES

Do you know the difference between wants, needs and desires? 'Wants' are short term. I want to go to a movie. I want a holiday. What other 'wants' can you name? Are there any wants we should not follow up on because of our Catholic **faith**?

Wants are not the same as needs. We all need a good night's sleep. We need an education. We need a balanced diet. 'Needs' are more important and more lasting than short-term wants. Our Catholic faith should help us to discern our true needs from the fleeting wants in our lives.

The third kind of yearning is a 'desire'. I desire success. I desire a family. I desire a career. 'Desires' are deeper, longer and more personal.

Sometimes there is a real cost involved in getting what you truly desire. It may require sacrifice, self-discipline and self-denial. Jesus said that no one could have a greater love than to lay down their life for a friend. Jesus made this ultimate sacrifice for us.

The deepest human desire is to know that we count for something, that we matter to someone

WHAT ABOUT YOU PERSONALLY?
- What sacrifices have you made for others?

LET'S PROBE DEEPER
- Recall times when you were really happy.
- How do you know that you were happy then?
- Explain the difference between things that give you lasting pleasure and those for which the happiness lasts only a short time.

WHERE DOES GOD FIT IN?
The deepest human desire is to know that we count for something, that we matter to someone. This is what 'meaning' is all about.

People of faith find meaning in God. The Church teaches us that we matter to God, that God loves us unconditionally and that he is the only true answer to our search for meaning in life. We give glory to God just by being alive, precisely because we are made in the **image of God**. St. Irenaeus (c. 125–c. 200) summarized it in this way: 'The glory of God is the human person fully alive.'

The **human person** is meant for God. Within each of us is a need or desire to know God. Through Sacred Scripture and the teaching of the Church we discover the Good News that God loves us more than any human parent loves their child, and he wants us to know this.

From the moment we are born, we yearn to relate to God who created us, to God who constantly says 'I love you'. We need to believe this truth, otherwise we will miss the meaning of our entire lives.

OVER TO YOU
- Do you believe that God wants you to be happy? Why or why not?
- How or where do you think you might find true happiness in life?

THE DESIRE FOR GOD IS UNIVERSAL

The belief that God made all human beings to share in his love and life, and that the desire for God is inherent in our human nature, is not just true for Christians. Followers of other religions have similar beliefs and desires. Rabindranath Tagore (1861–1941), a Hindu sage and Nobel prize-winning writer, wrote a poem about the desire to be connected to God's love. The following **prayer** by Father Donal Neary is based on that poem.

> Loving God, may your love play upon my
> voice,
> and rest in my silence.
> Let it pass through my heart,
> into all that I do.
> Let your love shine like stars in the darkness of
> my sleep,
> and in the dawn at my awakening.
> Let it burn in all the flames of my desires,
> and flow in all the currents of my love.
> Let me carry your love in my life,
> as a harp does its music,
> and give it back to you at last with my life.

WHAT ABOUT YOU PERSONALLY?

⊙ Which line of this prayer do you identify with most, and why?

JOURNAL EXERCISE

⊙ Have a go at writing your own prayer describing this particular time in your life. You might also like to draw a picture or an image.

In this chapter we explore how we share in God's life and love and what it means to be made 'in the image and likeness of God'.

The desire for God is inherent in our human nature and is not just true for Christians

Human life is special

OPENING CONVERSATION

On the last weekend of August 2005, eight people, five women and three men, spent three days in a cage in London Zoo alongside the apes. Their cage had the usual explanatory notice outside it, except that it listed 'Human Beings' as the exhibit, and gave details of their diet, habitat, world distribution and threats to the species. A spokesperson for the zoo explained that the purpose of the experiment was to show that 'human beings are animals, just like the apes'.

- ⊙ What are your thoughts about this experiment?
- ⊙ What would you think the people in the cage learned from their weekend?
- ⊙ What do you think visitors to the zoo, who stopped at their cage, learned?
- ⊙ In your opinion, are human beings animals 'just like the apes'? Explain.

WHAT MAKES US DIFFERENT?

- ⊙ *Brainstorm:* What are the things that make humans different from other animals?

It is clear that human beings have bodies that are similar in many ways to those of animals. We have arms, legs and heads quite like those of apes and chimpanzees. Some people think that we are merely intelligent and resourceful primates.

Others believe that we are different from animals because we think and imagine. Human beings can communicate in ways that animals cannot. Human beings have been created with a body and a **soul**, a physical and a spiritual dimension. We have an **intellect** and imagination. We have the power to think abstractly and invent things. For example, try to imagine what your life will be like in ten years' time. Do you think your pet dog or cat can use imagination in this way?

God has revealed and the Catholic Church teaches that every person has a 'sacred' dignity because God has created human beings in the divine image and likeness and put us over the rest of creation. We have an intellect and will; we can know and love. This truth is clearly revealed and taught in the first two chapters of the very first book of the **Bible**, the Book of Genesis. Read those chapters now.

THE BOOK OF GENESIS—A FAITH ACCOUNT

The Book of Genesis is not an eyewitness account of what happened billions of years ago. It presents the truth of Revelation written by human authors who were inspired by the **Holy**

Spirit to teach what God, the principal author of Scripture, wanted to reveal about the divine plan of **Creation** and **Salvation**. The inspired accounts of Creation in the first two chapters of Genesis are not meant to teach *scientific truths* about the origins of the world and the universe, questions that scientists and others continue to explore.

The inspired biblical texts teach some of the great *truths of our faith* that God has revealed. The task of the inspired human authors was to respond to the question 'Where did it all come from?' They did this by teaching 'firmly, faithfully, and without error. . . . [the] truth which God, for the sake of our salvation, wished to see confided to the Sacred Scriptures' (Vatican II, *Constitution on Divine Revelation*, quoted in CCC, no. 107). In other words, they taught *truths of faith* and did not intend to teach *truths of science*.

The Creation accounts in Genesis teach us the truth about the world, about ourselves and about God. They teach that God made the universe and everything in it. They tell us that God made the trees and plants and everything that grows on the earth; that he made the animals, insects and all the creatures that live upon the earth; and that he made the fishes and all creatures that live in the seas. Most importantly, they tell us that God made human beings and that he saw human beings as the pinnacle of all Creation.

We read in Genesis that when God looked back at the work of Creation he found that it was good.

And God said, 'Let the earth bring forth living creatures of every kind: cattle and creeping things and wild animals of the earth of every kind. And it was so. God made the wild animals of the earth of every kind, and the cattle of every kind, and everything that creeps upon the ground of every kind. And God saw that it was good.

—Genesis 1:24–25

CREATION | BAPTISTERY OF ST JOHN, FLORENCE, ITALY

But when God had made man and woman, he found that it was *very* good. Then God gave man and woman responsibility for all creation.

Then God said, 'Let us make [man] in our image, according to our likeness; and let them have dominion over the fish of the sea, and over the birds of the air, and over the cattle, and over all the wild animals of the earth, and over every creeping thing that creeps upon the earth.'
    So God created [man] in his image,
      in the image of God he created them;
      male and female he created them.

ELOHIM CREATING ADAM | WILLIAM BLAKE

God blessed them, and God said to them, 'Be fruitful and multiply, and fill the earth and subdue it; and have dominion over the fish of the sea and over the birds of the air and over every living thing that moves upon the earth.' . . . . And it was so. God saw everything that he had made, and indeed, it was very good.
—Genesis 1:26–28, 30–31

As you read the first account of Creation in the Book of Genesis, note the following:

- God created darkness and light on the first day but the sun and moon on the fourth day. Clearly, this is not a scientific account and cannot be interpreted literally. What this story teaches from a faith point of view is that God is the living **Creator** and Sustainer of all that exists.
- God created man and woman 'in the image of God'. In the eyes of God, men and women are equal; both fully reflect the divine image.
- According to the first account of Creation, God gave humankind 'dominion' over the rest of creation. The second account of Creation will make it clear that God, therefore, has made us responsible for all of creation and he demands that we be good stewards of creation.

- The first account of Creation (Genesis 1:1—2:4a) teaches that God rested on the seventh day and made it holy. Christians rest on the seventh day, which is the **Sabbath** for Jews and the **Lord's Day** for Christians. In the **New Covenant** the Lord's Day is observed not on the seventh day but on the first day of the week in remembrance of Christ's Resurrection. Catholics keep the Lord's Day holy primarily through our participation in the Eucharist, in our offering thanksgiving and praise to God. The Lord's Day is also a time to disengage from our normal daily routines, so that we have an opportunity to think about our lives, what we really want, and to ask God's help in achieving this.

TALK IT OVER

- The Book of Genesis teaches that men and women are made in the image and likeness of God. Which aspects of human beings do you think point most strongly to the truth of this statement?

WHAT ABOUT YOU PERSONALLY?

- What do you think it is about you personally that shows you are made in the image of God?

Human beings share in God's divine life

OPENING CONVERSATION

⊙ How and where do you see God's love in the world around you?

THE SECOND ACCOUNT OF CREATION

In chapter 2 of Genesis there is a second account of the Creation of man (Genesis 2:18–25), which is much older than the account in chapter 1 (Genesis 1:26–27). In Genesis 2 the inspired sacred writer presents God the Creator as a modeler in clay, shaping 'man' out of the red Near Eastern mud. It is a very different kind of story and yet one that reaffirms and elaborates on the truths in the first account of Creation.

As you read this account, focus on: The 'person of the earth' (in Hebrew 'Adam') becomes alive by the breath of God. 'The LORD God formed man from the dust of the ground, and breathed into his nostrils the breath of life; and the man became a living being' (Genesis 2:7).

God breathed 'the breath of life' into the man and the man became a living person. The Hebrew word *ruach*, which is translated as 'the breath

of life', can also be translated 'spirit'. As human beings, we receive from God both the gift of physical life and existence (nature) and the life of our 'spirit' (grace). We are temples of the Ruach of God, the Holy Spirit—the Third Divine Person of the Blessed Trinity.

The dignity of human beings comes from God creating us to share in the life of the **Holy Trinity**, both now and in eternity. Our desire for God is part of our very being. It is written in our heart. Only in God can we find lasting joy and peace in this life and in life after death, the life everlasting.

God saw that it was not good for 'the person of the earth' to be alone, and so he made the animals and the birds and all the other creatures, but none of them was a suitable companion for the man. And so God formed another human being.

The LORD God caused a deep sleep to fall upon the man, and he slept; then he took one of his ribs and closed up its place with flesh. And the rib that the LORD God had taken from the man he made into a woman and brought her to the man. Then the man said,

'This at last is bone of my bones
 and flesh of my flesh;
this one shall be called Woman,
 for out of Man this one was taken.'
—Genesis 2:21–23

The story now refers for the first time to *ish* and *isha* (the terms for 'man' and 'woman'). And, as in the first account, both are equally created in the divine image.

So, we learn that human beings are specially created, individually. Each human being is unique and different. Just as each one of us has different fingerprints, so too every heart, every mind, every soul is different. 'For we are what God has made us' (Ephesians 2:10).

⊙ The Book of Genesis teaches us that our life is a share in God's own life. What conclusions does this lead you to make about your own life and about human life in general?

WHAT ABOUT YOU PERSONALLY?

⊙ How does this make a difference to you in your own life?

WE SHARE IN GOD'S LIFE AND LOVE

We are made to love and to be loved. This is why our deepest desires are fulfilled when we live as a loving person: loving God, loving ourselves, loving others and loving all creation.

Your experience of love comes first from your life with your parents or the other adults who love and care for you. You also experience love from your friends. You can probably think of many instances in your life to date when you knew that you were loved.

The love that we experience from those around us gives us some idea of what the love of God is like, but God loves us more than any human being could ever love us. In the Book of Genesis we find the great truths that we are made in the image of God and that our life is a share of God's own life. In the First Letter of St. John, one of the final and most moving books of the Bible, we read, 'God is love' (1 John 4:8). It is as if the revelation of God's love has been emerging for thousands of years—the length of time it took for the Bible to be written—and now, at last, it is proclaimed in these final verses:

Beloved, let us love one another because love is from God; everyone who loves is born of God and knows God. Whoever does not love does not know God, for God is love.

In this is love, not that we loved God but that he loved us and sent his Son to be the atoning sacrifice for our sins.

—1 John 4:7–8, 10

We know for certain that we are 'made out of love'. God, who is Truth, has revealed this truth about who we are.

THE GARDEN OF EDEN | LUCAS CRANACH THE ELDER

OVER TO YOU

⊙ When have you noticed that God loves you?
⊙ How do you recognize God's love?
⊙ Think of an image that captures for you what God's love is like.

GOD PROMISES US SALVATION

God's loving plan of goodness, however, did not satisfy the hearts of Adam and Eve. They heard what God said, 'You may freely eat of every tree of the garden; but of the tree of the knowledge of good and **evil** you shall not eat, for in the day that you eat of it you shall die' (Genesis 2:16), but they did not listen and take it to heart. They trusted more in their own wisdom and disobeyed God. In other words, they refused to listen and accept the wisdom of God's plan of goodness. They turned their backs on God and his love. They sinned. They disobeyed God and freely and knowingly chose to live a self-centered life rather than a God-centered life. This **sin** of our first parents is called **Original Sin**.

After the **Fall**, Original Sin, God makes a promise, speaks his word of hope. It is the first announcement of good news that points to the Savior. God tells the serpent, 'I will put enmity between you and the woman, and between your offspring and hers; he will strike your head, and you will strike his heel.' This is the first promise of salvation, the restoration of God's original plan, to be found in the Bible. It will be fulfilled in the Person and ministry of Jesus Christ, the Incarnate **Son of God**, whom the Father sent to restore his original plan and reconcile humanity and all creation with him.

TALK IT OVER

⊙ After our first parents sinned, God the Father promised to send Jesus, the Incarnate Son of God, to restore his original plan and to reconcile humanity and all creation with him. What does this tell us about God and his relationship with humankind? How does this make you feel?

GOD'S LOVE IS ALL AROUND US

God's love is all around us in the majesty and beauty of the created world. We see God's love, too, in the depths of the human person, including in our own self, especially in our own capacity to love others. Human beings continually surprise us by showing extraordinary levels of courage and care for others. Human love is a reflection of God's love. When we witness human love at its best, we get a sense of what God and the love of God is like. Think of the compassion shown by people like Blessed Mother Teresa of Calcutta, or the courage of the firefighters in the aftermath of the attack on New York's Twin Towers in 2001.

Many Christians have come to realize the love of God for them through reading the Bible, both the stories, prophecies and prayers of the Old Testament and the Good News of Jesus in the New Testament. The Word of God is passed on to us through the teaching of the Church, the prayer of people in worship, the preaching of the Gospel and the example of the lives of Christians through the ages.

REFLECT AND SHARE

⊙ Think of examples of great love and courage from your own family or your local community. Share your stories.

WHAT ABOUT YOU PERSONALLY?

⊙ What do you regard as the greatest evidence of God's love in your life? For example, where can you see God's love at work in your own efforts to be kind and compassionate to people in need?

MOTHER TERESA WITH MOTHERS AND CHILDREN AT HER MISSION IN CALCUTTA, INDIA

How do we recognize our desire for God?

OPENING CONVERSATION

Sometimes we can fail to see that someone loves us or that we love someone deeply. This can happen between parents and children, between husband and wife, between brothers and sisters, between friends. But it can also happen between ourselves and God.

- ⊙ Has this ever happened to you? Have you ever been slow to recognize someone's love for you; for example, the love your parents have for you? Think about what helped you to realize their love for you.
- ⊙ What about your love for God and God's love for you? What has helped you to know God's love in your life? What has helped you to love God?

THE DESIRE FOR GOD IS WRITTEN IN THE HUMAN HEART

Human beings are continually looking for more or better. As soon as children are able to ride a bike, they want to ride it without using their hands. That's how human beings are. We are rarely satisfied to leave things be. As adults, we want to stretch ourselves to the limit. We yearn for something or someone that is always beyond us. Nothing can fulfill our human desires and needs except God. The more we experience and realize God's love for us, and the better we respond to that love by loving our neighbor as ourselves, the more we will be truly happy. St. Augustine (354–430), a convert to Christianity, put it best in his memorable statement: 'Our hearts are restless until they rest in you' (*Confessions*, Book 1, Chapter 1).

The *Catechism of the Catholic Church* sums it up like this: 'The desire for God is written in the human heart, because man is created by God and for God' (CCC, no. 27). This means that we are made to be happy with God, in his love, now and for all eternity. Any other pleasure or delight that we experience in life is fleeting and a pale imitation of the lasting joy and peace that God alone can give us.

The French philosopher Blaise Pascal (1623–62) also wrote about this. He said: 'There is a God-shaped hollow in the human heart that only God can fill.'

Why does the *Catechism* say that the desire for God is 'written in the human heart'? It is because the heart is the real core of the human being. If the heart ceases to function, the human being dies. It is not surprising, therefore, that when we want to talk about something that is really important to human well-being, we use the heart as a symbol. We speak of being 'heartbroken', of thoughts 'deep in our heart', of talking with another 'heart to heart'. The image of the heart is used frequently when we speak of human love. So the heart is a good image for our dearest desires and deepest longings. Our hearts really 'make us tick'!

FAITH WORD

Faith

Faith 'is both a gift of God and a human act by which the believer gives personal adherence to God (who invites his or her response) and freely assents to the whole truth that God has revealed'.
—*United States Catholic Catechism for Adults*, 512

TALK IT OVER

⊙ If a person doesn't have any belief in God, how do you think that leaves a 'hollow' in their heart?

⊙ In the absence of believing in God, what might fill this hollow?

WHAT ABOUT YOU PERSONALLY?

⊙ Do you think you could be totally happy without God being a part of your life? Why or why not?

⊙ In what situations or places do you feel closest to God? And why do you think this is the case?

⊙ Are there times when you feel that God is far from you, or no longer in your life? What kind of situations lead you to feel like this?

REFLECTIVE ACTIVITY

⊙ With a partner, read psalm 42, in which the psalmist recognizes and describes his desire for God.

⊙ Identify the various images for God that the psalmist uses.

⊙ Pick out and discuss the lines that reflect the psalmist's belief that the longings of the human heart are satisfied in God alone.

⊙ What is your personal response to this psalm? How do the sentiments expressed in it mirror your own feelings?

OUR CATHOLIC FAITH GUIDES US

God loves us and gives us life. Only God can fulfil our true longings and give us lasting joy.

Of course, we may not recognize our restlessness for what it is. We may fail to identify the vacuum in our lives as a longing or desire for the love of God, just as we can fail to see the love of others for us. The immediate wants and needs in our lives can very easily swamp our deeper (or higher) desires. Our Catholic faith should help us to keep in mind just what our really important desires are and how best to fulfil them.

JUDGE AND ACT

REVIEW WHAT YOU HAVE LEARNED

- ⊙ What are the best things you have learned from this chapter about yourself? About God? About what God desires for you?
- ⊙ What have you learned about the Christian life and the wisdom it can bring to your own life?

JUDGE AND DECIDE

- ⊙ Think of one thing that you really desire, that you feel would make you happy for a long time to come. Make sure to choose something that will last, that your heart really wants.
- ⊙ Once you have identified the thing you really desire, consider for a moment whether your awareness of God, your Christian faith, your friendship with Jesus, your listening to the Holy Spirit, played any part in your choice. Did these factors play a role in your choices in the past?
- ⊙ What *will* you do so that these things will have a greater influence on your choices from now on?

JOURNAL EXERCISE

- ⊙ Write down ten words that describe what you feel God desires for you. Are these things that you would desire for yourself? Has anything you have learned in this chapter caused you to change what you wish for?

LEARN BY EXAMPLE

The story of St. Augustine of Hippo

Augustine was born in North Africa in AD 354. As a young man he lived a wild life and had little time for God or for the teachings of Christianity. He followed his every want and sampled all the pleasures that came his way. He was the despair of his mother, Monica, who prayed continuously for his conversion to the way of Jesus Christ.

Eventually, at the age of thirty-three, after much inner struggle and soul-searching, Augustine converted to Christianity. He describes his journey toward faith in his book *The Confessions*, which is a moving and powerful account of his change of life. Apart from his mother's prayers, the key to Augustine's conversion to Christian faith was that he listened to the promptings of his own heart. As he identified his deepest desires, he gradually found himself talking to God and recognizing God's unconditional love for him. His famous phrase sums up his experience: 'Our hearts are restless until they rest in you.'

Augustine became a priest in 391 and Bishop of Hippo in 396. Over the course of his lifetime he wrote a great number of very influential theological books, sermons and writings. He died in 430.

ST. AUGUSTINE | FRESCO IN ST. MARK'S CHURCH, MILAN

TALK IT OVER

⊙ Reflect on St. Augustine's story for a moment. How did he discover God's love for him and his love for God?

⊙ With a partner, try to think of other examples—from movies or television or real life—of people who changed their life for the better. Share your best examples.

WHAT ABOUT YOU PERSONALLY?

⊙ What have you learned from St. Augustine's story about the key to human happiness? How does this apply to your own life?

⊙ How often do you listen to the promptings of your own heart?

⊙ How often do you talk to God about your deepest desires?

⊙ How do you think you would live your life if you were deeply aware of God's unconditional love for you?

RESPOND IN YOUR HOME

Sometimes we can take people for granted or we think others take us for granted, especially the people closest to us. Hopefully, all of us can remember times when we just knew that our parents, or those close to us, love us. It may be a childhood memory of being hugged when we were afraid. But sometimes we don't realize how much our parents and family love us. We even misunderstand them at times, or we get distracted or are thrown off course, or we are just too busy to listen or hear what people are saying.

⊙ How do your parents and family know that you love them? What are the distractions that make you forget those people whom you love? What will you do to rectify this? How can your Catholic faith help?

A PRACTICAL GESTURE

⊙ Write a letter of appreciation to your family or close friends for the support and love that they have given you. Make sure that you include an example or two of what they have done for you. Might you mention that their love for you is one way that you experience God's love for you? Will you send the letter now, or at some suitable occasion in the near future? Or would you prefer to say those things face to face?

WHAT WILL YOU DO NOW?

⊙ Do you feel that God loves you? How do you show your love for God? Will you decide to dedicate more of your time to talking and listening to God from here on? What commitments are you prepared to make in order to do this?

⊙ Sometimes it is difficult to stick to the decisions we make when others disagree with us and want something different. Do you think you have the backbone and determination to stand out against the crowd? How can your Catholic faith give you the courage you need to make good choices?

LEARN BY HEART

God blessed them and said to them, 'Be fruitful and multiply, and fill the earth and subdue it, and have dominion over the fish of the sea and over the birds of the air and over every living thing that moves upon the earth.'

GENESIS 1:28

CREATION OF ADAM | ANDREA PISANO

PRAYER REFLECTION

Pray the Sign of the Cross together.

LEADER
Jesus said, 'Where two or three are gathered in my name, I am there among them' (Matthew 18:20). Whenever we gather in prayer, the risen Jesus is with us.

Conflicting Desires
I have so many conflicting desires, Lord,
Or that's how it seems.
One moment I'm all for good,
Then I turn nasty and selfish.
At other times I really want to help another,
A friend or a parent,
And I'm loving and tolerant.

Then again I'm filled with prejudice
And I want to throw my weight around.
Why have I conflicting desires?
Loving God, nourish within me the good desires,
The desires for a wholesome love,
Concern for the needy,
Desire for prayer with you;

And in the silence of my personality, O God,
Make strong my good desires.

LEADER
We pray together now in the words Jesus taught us.

ALL
Our Father. . . .

LEADER
We pray for peace.

Lord Jesus Christ,
who said to your Apostles,
Peace I leave you, my peace I give you;
look not on our sins,
but on the faith of your Church,
and graciously grant her peace and unity
in accordance with your will.
Who live and reign for ever and ever.

ALL
Amen.

Pray the Sign of the Cross together.

Where two or three are gathered in my name, I am there among them.

MATTHEW 18:20

CHAPTER 2

God Reaches Out to Us in Many Ways

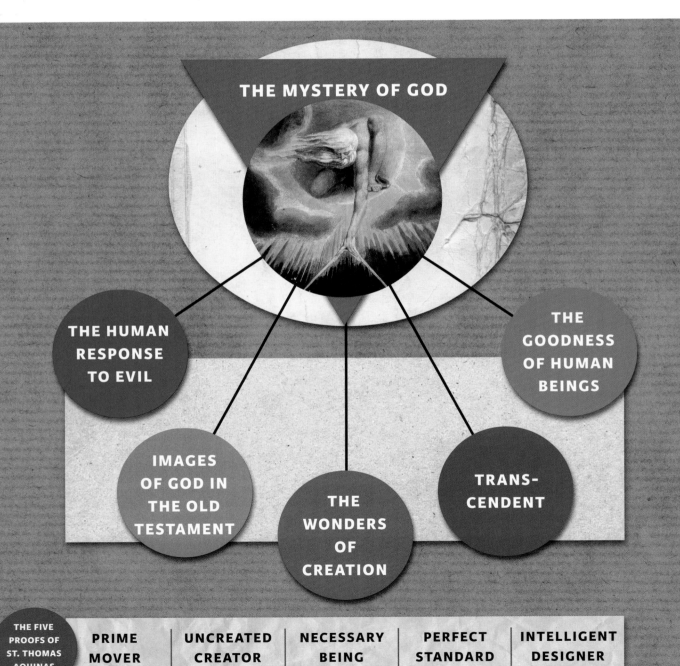

THE MYSTERY OF GOD

THE HUMAN RESPONSE TO EVIL

THE GOODNESS OF HUMAN BEINGS

IMAGES OF GOD IN THE OLD TESTAMENT

THE WONDERS OF CREATION

TRANS-CENDENT

THE FIVE PROOFS OF ST. THOMAS AQUINAS

| PRIME MOVER | UNCREATED CREATOR | NECESSARY BEING | PERFECT STANDARD | INTELLIGENT DESIGNER |

IN THIS CHAPTER WE DISCUSS SOME OF THE reasons why people believe in God. In particular we explore how the world of nature can reveal God to us. We also explore the teaching of the Church which says that, through our human reason, we can begin to know God

HUMAN ATTRIBUTES THAT POINT TO GOD'S EXISTENCE

OUR OPENNESS TO TRUTH AND BEAUTY

OUR SENSE OF MORAL GOODNESS

OUR FREEDOM OF CONSCIENCE

OUR LONGINGS FOR THE INFINITE AND FOR HAPPINESS

Faith Focus: These teachings of the Catholic Church are the primary focus of the doctrinal content presented in this chapter:

- ⊙ The existence of God can be known with certainty from the natural light of human reason.
- ⊙ Creation manifests the existence and glory of God.
- ⊙ God is transcendent; it is not possible for us to comprehend fully the Mystery of God by the use of our intellect and natural reason.
- ⊙ The gift of faith enables us to come to know God and all that he has revealed in a way that the natural light of human reason cannot do;
- ⊙ The human person participates in the wisdom and goodness of God and shares in the very life and love of God.
- ⊙ God gives the human person the ability to know and to choose the true and the good.
- ⊙ The natural moral law is the foundation of the law that God has revealed.

Discipleship Formation: As a result of studying this chapter and discovering the meaning of the faith of the Catholic Church for your life, you should be better able to:

- ⊙ reaffirm your belief in God and his existence;
- ⊙ be open to seeing the power and wonder of God in the created universe;
- ⊙ develop a deeper confidence in your belief in the existence of God through the use of your own intellect and reason;
- ⊙ recognize the goodness you see in the lives of human beings as manifestations of the goodness of God;
- ⊙ be more aware of the presence of God in your life and of how you can respond to his presence.

Scripture References: These Scripture references are quoted or referred to in this chapter:
OLD TESTAMENT: Deuteronomy 32:11; **Psalms** 8:3–9, 18:2, 19:1–4, 23:1–3, 29:7–8; **Wisdom** 13:1–3, 5
NEW TESTAMENT: Romans 1:20

Faith Glossary: Familiarize yourself with the meaning of these key faith terms. Definitions are found in the Glossary: **Creation, Divine Revelation, faith, human person, intellect/reason, Magisterium, moral law, Mystery of God, Sacred Scripture, Sacred Tradition, transcendence**

Faith Word: transcendence
Learn by Heart: Psalm 19:1; Psalm 23:1–3
Learn by Example: St. Katharine Drexel

Is it reasonable to believe in God?

On September 21, 1897, an editorial appeared in the *New York Sun* which has since become a classic of Christmas lore. It was written in response to the following letter:

> Dear Editor. I am 8 years old. Some of my little friends say there is no Santa Claus. Papa says,

'If you see it in *The Sun* it's so.' Please tell me the truth, is there a Santa Claus?
Virginia O'Hanlon, 115 West Ninety-Fifth Street

The editorial, entitled 'Is There a Santa Claus?', was written by Francis Church. Here are some extracts from it.

Is there a Santa Claus?

Virginia. Your little friends are wrong. They have been affected by the skepticism of a skeptical age. They do not believe except [what] they see. They think that nothing can be which is not comprehensible by their little minds. All minds, Virginia, whether they be men's or children's, are little. In this great universe of ours, man is a mere insect, an ant, in his intellect, as compared with the boundless world about him, as measured by the intelligence capable of grasping the whole of truth and knowledge.

Yes, Virginia, there is a Santa Claus. He exists as certainly as love and generosity and devotion exist, and you know that they abound and give to your life its highest beauty and joy. Alas! how dreary would be the world if there were no Santa Claus. It would be as dreary as if there were no Virginias. There would be no childlike faith then, no poetry, no romance to make tolerable this existence. We should have no enjoyment, except in sense and sight. The eternal light with which childhood fills the world would be extinguished.

Not believe in Santa Claus! You might as well not believe in fairies! Nobody sees Santa Claus, but that is no sign that there is no Santa Claus. The most real things in the world are those that neither children nor men can see. Did you ever see fairies dancing on the lawn? Of course not, but that's no proof that they are not there. Nobody can conceive or imagine all the wonders there are unseen and unseeable in the world. . . .

No Santa Claus! Thank God! He lives, and he lives forever. A thousand years from now, Virginia, nay, ten times ten thousand years from now, he will continue to make glad the heart of childhood.

⊙ What do you think are the 'most real things in the world' that we cannot see?

A QUESTION OF FAITH

Many people in the past and in the present have given 'reasons' for their belief in God's existence. Many of these reasons come from the use of their '**intellect**', or God-given natural ability to come to know 'truth'. We can look at these reasons and ask, 'Do they make sense?' But coming to know God is about more than using our 'intellect' and reasoning powers. Coming to know and believe in God and in all that he has revealed is a gift, the gift of **faith**, which, with the help of God's grace, we will accept.

We can come to grasp with certainty that God exists from the use of our intellect, by the 'natural light of human reason'. The Church teaches that 'man can come to know that there exists a reality which is the first cause and final end of all things' (*Catechism of the Catholic Church* [CCC], no. 34). St. Thomas Aquinas and other great teachers of the Church have taught 'that everyone calls [that reality] "God"' (St. Thomas Aquinas, *Summa Theologiae*, 1, 2, 3, quoted in CCC, no. 34). *(We explore St. Thomas' proofs for the existence of God in more detail later in this chapter.)* The Church affirmed this teaching of the Fathers of the Church at Vatican Council I (December 8, 1869—September 1, 1870). The Council taught:

'Our holy mother, the Church, holds and teaches that God, the first principle and last end of all things, can be known with certainty from the created world by the natural light of human reason' [Vatican Council I, *Son of God* (*Dei Filius*), 2]. Without this capacity, man would not be able to welcome God's revelation. Man has this capacity because he is created 'in the image of God' [see Genesis 1:27].

—CCC, no. 36

The gift of faith enables us not only to know that God exists, but also to come to *know* God, who is Father, Son and Holy Spirit—the Holy Trinity—and all that he has revealed, in a way that the natural light of human reason could never do on its own. 'What moves us to believe is not the fact that revealed truths appear as true and intelligible in the light of natural reason: we believe "because of the authority of God himself who reveals them, who can neither deceive nor be deceived"' (Vatican I, *Son of God*, 3, quoted in CCC, no. 156).

No one can *see* God, but we can *experience* God through other people and through the world around us. From these experiences we can also come to *know* that God is really present in our lives and in the world. For all creation is a manifestation of the Creator. This knowledge can lead us to respond in faith to God, who reveals himself to us. 'In faith, the human intellect and will cooperate with divine grace: "Believing is an act of the intellect assenting to the divine truth by command of the will moved by God through grace"' (CCC, no. 155, quoting St. Thomas Aquinas, *Summa Theologiae* II–II, 2, 9).

TALK IT OVER

⊙ Do you know people who really believe in God? Why do you think they do?
⊙ Have you ever had a conversation with your friends about whether they believe in God or not? What were their reasons for believing or not believing in God?

JOURNAL EXERCISE

⊙ Why do you believe in God? Write about the last time you really/sincerely prayed to God.

The heavens proclaim the glory of God

On Christmas Eve, December 24, 1968, three men, for the very first time in human history, circled just above the moon in the *Apollo 8* spacecraft. The three, Frank F. Borman, James A. Lovell and William A. Anders, then made a TV broadcast of Christmas greetings to Earth, during which they read the first ten verses of the Book of Genesis, which begins: 'In the beginning, God created the heavens and the earth. . . .'

REFLECT AND DISCUSS

⊙ Imagine what it would feel like to read these verses if you were looking out the window of a spacecraft onto the surface of the moon and into empty space.

⊙ How do you think you would feel looking down on Earth from space?

THE STORY OF GOD IS WRITTEN IN THE NATURAL WORLD

The *Catechism* presents three paths through which every person can come to know God: **creation**, the **human person** and **Divine Revelation**. (See *United States Catholic Catechism for Adults* [USCCA], 3.) In this chapter we explore the first two.

Both the Old and New Testaments repeatedly state that God and his glory is reflected in creation.

> For from the greatness and beauty of
> created things
> comes a corresponding perception of
> their Creator.
> —Wisdom 13:5

> Ever since the creation of the world God's eternal power and divine nature, invisible though they are, have been understood and seen through the things he has made.
> —Romans 1:20

The author of Psalm 19 imagines how it would be if the sky itself, and even the days and nights, could talk to one another and proclaim out loud that God is their Creator. The psalmist then goes on to recognize that, even though these works of Creation can't use words to communicate, still, by their very existence, they proclaim the glory of God.

> The heavens are telling the glory of God;
> and the firmament proclaims his
> handiwork.
> Day to day pours forth speech,

'EARTHRISE': EARTH PHOTOGRAPHED FROM LUNAR ORBIT BY *APOLLO 8*

and night to night declares knowledge.
There is no speech, nor are there words;
    their voice is not heard;
yet their voice goes out through all the earth,
    and their words to the end of the world.

—Psalm 19:1–4

People have always had difficulty describing God; he is Ultimate Mystery and far more than our human mind, our intellect and reason, can ever comprehend on its own. The biblical authors had to try to find words to help people to understand and know God. So they used words that described things they had experienced and did know about. They said, for example, that God speaks like thunder or like a soft gentle whisper. They said that God's action is like the storm, the earthquake, the flood or the avalanche. They described God as a mighty king, a stern judge, a gentle midwife, a loving father or mother. They spoke of God using figurative language and by analogy. Starting from the many and diverse reflections of God manifested in his creatures, we can really begin to name God. These characteristics of creatures are likenesses of and point to, in a limited way, the infinite God.

The Bible uses all these words and images to talk about God. Here are some more of the images we find in the Bible:

When talking about how God looked after Jacob:

As an eagle sits upon its nest
    and hovers over its young;
as it spreads its wings, takes them up,
    and bears them aloft on its pinions,
the LORD alone guided him.

—Deuteronomy 32:11

The psalmist wrote:

The LORD is my rock, my fortress, and my
        deliverer,
    my God, my rock in whom I take refuge,
    my shield, and the horn of my salvation, my
        stronghold.

—Psalm 18:2

The LORD is my shepherd, I shall not want.
    He makes me lie down in green pastures;

he leads me beside still waters,
    he restores my soul.

—Psalm 23:1–3

The voice of the LORD flashes forth flames of
    fire.
The voice of the LORD shakes the wilderness;
    the LORD shakes the wilderness of Kadesh.

—Psalm 29:7–8

Through the use of our intellect and reason we can come to know both that God exists and certain qualities of God. We can get a glimpse into the inner life and reality of the divine **Mystery** who is God. But our minds, or intellect and will, are limited in what they can come to know about who God is; namely, that God is Trinity—there is one God in three divine Persons, God the Father, God the Son and God the Holy Spirit.

TALK IT OVER

⊙ Which of the above quotations appeals most to you? Discuss your choice, explaining why you chose it.

LET THOSE WHO HAVE EYES SEE, AND THOSE WHO HAVE EARS HEAR!

Do you think that the elements of nature, by their very existence, communicate something of God to us today in the twenty-first century? In Old Testament times, long before our technological age, people's lifestyles and modes of transport meant that they were physically closer to nature than people are today. Could it be that we have become so distant from the natural world and so surrounded by city streets and the trappings of modern living that we are insulated from the processes of nature? We are no longer familiar enough with the stars and the planets. Could this mean that nature does not speak to us and that we are, therefore, somewhat isolated from God and his Revelation in the natural world?

Novelists, poets and playwrights have always spoken to the deepest realities of life. Your study of literature throughout high school will provide you with many opportunities to listen to both the hearts and minds of those whose writings have inspired readers to reflect on the deeper meanings of their experiences. Read and

reflect on this example from the opening lines of the well-known poem 'Leisure' by W. H. Davies (1871–1940):

> What is this life if full of care
> we have no time to stand and stare?

WHAT ABOUT YOU PERSONALLY?

- Have there been times when you wished that you had more time just to 'stand and stare'? Explain.
- When was the last time that you did 'stand and stare'? What did you 'see'? What thoughts were in your mind at that time?
- Have you ever just stopped and thought 'AWESOME!'? Did the idea of the Creator, of God, come to you? Explain.
- What particular aspect of the world of nature speaks to you most eloquently of God's power and grandeur?
- How do you respond to 'seeing' God in nature? What responsibilities does this give you?

WHAT DOES IT ALL MEAN?

The author of the Book of Wisdom, writing about a hundred years before the time of Jesus, reflected on how pagans thought that parts of the visible universe were gods because they were so awesome:

> For all people who were ignorant of God were
>   foolish by nature;
> and they were unable from the good things that
>   are seen to know the one who exists,
> nor did they recognize the artisan while paying
>   heed to his works;
> but they supposed that either fire, or wind, or
>   swift air
> or the circle of the stars, or turbulent water,
> or the luminaries of heaven were the gods who
>   ruled the world.
> If through delight in the beauty of these things
>   people assumed them to be gods,
> let them know how much better than these is
>   their Lord.
>
> —Wisdom 13:1–3

Why do you think so many ancient people worshipped elements of nature as though they were gods? Are there any 'false gods' in our time? Like what? And why do people 'worship' them?

Today, some agnostics (those who can't decide if God exists) and some atheists (those who assert that there is no God) think that evolution is the *only* explanation for why everything exists. They assert that the universe and everything in it came into existence spontaneously; that is, without any help from an outside power. What do you think?

We can begin to know God through human reasoning

OPENING CONVERSATION

⊙ What prompts you to reflect on the existence of God?

THE MYSTERY OF GOD

Christian theologians, such as St. Augustine, point to the universe as evidence of God. Augustine is quoted in the *Catechism of the Catholic Church*:

Question the beauty of the sea . . . question the beauty of the sky. . . . These beauties are subject to change. Who made them if not the Beautiful One who is not subject to change?

—CCC, no. 32

JIM CARREY IN *BRUCE ALMIGHTY*

As human beings, with our human intellects, it is impossible for us to grasp *fully* what God is like or who God is. God is bigger than our understanding. St. Augustine once said that if you thought you could fully understand God, it would not be God that you understood.

When we talk about God, we are trying to talk about the One that we have never and can never experience fully through our human capacities. We can never experience or even imagine what it is like to be eternal or almighty. God is infinitely more than anything we can say. God is *beyond* anything we could ever imagine.

In the movie *Bruce Almighty*, Bruce 'becomes' Almighty God for a short period of time. It is a comedy with some good laughs, but how much can it tell us about what God is really like? God *transcends*, that is, goes beyond, all human thinking . . . or else, as Augustine said, we are not talking about God at all . . . just Bruce Almighty!

Our human intelligence is not able to grasp the Mystery who is God. But we can get *some* idea about who God is and what he is like from the various ways in which he makes himself known; for example, through the wonders and miracles of the natural world, and through people who, by their lives of love and service of God and others, show the divine love of God at work in and through them. We can come to know God most fully and clearly through the Person, life and teaching of Jesus, through divinely inspired **Sacred Scripture** and the teaching (**Sacred Tradition**) of the Church.

We can also begin to know God through human reasoning. Let's read now about one man who showed how we can use our reason to come to know God in this way.

ST. THOMAS AQUINAS

Thomas Aquinas was born in Aquino in Italy in 1225. As a young man he decided to join the newly founded Dominican order. His family objected strongly and tried to dissuade him, even going so far as to imprison him for more than a year. When free again, he studied first in Paris and then in Cologne, where his teacher was St. Albert the Great. Thomas was a big man, but very quiet and usually silent in class. Albert called him 'the dumb ox, whose bellow would astonish the world'. (By 'dumb', he did not mean 'stupid' but 'one who does not talk'.)

At that time, knowledge of ancient Greek philosophy, especially of Aristotle, was coming into Europe through Muslim authors. Thomas took on the challenge of reconciling this new learning with Christian theology. His great work, the *Summa Theologica*, used human reasoning to explore the divinely revealed truths of the Bible and bring them and the new ideas from Greek philosophy into harmony. His 'solution' has lasted into our own day, though it was challenged by scientists like Isaac Newton in the seventeenth century.

Through the use of his own intellect, Thomas Aquinas worked out 'five proofs' for the existence of God. While they are not scientific proofs, they give us sound and compelling reasons for God's existence. In many ways, they all boil down to 'the argument from causality', as Aquinas called it. The argument from causality states that everything that exists must have a cause, so there must be an Original Cause of all that is. As the Church teaches: 'God, the first principle and last end of all things, can be known with certainty from the created world by the natural light of human reason' (CCC, no. 36).

Near the end of his life, Thomas Aquinas had a mystical experience, after which he abruptly stopped writing. He said that anything he had written up to then was just straw, because now he had had a glimpse of the reality of God. Thomas Aquinas died in 1274, was canonized a saint and named a doctor or teacher of the Church. He is the patron of Catholic schools.

TALK IT OVER

⊙ St. Thomas Aquinas' 'five proofs' are given below. Think about these arguments for a few minutes. Then discuss which one makes most sense to you and which is the most difficult to understand.

WHAT ABOUT YOU PERSONALLY?

⊙ What are some of your own best 'reasons' for believing in God?

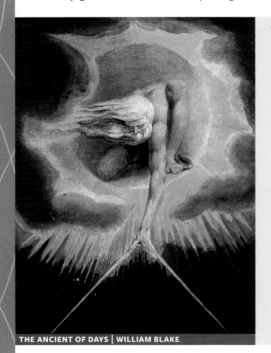

THE ANCIENT OF DAYS | WILLIAM BLAKE

The five proofs of St. Thomas Aquinas

⊙ The existence of a **prime mover**—nothing can move itself; there must be a first mover. The first mover is called God.

⊙ Cause of existence—things that exist are created by other things; nothing can create itself. There must be, at the beginning, an **uncreated creator**, called God. God is the first cause of everything that is.

⊙ The existence of a **necessary Being**, which causes the existence of others. This necessary Being is called God.

⊙ Degrees of perfection—for any given quality (for example, beauty, goodness) there must be a **perfect standard** by which all such qualities are measured. This perfect standard is called God.

⊙ Intelligent design—we can see that the universe has intelligence and intelligent beings, and there is one **intelligent Being, God**, who directs them to their end.

Consider other arguments for God's existence

We live in a time when many are arguing that there is no God. Looking at the chaos in the world, they maintain that the existence of evil—the violence, the suffering—simply negates any arguments, or proofs, for God's existence. Some thinkers actually point to the negative reaction of the vast majority of people to such violence and suffering as an argument for the existence of God.

REFLECT AND DISCUSS

⊙ Remember the outrage at what happened on 9/11? Or can you recall how people reacted to any of the high school massacres of recent years? Do you remember a time in your own life when you just knew that what you saw happening was wrong? For example, have you ever seen someone being bullied or being treated unfairly, or someone taking something that didn't belong to them, or have you ever heard someone saying something that you just knew was untrue? Can you remember how you felt at these times? What words would you use to describe those feelings?

⊙ Where do you think such feelings come from?

CONSIDER THE HUMAN RESPONSE TO EVIL

Some philosophers propose that we can know of God from the reaction of most humans to evil. This is evidence of the fact that there is a **moral law** deeply embedded in the heart of people. This law is 'natural' to man, embedded in his very nature and rooted in the reality that the human person is created in the image and likeness of God and shares in the very life of God. Its origin is God. It is immutable and permanent and cannot be removed from the human heart.

Man participates in the wisdom and goodness of the Creator who gives him mastery over his acts and the ability to govern himself with a view to the true and the good. The natural law expresses the original moral sense which enables man to discern by reason the good and the evil, the truth and the lie: . . .

—CCC, no. 1954

Even if no one ever said anything to us about right and wrong, what is good and what is evil, there are things that we as human beings would automatically recognize and acknowledge as being good or evil. This innate sense comes from God. The natural moral law 'provides the solid foundation on which man can build the structure of moral rules to guide his choices' (CCC, no. 1959) and it is the foundation of the law revealed by God.

Obviously, how you judge the rightness or wrongness, the good or evil, of something is influenced by the things you have learned and by the things people have told you about right and wrong. It is the responsibility of the **Magisterium** of the Church to interpret and teach the moral law, both natural and revealed.

TALK IT OVER

⊙ Does this argument for the existence of God make sense to you? Explain.

DEBATE

⊙ Have a debate on the argument outlined above for the existence of God, with one side finding this argument convincing, the other finding it unconvincing.

The following are extracts from private reflections written by Mother Teresa of Calcutta (1910–97). Mother Teresa's life of dedicated service to the abandoned and forgotten poor of Calcutta was acknowledged not only by the Church, who has named her Blessed Mother Teresa, but also by the world community, who honored her with the Nobel Peace Prize. In these reflections she recalls her initial experiences of ministering with the poor as a Missionary of Charity. Read them and see if you think they further support the argument that human beings have an in-built and God-given sense of right and wrong.

The dark holes of the poor

We started at Taltala and went to every Catholic family.—The people were pleased—but the children were all over the place—and what dirt and misery—what poverty and suffering—I spoke very, very little, I just did some washing of sores, and dressings, and gave medicine to some.—The old man lying on the street—not wanted—all alone just sick and dying—I gave him carbonsone and water to drink and the old man was so strangely grateful. . . .

Then we went to Taltala Bazaar, and there was a very poor woman dying of starvation more than TB. What poverty. What actual suffering. I gave her something which will help her to sleep—but the woman was longing to have some care. I wonder how long she will last—she was just 96 degrees at the time. She ask a few times for confession and Holy Communion.—I felt my own poverty there too—for I had nothing to give that poor woman.—I did everything I could but if I had been able to give her a hot cup of milk or something like that, her cold body would have got some life. . . .

I believe that some are saying what use of working among these lowest of the low, that the great—the learned and the rich are ready to come [so] it is better to give full force to them. Yes, let them all do it.—The Kingdom must be preached to all. If the Hindu and Muslim sick people can have the full service and devotion of so many nuns and priests, surely the poorest of the poor and the lowest of the low can have the love and the devotion of us few. 'The Slum Sister,' they call me, and I am glad to be just that for His glory and love.

- How do you think you would have felt had you seen what Mother Teresa saw in Calcutta?
- Where do you think your reaction to such poverty and suffering might come from? Could it come from God?

The *Catechism of the Catholic Church* lists the following attributes of human beings as pointers toward God's existence: our openness to truth and beauty; our sense of moral goodness; our freedom for the voice of our conscience; our longings for the infinite and for happiness. (See CCC, no. 33.)

The poet Patrick Kavanagh wrote:

> God is in the bits and pieces of
> Everyday—
> A kiss here and a laugh again, and sometimes tears,
> A pearl necklace round the neck of poverty.

Kavanagh could see God in the ordinary, everyday world around him. Likewise, a wise man was once asked, 'Do you believe in miracles?' He responded, 'How could I dispute what I see happening in front of my eyes every moment of every day?'

REFLECT AND DISCUSS
- What do you think of Kavanagh's argument that God is manifested in the 'Everyday'?

JOURNAL EXERCISE
- Think about a time when you were very aware of God's presence in the 'bits and pieces' of your own life. Write about your experience.

JUDGE AND RECORD
- Discuss and then write the two best arguments for God's existence that you can come up with.

FAITH WORD

Transcendence

Transcendence refers to the idea that God is so 'beyond' the universe, and so different from anything else that exists, that God cannot be directly experienced by human beings. A shorthand way of saying that God is transcendent is: 'God is the absolute Other.'

GOD THE FATHER | COLEGIO MAYOR DE SAN ILDEFONSO, MADRID

JUDGE AND ACT

REFLECT ON WHAT YOU HAVE LEARNED

This lesson has outlined evidence and arguments, ancient and contemporary, for the existence of God. Yet there are people who do not believe in God, who deny the existence of God (atheists) or who cannot decide whether or not God exists (agnostics). They argue that faith in God is not reasonable or scientific.

◉ Think for a few moments about what you have learned in this chapter concerning the Mystery of God and the various ways in which human beings can come to know him.

DECIDE FOR YOURSELF

◉ 'The more we know about God, the more we realize that we will never know him fully in this life.' Do you agree with this statement? Explain.

◉ What real difference will your faith make to your everyday life from here on?

◉ Think of someone with whom you can share your faith in God, perhaps a person who needs a bit of reassurance or encouragement.

The more we know about God, the more we realize that we will never know him fully in this life

The story of St. Katharine Drexel

If God is 'in the bits and pieces of Everyday' (Kavanagh), we must pay attention to all that happens around us so that we will hear what he is revealing to us. Katharine Drexel, now a saint, is an example of someone who did just that. By looking carefully at the world around her and by reflecting on her experiences, she became aware that God was calling her to change her direction in life.

Katharine Drexel was born in Philadelphia in 1858. Her father was an international banker, so her family was very rich. She had an excellent education and enjoyed all the privileges that came with wealth at that time. However, when she nursed her stepmother through a terminal illness, she came to realize that all the money in the world could not buy immunity from pain or death.

Katharine had read a book entitled *A Century of Dishonor* by Helen Hunt Jackson, which explored the plight of Native Americans. While on a European tour, she met Pope Leo XIII and asked him to send some missionaries to Wyoming to help the needy Native Americans there. His answer was: 'Why don't you become a missionary?'

Katharine thought seriously about the Pope's suggestion. When she returned home, she met the Sioux leader Red Cloud and began her systematic aid to Native American missions. She decided that she would found a religious order and dedicate her life and inheritance to working on behalf of oppressed Native Americans and African Americans in the West and Southwest US. In 1889 she wrote: 'The feast of St. Joseph brought me the grace to give the remainder of my life to the Indians and the colored.' The newspaper headlines screamed 'Gives Up Seven Million'.

After three years of training, Katharine and her first band of nuns (Sisters of the Blessed Sacrament) opened a boarding school in Santa Fe. By 1942 she had a string of Catholic schools in thirteen states, plus forty mission centers and twenty-three rural schools. Her greatest achievement was the founding of Xavier University in New Orleans, the first US university for African Americans.

At seventy-seven, Katharine suffered a heart attack and had to retire. However, she spent the next twenty years in prayer. Small notebooks and slips of paper record her various prayers and meditations. She died in 1955. Because of her lifelong dedication to her Catholic faith and her selfless service to the oppressed, she was canonized by Pope John Paul II in 2000.

OVER TO YOU

⊙ What might you learn from Katharine Drexel for your own life?

⊙ When have you ever had the sense that God was calling you to do something special with your life? Share your story.

RESPOND IN YOUR HOME

⊙ Does your family say 'Grace' before and after meals? If not, might you be able to encourage them to do so?

⊙ The word 'grace' in this context means 'thanks'. To say 'Grace' before and after meals is to offer a prayer to God in gratitude for creation, which includes our food and drink, and, of course, the wonderful people who

The heavens are telling the glory of God; and the firmament proclaims his handiwork.

PSALM 19:1

The LORD is my shepherd, I shall not want. He makes me lie down in green pastures; he leads me beside still waters; he restores my soul. He leads me in right paths for his name's sake.

PSALM 23:1—3

harvested the food, transported it, cooked it and served it on our table. Traditionally, people pause for a moment before saying Grace in order to reflect on what God and other human beings have done for us. We also remember those who are not so blessed, who may lack food or drink, who are sick and suffering and who today need our support and prayers.

⊙ Here is a commonly used 'Grace' for mealtimes:

Before meals: Bless us, O Lord, and these your gifts, which we are about to receive from your bounty, through Christ our Lord. Amen.
After meals: We give you thanks for all your benefits, almighty God, who lives and reigns forever. And may the souls of the faithful departed, through the mercy of God, rest in peace. Amen.

⊙ Write your own 'Grace' for mealtimes. Invite your family to pray this at some of your mealtimes.

JOURNAL EXERCISE

⊙ Write an account for yourself, that you will be able to look back on and remember when you are older, of any awesome experiences you have had in your life, especially ones that helped to turn your mind and heart toward God. What, for instance, was the most wonderful thing you ever saw? (Things seen in the movies or on television or video do not count! You must have been there and seen it yourself.) Where was it? When did you see it? How long did it last? Who was with you? Was anything said? What were your thoughts at the time? Did you do anything? Did you tell people later? Would you like to share this experience with the group now? Did these experiences make you think of God or lead you to question whether he was behind them? If not, might you be asking yourself such questions now, especially in light of what you have learned in this chapter?

PRAYER REFLECTION

Pray the Sign of the Cross together.

LEADER
Together let us give thanks for the many ways in which God's presence is made known to us:

For the vastness of the ocean. . . .
All: We give you thanks, Almighty God.

For the beauty of the sky. . . .
All: We give you thanks, Almighty God.

For the bounty of the fields. . . .

All: We give you thanks, Almighty God.

For the majesty of the mountains. . . .
All: We give you thanks, Almighty God.

For gentle breezes. . . .
All: We give you thanks, Almighty God.

For the creativity of humanity. . . .

All: We give you thanks, Almighty God.

For the nurture of parents. . . .
All: We give you thanks, Almighty God.

LEADER
Loving God, in the presence of these and the many other wonders of our world, we praise and thank you. Open our eyes so that we may be ever more aware of your presence in our lives and in our world. Open our hearts to respond and live as your own people, a people of God.

Let us now recite this heartfelt prayer from the Book of Psalms:

ALL *(either together or individually)*
When I look at your heavens, the work of your
    fingers,
    the moon and the stars that you have
    established;

what are human beings that you are mindful of
    them,
    mortals that you care for them?
Yet you have made them a little lower than God,
    and crowned them with glory and honor.
You have given them dominion over the works
        of your hands,
    you have put all things under their feet.
all sheep and oxen,
    and also the beasts of the field,
the birds of the air, and the fish of the sea,
    whatever passes along the paths of the seas.
O LORD, our Sovereign,
    how majestic is your name in all the earth!
                                    —Psalm 8:3–9

LEADER
Ever-loving God, you called Blessed Katharine Drexel to teach the message of the Gospel and to bring the life of the Eucharist to the African American and Native American peoples. By her prayers and example, enable us to work for justice among the poor and the oppressed and keep us united in love in the eucharistic community of your Church. Grant this through our Lord Jesus Christ, your Son, who lives and reigns with you and the Holy Spirit, one God, for ever and ever.

ALL
Amen.

LEADER
As we end our prayer reflection, let us ask God to bless us and all those whom we love.

ALL
Amen.

Pray the Sign of the Cross together.

CHAPTER 3

God's Revelation through the Bible

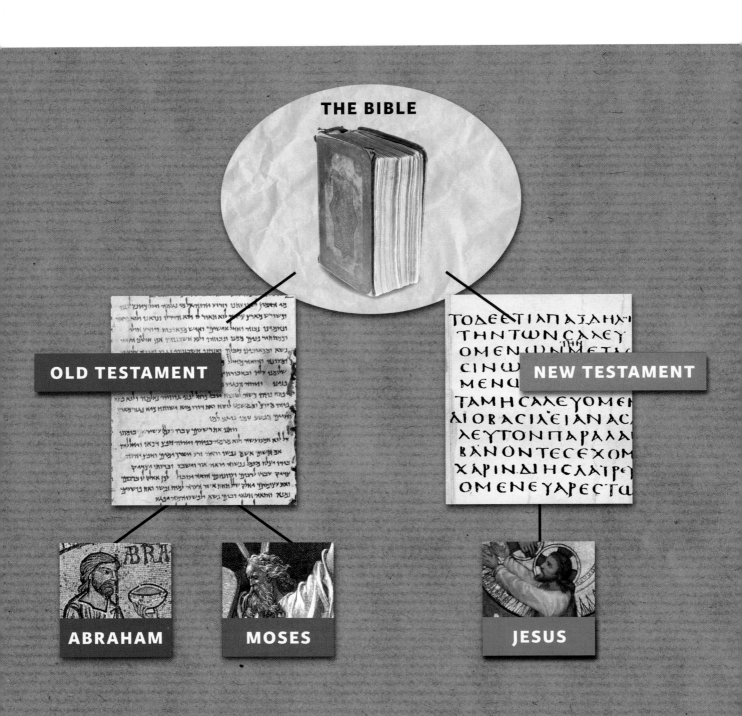

THE BIBLE

OLD TESTAMENT

NEW TESTAMENT

ABRAHAM

MOSES

JESUS

IN THIS CHAPTER WE EXPLORE HOW GOD'S Revelation through the Bible enables us to understand who we are and how to live as the Church, the new People of God. Understanding the past can help us to understand the present and shape our future. We learn how the Bible helps us to know and appreciate the foundations of our faith as Catholics.

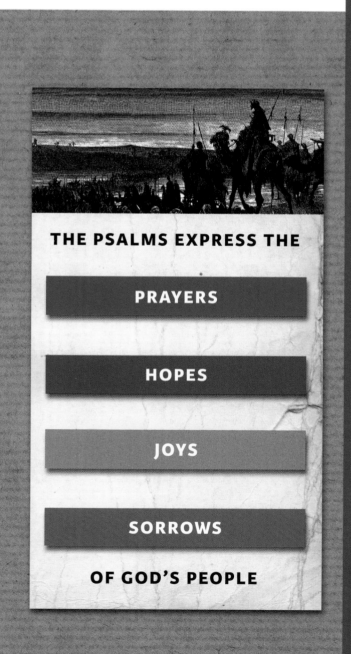

THE PSALMS EXPRESS THE

PRAYERS

HOPES

JOYS

SORROWS

OF GOD'S PEOPLE

Faith Focus: These teachings of the Catholic Church are the primary focus of the doctrinal content presented in this chapter:
⊙ The Bible reveals God's will and plan for humankind.
⊙ The Old Testament prefigures Jesus.
⊙ Jesus, the Messiah, is the fulfillment of God's promises in the Old Testament.
⊙ The Psalms are an expression of the prayers, hopes, joys and sorrows of the Israelite people.

Discipleship Formation: As a result of studying this chapter and discovering the meaning of the faith of the Catholic Church for your life, you should be better able to:
⊙ understand the importance of the Bible in your life;
⊙ recognize God's call in your life at this time and decide how you can respond to it;
⊙ indicate where you believe God has been active in your life to date;
⊙ consider how you might live the Great Commandment;
⊙ experience the Psalms as sources for prayer in your life;
⊙ listen more attentively to the Bible readings proclaimed during the Liturgy and read the Bible more frequently on your own.

Scripture References: These Scripture references are quoted or referred to in this chapter:
OLD TESTAMENT: Genesis 12:4, 17:4–7; **Exodus** 3:4–5, 7 and 10; **Deuteronomy** 6:5; **Leviticus** 19:18; **Psalms** 17:8–9, 20:4–5, 22:1, 4–5, 25:6–7, 51:1–2, 139:1–2 and 13–14, 144:9
NEW TESTAMENT: Matthew 5:17–18, 22:34–40, 28:19; **Mark** 1:14–15, 12:28–31; **Luke** 4:16–21, 10:25–28; **John** 13:1 and 34, 15:9 and 12, 16:22, 20:22–23; **Acts of the Apostles** 1:8, 2:4; **Philippians** 2:6–11; **1 Timothy** 4:14; **2 Timothy** 1:6–7; **Hebrews** 1:1–2; 1 John 4:7–13

Faith Glossary: Familiarize yourself with the meaning of these key faith terms. Definitions are found in the Glossary: **Ascension, Bible, charity (love), Church, Covenant, grace, Great Commandment, Hebrews, Jesus, Jesus Christ, Kingdom of God, Law of Love, Messiah, New Commandment, New Covenant, New Testament, Old Testament, People of God, prophets, Resurrection, Word of God**

Faith Word: grace
Learn by Heart: Hebrews 1:1–2
Learn by Example: St. Frances Xavier Cabrini

How does understanding the past help us to understand the present and shape our future?

More and more people today want to find out about their past, their family history. When people discover what happened to their great grandparents more than a century ago, for example, they begin to understand a little more about their own life.

Events in which your family participated over the years, people whom they encountered, challenges that they faced, successes and failures that they enjoyed or endured, beliefs, practices and values that they held dear, the culture and religion that they clung to through thick and thin, all tell you something not only about who you are but about why you and your family are as

you are today. Your identity is inextricably linked to your family's story.

TALK IT OVER
- What do you know about the history of your family or where your ancestors came from?
- What do you know about the role that God or religion played in their lives?

The following extract from a book entitled *Playing Poker with Nana* by Megan McKenna reflects how her relationship with her grandmother influenced the person she is today.

A visit with Nana

A visit with Nana! Every summer it was two weeks to remember, mull over, reflect on, and look forward to the following year. . . . I never knew my grandfather, and only knew my father's mother, Nana. . . . We didn't talk about stuff much at home, but here, for two or three weeks you could ask anything. She always answered with authority, sometimes looking stern . . . talking to me as an equal (not as an adult so much, but as someone of worth deserving an answer, honesty). Being treated this way opened doors:

to think, to wonder, to question, to disagree, to play with words, ideas, and fantasize. There was drawing, tracing pictures, writing—it all started there.

It's amazing how often her voice returns to me, and I hear her saying one-liners, or see her in my head—blue eyes dancing, looking at me over her wire-rimmed glasses—as though to say—What? Do you really believe that? Why are you doing that now? This is the woman that would say to us kindly: 'God never takes his eye off of you. God watches you every single moment, but that's because God loves you so much! Just like I do.' Being loved by Nana was grand. I'd have to check out this God that seemed to accompany her all the time, like an invisible friend that I couldn't see yet. I was intrigued early though, maybe when I was six or seven years old.

How do you think you have been shaped by people in your family?

OVER TO YOU

- How do you think Megan McKenna was influenced by her Nana?
- Now look at yourself. From what you know about your parents, grandparents and other elderly members of your family, how do you think you have been shaped by people in your family?

REFLECTIVE EXERCISE

- Look back over the ups and downs, the twists and turns in your life to date. Pick out the decisive events, the things that happened to you that have made a big difference to your life. Maybe you moved home, changed school, suffered an accident or an illness, enjoyed a great success, endured the loss of someone you loved? Or perhaps your life so far has had little incident, no real changes, and seems to have proceeded at a steady pace in the one direction?

- Where do you see God as active in the events of your life? What role has God played in your life, though perhaps hidden behind the events and people who filled your world?
- Now take a 'big' sheet of paper. Across the page, draw a line from which you will label all the significant things that have happened to you in your life so far. The line should include changes of direction, corners and curves, each identified by the life-changing events that you can remember. Mark the places where you think God was active in your life.

What is true of our own family is also very true of our Christian family. In the following section we will study how the great story of God's family is reflected in our **Bible**, the foundation of God's Revelation to our lives, and how it sustains our identity in Catholic faith today.

The Bible tells the story of God's action in human history

The Bible is the Christian Sacred Scripture (which means 'holy writing'). It is cherished by Christians as what the Second Vatican Council called the **Word of God** in human language. It reflects God's Revelation through his action in human history, in the Israelite people and in Jesus Christ, God's own Son. Just as finding out about our ancestors teaches us something about who our family is and what it values and stands for, so the story of God's interaction with people down through the ages, as revealed in the Bible, helps us to understand where we have come from in terms of our Christian faith. As Sacred Scripture shaped the faith of those who have lived before us, so it should shape us today and how we are to live as the **People of God** in imitation of Jesus Christ.

REFLECT AND DISCUSS

◉ What is your own attitude toward the Bible?

THE BIBLE

The story told in the Bible covers many centuries. The Bible is not, in fact, a single book but a library of seventy-three books—the forty-six books of the **Old Testament** and the twenty-seven books of the **New Testament**. *(See introduction for a description of the books of the Old Testament and the New Testament.)*

The earliest parts of the Bible come from four thousand years ago, while the last books were written around nineteen hundred years ago. All the books are closely linked because, when put together, they tell a single story, the Greatest Story ever told, of God's unconditional love and plan for humankind since the beginning of time.

The *Catechism of the Catholic Church* states:

The unity of the two Testaments proceeds from the unity of God's plan and his Revelation. The Old Testament prepares for the New and the New Testament fulfills the Old; the two shed light on each other; both are the true Word of God.

—CCC, no. 140

THE OLD TESTAMENT

The first part of the Bible, the Old Testament, tells the story of God's covenantal relationship with the Israelites—now the Jewish people—before the coming of Jesus. ('Testament' means covenant, and refers to the agreement or treaty that God and the People of God have entered into.) The Old Testament also contains the Sacred Scripture of the Jewish people today, as well as other holy writings of the ancient people of Israel; Christians and Jews share this first Testament of the Bible. Jesus himself was very familiar with the books of the Old Testament. As a child and young man, he would have studied them and heard them read in the synagogue; they shaped his trust in his Father and how he fulfilled his mission on earth. As an adult, Jesus quoted from them frequently. Here is a reference to Jesus reading and teaching from Sacred Scripture in Luke 4:16–21:

When he came to Nazareth, where he had been brought up, he went to the synagogue on the sabbath day, as was his custom. He stood up to read, and the scroll of the prophet Isaiah was given to him. He unrolled the scroll and found the place where it was written:
'The Spirit of the Lord is upon me,
      because he has anointed me
         to bring good news to the poor.
He has sent me to proclaim release to the captives
         and recovery of sight to the blind,
            to let the oppressed go free,
   to proclaim the year of the Lord's favor.'
And he rolled up the scroll, gave it back to the attendant and sat down. The eyes of all in the synagogue were fixed on him. Then he began to say to them, 'Today this scripture has been fulfilled in your hearing.'

TALK IT OVER

⊙ Consider for a moment why you think Jesus chose to read this passage from Isaiah. Then discuss what this tells us about how Jesus viewed his mission.

THE NEW TESTAMENT

The second main part of the Bible, the New Testament, is the story of **Jesus Christ**, the founder of the **Church**, his life and teachings, Passion, **Resurrection** and **Ascension**. It is also the story of the early Church, whose members, after Jesus' Ascension, came to be known as Christians.

REFLECT AND DISCUSS

⊙ The Bible is the most widely published and read book in the history of the world; why do you think this is so?

WHAT ABOUT YOU PERSONALLY?

⊙ How carefully do you listen to the readings from the Bible in church?
⊙ Explain the effect, if any, that these readings have on you.
⊙ Think of powerful words from the Bible that have influenced your life; that gave you courage or hope or direction. Share these.

The Bible reveals God's plan for humanity

THE BIBLE IS OUR STORY, THE STORY OF THE PEOPLE OF GOD

The Bible is our story. It tells us where we have come from as the Church, the new People of God. It recounts not just the actions of our ancestors and the understandings they had of the world in which they lived; more importantly, it tells the story of the action and plan of God for our ancestors in faith and, ultimately, for us. God is the central agent in this story. This was true in biblical times and it is still true today. God is still active in our stories, in our own lives, in the Church and in our world.

REFLECT AND DISCUSS

- What major events have happened in the years since you were born in your country/ state and in the world?
- How has the story of your life so far been influenced or guided by the story of the world you live in?
- Has God's care and love for human beings— and for you—played a part in your life? What story would you tell to show that it has?
- Do you believe that God continues to act within human history? How? Why?

In the beginning God created human beings from nothing, rescued them from evil, protected them and promised them the peace and happiness of his love. The story of Noah and the Great Flood shows us that even in the midst of the dangers and perils of life, human beings believe that the Creator loves them and has agreed never to let the world or the human race be totally destroyed.

As we read the Old Testament, we see that God's people did not always listen to his promises. Nor did they live by the **Covenant** that God had entered into with them. Even when the **prophets** tried to teach them God's ways and chastised them for some of the things they were doing, often the people did not listen. Meanwhile, through the prophets, God constantly promised to send a **Messiah**, an Anointed One, who would be the Savior of the world.

God the Father sent his Son, Jesus Christ, to save humankind, to make known God's love for all people and to establish the **New Covenant**, open to all humanity. Jesus was the Messiah and Savior and he fulfilled that mission by what he preached, by how he lived and treated people, by how he died and rose again to raise up all

HOUSE DESTROYED BY HURRICANE SANDY, UNION BEACH, NEW JERSEY

humankind. Jesus Christ came to save all of humanity from sin, to show us the way to God, and to make it possible for us to live as the People of God. Through Jesus, God the Father extended the promise of divine love to all people in the world. After Jesus' Death and Resurrection and Ascension, God the Father sent the Holy Spirit in the name of Jesus to continue Jesus' work of saving the world. Now, through the Holy Spirit, we receive the power, or **grace**, to live as disciples of Jesus, who is 'the Way' that he modeled and made possible for us to live. And God now sends us out to bring the Good News of his saving love to everyone until the end of time.

ABRAHAM TRAVELS TO THE LAND OF CANAAN | GUSTAVE DORÉ

GOD REVEALED HIS PLAN TO ABRAHAM

The Bible tells us that God invited Abraham to have faith in him and revealed to Abraham that he had chosen him to be the founder of a great nation, who would be God's people. God challenged Abraham to leave his country and his home and travel with his wife Sarah and family to the land that God would show them. That land was Canaan, later known as Palestine, and today is in Israel. God promised to make the descendants of Abraham and Sarah into a great nation, a people whom God would bless.

The Book of Genesis says that 'Abram [his original name] went as the Lord had told him' (Genesis 12:4). For his great act of faith—setting out for the unknown at God's command—God later said to Abraham:

You shall be the ancestor of a multitude of nations.... I will establish my covenant between me and you, and your offspring after you throughout their generations, for an everlasting covenant, to be God to you and your offspring after you.

—Genesis 17:4–7

This was how the Covenant between God and the Israelites (the **Hebrews**) was first established. The Israelites promised to obey God's law and, in return, they would be God's own chosen people. (You will find the full story of Abraham and Sarah in the Book of Genesis, chapters 12 through 25.)

WHAT ABOUT YOU PERSONALLY?

- ⊙ Do you ever feel that God is calling you to do some great (or small) act of faith? What might this be?
- ⊙ What can you learn from Abraham and Sarah about responding to God's invitations in your life?
- ⊙ Abraham and Sarah were first migrants and then immigrants in the land of Canaan. Many of our ancestors were also migrants and immigrants, leaving their homeland and traveling to this country in search of a livelihood, safety, adventure, challenge and prosperity.
- ⊙ Share any stories you know of such courageous people in your family history. How did *their* faith sustain them?
- ⊙ What can you learn from their story as well as from the story of Abraham and Sarah?

GOD CALLS MOSES AT THE BURNING BUSH | PFARRKIRCHE ST. JOHANNES DER TÄUFER, HAMBUCH, GERMANY

GOD CALLED MOSES TO LEAD THE ISRAELITES TO THE PROMISED LAND

The descendants of Abraham and Sarah eventually had to flee from Canaan, the land to which God had brought them, and were forced into slavery by the Egyptians. God called Moses to lead the people out of slavery and on to freedom in their own land once again. God revealed to Moses that he, the God of Abraham, alone is the only living and true God and that the oppressed Israelite slaves were God's chosen people. Opposed to all injustice, God would intervene to set them free.

God called to him out of the bush, 'Moses, Moses!' And he said, 'Here I am.' Then he said, 'Come no closer. Remove the sandals from your feet, for the place on which you are standing is holy ground. . . . I have observed the misery of my people who are in Egypt. . . . I will send you to Pharaoh to bring my people, the Israelites, out of Egypt.'

—Exodus 3:4–5, 7, 10

God called the scattered tribes of Israelites under Moses' leadership. While they were on their journey through the desert, God appeared to Moses on Mount Sinai, revealed the Ten Commandments written on two tablets of stone, and entered into the Covenant with them. (Read the full story of Moses in the Book of Exodus, chapters 2 through to 20.)

Later, when the Israelites had settled again in the land God promised them, Canaan, they sometimes were not faithful to their promise to live the Covenant. Like us, they often neglected the Ten Commandments that God had revealed to Moses. God called the prophets to remind the Israelites that God never stopped loving them and to call them to return to living the Covenant more faithfully. We still need to hear the call of the great prophets of the Bible today.

OVER TO YOU

⊙ Why do we still need to hear the message of the prophets in our world today?

JESUS, THE MESSIAH, THE CLIMAX OF GOD'S ACTION AND REVELATION IN HISTORY

Through the prophets God continued to promise to send a Savior, a Messiah (meaning 'anointed one'), to establish the New Covenant. At the time appointed by God, God the Father sent **Jesus**, God's own Son. Jesus, the Incarnate Word of God, is the fulfillment and summation of God's Revelation.

Through his actions, through the way he lived, through the way he treated people, through the words he spoke, through how he died and rose from the dead—through the mysteries of his whole life on earth—Jesus Christ (the Greek for 'anointed' is *Christos*) revealed what God is like and how the people were to live as God's People.

The central message of Jesus' life and preaching was the announcement and inauguration of the coming of the **Kingdom of God**. (See Mark 1:14–15.) This Kingdom will be realized only at the end of time when Jesus comes again in glory. Jesus' disciples prepare for the coming of the Kingdom by doing God's will 'on *earth* as it is in heaven'.

The supreme law of God's Kingdom, or reign, is the **Great Commandment** (see Matthew 22:34–40, Mark 12:28–31 and Luke 10:25–28). In this Commandment Jesus combined the Old Testament teaching of the Law of Love that is succinctly revealed in Deuteronomy 6:5 and Leviticus 19:18. This Law of the Old Covenant has been fulfilled in Jesus Christ, who taught, 'Do not think that I have come to abolish the law or the prophets; I have come not to abolish but to fulfill. For truly I tell you, until heaven and earth pass away, not one letter, not one stroke of a letter,

will pass from the law until all is accomplished' (Matthew 5:17–18).

Jesus is the definitive Word of God, the fulfillment and summation of God's Revelation. He is the climax of God's saving action in history; in Jesus God 'has said everything; there will be no other word than this one' (CCC, no. 65). His whole life revealed the way we are to live this Great Commandment. We are to love God, others and ourselves as Jesus lived the Law of Love.

The 'Law of Love' first revealed in the Old Testament and fulfilled in Jesus is this: We are first and above all to love God with all our mind, heart and strength. Our love of God flows over and moves us to love our neighbor and ourselves as God himself does. The First Letter of John teaches:

Beloved, let us love one another, because love is from God; everyone who loves is born of God

ST. JOHN THE EVANGELIST | LINDISFARNE GOSPELS, 7TH–8TH CENTURY

> # Beloved, let us love one another, because love is from God.
>
> 1 JOHN 4:7

and knows God. Whoever does not love does not know God, for God is love. God's love was revealed among us in this way: God sent his only Son into the world so that we might live through him. In this is love, not that we loved God but that he loved us and sent his Son to be the atoning sacrifice for our sins. Beloved, since God loved us so much, we also ought to love one another. No one has ever seen God; if we love one another, God lives in us, and his love is perfected in us.

By this we know that we abide in him and he in us, because he has given us of his Spirit.

—1 John 4:7–13

THE RESURRECTION | MOSAIC IN RED SQUARE, MOSCOW, RUSSIA

Throughout his public ministry, Jesus constantly called disciples to follow his *new* 'way' of living as the People of God. Surely there could be no greater commandment than the Law of Love fully revealed in the Incarnate Son of God, Jesus Christ. The **New Commandment** that Christ gives is *new* precisely because it is given by Christ, who is the Son of God made man. The Church sums up this teaching:

Jesus makes **charity** [love] the *new commandment* [see John 13:34]. By loving his own 'to the end' [John 13:1], he makes manifest the Father's love which he receives. By loving one another, the disciples imitate the love of Jesus which they themselves receive. Whence Jesus says: 'As the Father has loved me, so have I loved you; abide in my love.' And again: 'This is my commandment, that you love one another as I have loved you' [John 15:9, 12].

—CCC, no. 1823

THE WORK OF THE CHURCH BEGINS

After Jesus' Death, Resurrection and Ascension, his disciples carried on his saving mission, spreading his Good News of God's love. This is what the risen Christ had instructed them to do: 'Go therefore and make disciples of all nations' (Matthew 28:19).

At Pentecost the Holy Spirit descended upon the Apostles and other disciples, about 120 of them, including Mary the Mother of Jesus and the women disciples. (Read the story in Acts of the Apostles 1 and 2.) From there St. Peter and the other Apostles, anointed by the Holy Spirit, began the work of the Church, which was born 'primarily of Christ's total self-giving for our salvation . . . on the cross' (CCC, no. 766). For almost two thousand years now, that work has continued, proclaiming that the Church is the instrument—the sacrament of salvation—of God's saving work in Jesus Christ in the world.

To fulfill their exalted mission, 'the apostles were endowed by Christ with a special outpouring of the Holy Spirit coming upon them, and by the imposition of hands they passed on to their auxiliaries the gift of the Spirit, which is transmitted down to our day

Do you think it is possible to live the Great Commandment faithfully?

through episcopal consecration' [Vatican II, *Constitution on the Church*, no. 21; see also Acts of the Apostles 1:8, 2:4; John 20:22–23, 1 Timothy 4:14, 2 Timothy 1:6–7].

—CCC, no. 1556

WHAT ABOUT YOU PERSONALLY?

- What do you think you can learn from this brief summary of our 'salvation story' for your own life today?
- What do you honestly think of the Great Commandment?
- Do you think it is possible to live it faithfully? Why or why not?
- What challenges does it present to you? How willing are you to meet those challenges?

PREPARATION FOR THE PRAYER REFLECTION

Read the following ancient prayer from the early Church and then try to select an appropriate piece of music to accompany it during the Prayer Reflection at the end of this chapter. Alternatively, find another song or hymn or poem you know that expresses the power of your faith in the living risen Christ for your life today. Bring it in tomorrow and the class can select one to use in the Prayer Reflection.

[Jesus Christ], though he was in the form of God,
   did not regard equality with God
   as something to be exploited,
but emptied himself,
   taking the form of a slave,
   being born in human likeness.
And being found in human form,
   he humbled himself
   and became obedient to the point of death—
   even death on a cross.

Therefore God also highly exalted him
   and gave him the name
   that is above every name,
so that at the name of Jesus
   every knee should bend,
   in heaven and on earth and under the earth,
and every tongue should confess
   that Jesus Christ is Lord,
   to the glory of God the Father.

—Philippians 2:6–11

Poetry, music and song as storehouses of meaning

MUSIC AND SONG

It is often said that our music and song is a reflection of our emotional history. Old tunes remind us about the way we or our people felt in the past. Sometimes these songs can last for centuries because the feelings are so deep and so powerful that they go beyond individuals, and are remembered and sung by people of many generations.

REFLECT AND DISCUSS

⊙ Name some songs that express the way you feel now.
⊙ Are there songs that remind you of things that happened to you in the past? Explain.
⊙ What songs reflect events, struggles and feelings throughout American history?

One of the most powerful veins of feeling ever expressed in song is found in the music of black slaves in the plantations of the Old South. Drawing on their African tradition, combined with the hope and promise they found in the Bible story, they sang the gospel songs that have echoed through the years as anthems of liberation: 'We shall overcome. . . . '; 'Swing low, sweet chariot, coming for to carry me home. . . . '; 'Let my people go. . . . '. Can you name any more of these 'hymns of hope' that we call spirituals?

Then, after the Civil War, the dejection of the black population was expressed in the blues music of the early twentieth century. As white people came to share their experiences during the Great Depression, they also took up singing the blues. Hip hop and rap music provided an outlet and a 'voice' for disenfranchised youth when it started in the 1970s.

DAVID DICTATING THE PSALMS | 10TH/11TH-CENTURY IVORY

The Book of Psalms in the Bible is a record of the prayer and pain, the hopes and joys of the Israelite people through the centuries

THE PSALMS

The Book of Psalms in the Bible is a record of the prayer and pain, the hopes and joys of the Israelite people through the centuries. There are psalms of praise to God, psalms of thanksgiving, psalms imploring God for help and deliverance, psalms of hope and resistance, and psalms expressing sorrow for sin. Psalms were usually sung by people gathered into two groups, back and forth, side to side, one group being answered by the other. This was a characteristic style of Jewish singing. The Psalms are still sung or recited in this way today in monasteries or where people gather to pray the 'Liturgy of the Hours'. Listen to the following quotations from a few psalms. As you listen, be attentive to what they might be saying to your life today.

My God, my God, why have you forsaken me?
    Why are you so far from helping me, from
        the words of my groaning?
In you our ancestors trusted;
    they trusted, and you delivered them.
To you they cried, and were saved;
    in you they trusted, and were not put to shame.
                        —Psalm 22:1, 4–5

May the God of Jacob grant you your heart's
    desire,
    and fulfill all your plans.
May we shout for joy over your victory,
    and in the name of our God set up our
        banners.
May the Lord fulfill all your petitions.
                        —Psalm 20:4–5

O God, guard me as the apple of your eye;
    hide me in the shadow of your wings,
from the wicked who despoil me,
    my deadly enemies who surround me.
                        —Psalm 17:8–9

Be mindful of your mercy, O LORD, and of your
        steadfast love,
    for they have been from of old.
Do not remember the sins of my youth or my
        transgressions;
    according to your steadfast love remember
        me,
    for your goodness' sake, O LORD!
                        —Psalm 25:6–7

Have mercy on me, O God,
    according to your steadfast love;
according to your abundant mercy
    blot out my transgressions.
Wash me thoroughly from my iniquity,
    and cleanse me from my sin.

—Psalm 51:1–2

O LORD, you have searched me and you know
    me.
You know when I sit down and when I rise up;
    you discern my thoughts from far away.
For it was you who formed my inward parts;
    you knit me together in my mother's womb.
I praise you, for I am fearfully and wonderfully
    made.

—Psalm 139:1–2, 13–14

REFLECTIVE EXERCISE

◉ Which of these psalms connects best with your own feelings about life and about God at this time? What does it say to your heart? How will you respond? Explain.

◉ Find that psalm in the Bible and read the rest of it. You might like to write a version of it in your own words.

AMAZING GRACE

One of the most famous songs through the Civil War period, on both sides, was a hymn called 'Amazing Grace', written by John Newton. The hymn was directly connected with the fight for the emancipation of slaves. 'Amazing Grace' expresses the emotions of one snatched from destruction by the saving action of God—God's amazing *grace* at work in the world.

Read carefully and meditate on the words of this famous hymn.

ST. CECILIA: PATRON SAINT OF MUSICIANS AND CHURCH MUSIC

I will sing a new song to you, O God; upon a ten-stringed harp I will play to you

PSALM 144:9

Amazing Grace

JOHN NEWTON (1725-1807)

Amazing grace, how sweet the sound
that sav'd a wretch like me!
I once was lost, but now am found,
was blind, but now I see.

'Twas grace that taught my heart to fear,
and grace my fears reliev'd;
how precious did that grace appear,
the hour I first believ'd!

Thro' many dangers, toils and snares,
I have already come;
'tis grace has brought me safe thus far,
and grace will lead me home.

The Lord has promis'd good to me,
his word my hope secures;
he will my shield and portion be,
as long as life endures.

Yes, when this flesh and heart shall fail,
and mortal life shall cease;
I shall possess, within the veil,
a life of joy and peace.

The earth shall soon dissolve like snow,
the sun forbear to shine;

but God, who call'd me here below,
will be forever mine.

This verse was added later to the original wording:

When we've been there ten thousand years,
bright shining like the sun,
we've no less days to sing God's praise
than when we first begun.

OVER TO YOU

- Why do you think Newton described grace as 'amazing'?
- How do you experience the power of God's amazing grace at work now in your own life?

ACTIVITY

- Listen to a recording of the hymn 'Amazing Grace'. Or better, sing it yourself with your group.

JUDGE AND ACT

REFLECT ON WHAT YOU HAVE LEARNED

Since the beginning of time, people have wondered about life and its meaning, and whether God exists; and if so, what kind of God and what this means for our own lives.

In this chapter we reminded ourselves once again of the wonderful good news that God has revealed the answers to these ultimate questions; God has chosen to make known to us, through both ordinary and extraordinary events and people, who he is and what our lives are all about.

Reflect on what this means for you personally.

DECISION TIME!

- Looking back over the past week of study and our summary overview of the Bible, choose three of the great truths from God's Revelation that appeal to you.
- First, what are they and why did you choose them?
- What are the hopes and challenges that they offer you?
- How can you take these truths to heart and allow them to permeate your daily life from here on?

CLASS DISCUSSION

The Bible asks us to take care of what the Old Testament calls 'the stranger in the land' and reminds us that we are all immigrants, in one way or another. (The word 'stranger' in the Old Testament has the same meaning as 'immigrant' today.)

- If there are students in the class whose family immigrated to the United States, either recently or in the distant past, talk with them about the experience and the circumstances surrounding it. The following questions may be useful:
  - Where did the family come from?
  - What is their history?
  - Why did they come?
  - What religious community do they belong to?
  - Where do they worship?
  - What legal and social obstacles do they face?
  - To what extent do they feel accepted/at home in our country?
  - What can we do to make them feel welcome and included?

- Follow this with a general discussion of how best to welcome new arrivals to the country, emphasizing what each person will do to help.

The story of St. Frances Xavier Cabrini

Frances Saveria Cabrini (1850–1917), also called Mother Cabrini, was the first American citizen to be canonized by the Catholic Church.

Frances was born into a large family in Sant'Angelo Lodigiano, Lombardy, Italy in 1850. She was determined from childhood to become a missionary and she took her vows in 1877, adding Xavier to her name to honor the Jesuit saint, Francis Xavier.

Frances became the mother superior of the House of Providence orphanage in Codogno, where she taught. In 1880 the orphanage was closed and Frances, along with six others, founded the Missionary Sisters of the Sacred Heart (MSC), of which she was mother superior until her death. The order established seven homes and a free school and nursery in its first five years.

In 1889 Pope Leo XIII sent Mother Cabrini to New York City to work among Italian immigrants. There she founded the orphanage which today is located in West Park on the river Hudson and known as St. Cabrini Home. After this, Mother Cabrini embarked upon a tireless crisscrossing of the world, establishing a network of educational, health care and social service institutions for needy immigrants—institutions that today continue to provide services for people of all faiths and backgrounds. By 1917 her congregation numbered over 1,500 nuns in eight countries. In all, Mother Cabrini founded sixty-seven houses devoted to education, nursing and the care of orphans.

Mother Cabrini was naturalized as a US citizen in 1909. She died at age sixty-seven in Columbus Hospital in Chicago, Illinois. She was beatified in 1938 and canonized in 1946.

St. Frances Xavier Cabrini is the patron saint of immigrants.

TALK IT OVER

⊙ What can you learn from St. Frances Xavier Cabrini's example about reaching out to those in need?

⊙ What do you find most inspirational in her story?

EXTEND A PERSONAL WELCOME

⊙ Consider how you, as a member of your school or parish community, could welcome someone who has recently arrived in your school or parish.

RESEARCH YOUR FAMILY'S HISTORY

⊙ Begin this research now, or at least start the questioning. Many people wait until it is too late before they decide to find out about their family's history!
A good place to start. . . .

⊙ Why not take a look at the story of your family and its connection with the Catholic Church; for example, the parishes your family has lived in, where you were baptized, made your First Holy Communion and so on. Your parents or grandparents will be able to answer many of your questions.

WHAT WILL YOU DO NOW?

- In light of what you have learned in this chapter, where do you stand now in your attitude toward the Bible? In your understanding of how it functions in your faith life? In your appreciation for it?

- Among the central messages of the Bible is that God is always faithful in his love for us and he cares deeply for our well-being. If you really try to take this Revelation to heart, what difference might it mean for your life and how you live it?

- Decide now: What role do you want the Bible to have in your life?

PRAYER REFLECTION

Pray the Sign of the Cross together.

LEADER
We will begin by listening to the words of the prayer from Philippians 2:6-11 (or the words of a poem or song the class has selected).

Following the reading:

LEADER
Let us ask the Holy Spirit to guide us through the heights and plains, the deserts and the mountains we experience in everyday life, as we reflect on Jesus' words of promise made shortly before his arrest, trial, and his suffering and death:

'I will see you again, and your hearts will rejoice, and no one will take your joy from you.'
—John 16:22

(Pause)

LEADER
Let us pray for the grace to cherish the Bible and to place it at the heart of our Catholic faith. *(Pause)*
May it help us to see God's presence in our lives and in our world. *(Pause)*
We pray for the wisdom to hear what God is revealing to us through the Bible and at every moment of our lives. *(Pause)*
We pray for the courage to follow the promptings of the Holy Spirit and to live as disciples of Jesus, the glorified Lord and Savior, who will come again in glory.

Let us pray for the grace to cherish the Bible and to place it at the heart of our Catholic faith.

We ask this through our Lord, Jesus Christ, who lives and reigns for ever and ever.

ALL
Amen.

Pray the Sign of the Cross together.

CHAPTER 4

The Bible: The Inspired Word of God

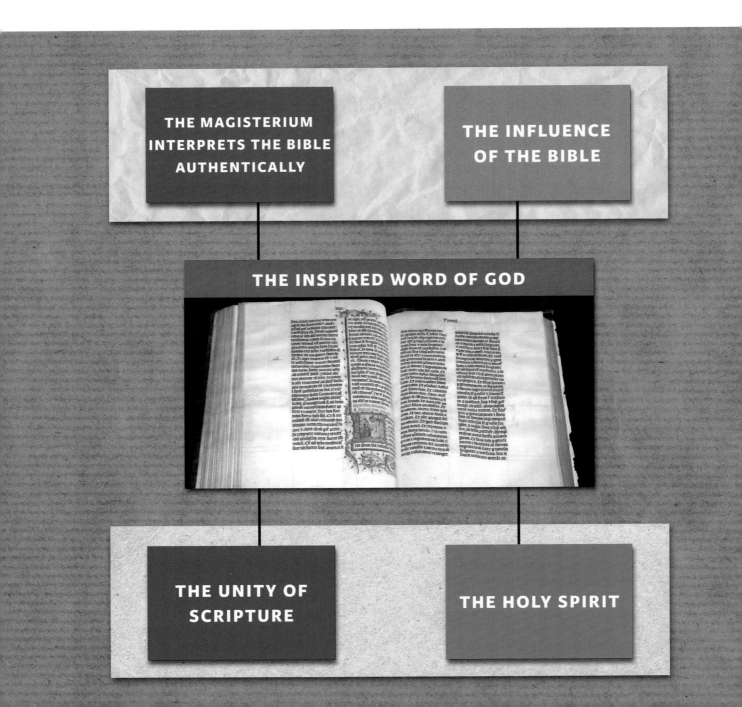

THE MAGISTERIUM INTERPRETS THE BIBLE AUTHENTICALLY

THE INFLUENCE OF THE BIBLE

THE INSPIRED WORD OF GOD

THE UNITY OF SCRIPTURE

THE HOLY SPIRIT

IN THIS CHAPTER WE STUDY WHAT IT MEANS TO say that the Bible is the inspired written Word of God. We also learn how the Bible can have a very positive and life-giving influence on us.

SACRED TEXTS

Jews
THE TANAKH

Muslims
THE QUR'AN

Christians
THE BIBLE

Faith Focus: These teachings of the Catholic Church are the primary focus of the doctrinal content presented in this chapter:

⊙ Sacred Scripture is the inspired written Word of God spoken through the words of human beings.

⊙ The Bible firmly, faithfully and without error teaches the truth that God, for the sake of our salvation, wished to see confided to the Sacred Scriptures.

⊙ We must strive to understand the language the human authors used, and be attentive to what they truly wanted to affirm and to what God wanted to reveal by their words.

⊙ The task of interpreting the Word of God authentically has been entrusted solely to the Magisterium of the Church.

⊙ Sacred Scripture and Sacred Tradition make up a single sacred deposit of the Word of God.

⊙ Jesus Christ is center and heart of Sacred Scripture and the fullness of Revelation.

Discipleship Formation: As a result of studying this chapter and discovering the meaning of the faith of the Catholic Church for your life, you should be better able to:

⊙ recognize moments of inspiration in your life;

⊙ come to a deeper sense of the Bible as the Word of God;

⊙ develop greater confidence in your ability to find meaning in the Bible;

⊙ have a deeper respect for the Bible;

⊙ strengthen your commitment to read the Bible frequently and regularly with an awareness of its importance for your life.

Scripture References: These Scripture references are quoted or referred to in this chapter:
OLD TESTAMENT: **Psalms** 9:1–2, 9–10, 18; **Isaiah** 40:4–5
NEW TESTAMENT: **Matthew** 5:5; **Luke** 4:16–21, 9:48, 25:27; **John** 15:5

Faith Glossary: Familiarize yourself with the meaning of these key faith terms. Definitions are found in the Glossary: **Apostolic Tradition, Bible, Divine Inspiration, Gospel/Gospels, Holy Spirit, inerrancy (of the Bible), inspiration, literary genre, Magisterium, Word of God**

Faith Word: Magisterium; inerrancy; Divine Inspiration
Learn by Heart: From Vatican II, *Constitution on Divine Revelation*, no. 13
Learn by Example: Dr. Martin Luther King, Jr.

What does it mean to be inspired?

In the following story, a teenager recalls how he felt a special influence helping him in a challenging situation.

Farewell Chuck

Tom was quite nervous as he made his way to the podium to speak at the memorial service for his friend, Chuck. Chuck and Tom had been best friends since early grade school and their families had become friends as well in recent years. Now Chuck was dead, after a long battle with leukemia, and Tom had been nominated to speak about him on behalf of his class.

Tom glanced at his notes and began to speak falteringly. . . . 'Chuck Falwell was a great guy . . . he was the best friend anyone could have . . . and now he's dead.'

Tom could feel the emotion welling up in his voice and he didn't know if he could continue. Then suddenly, he could see Chuck's smiling face in front of his eyes, and some of his friend's last fun posts to the blog he had set up in his final months crossed Tom's mind. He couldn't repress a smile and, without further hesitation, he knew what he wanted to say.

Tom went on to speak for a full ten minutes, recalling in vivid detail the aspects of Chuck's personality that had made him such a well-loved and popular character. He spoke of Chuck's bravery during his illness and how he was always more concerned about hearing his friends' stories or troubles than dwelling on his own. In spite of his illness, Chuck's blog had never failed to entertain, and his courage in the face of death had helped everyone to come to terms with his loss.

After Tom's speech, the applause was heartfelt and sustained.

The school principal, Mr. Matthews, was warm in his congratulations: 'You really brought Chuck to life there, Tom.'

'To be honest, Sir,' Tom replied, 'it felt as if I was inspired by Chuck. Does that sound stupid?'

Later that evening, talking to another friend, Tom tried to analyze what had happened: 'One moment I was tongue-tied, and then the words just seemed to come from somewhere . . . it was as if someone was helping me. Could it have been Chuck?'

REFLECT AND DISCUSS

- What do you think Tom meant by the word 'inspired'?
- Does this story remind you of something similar in your own life? If so, share your story.
- Most of us, when faced with a task that involves writing or composing original material, find it difficult to come up with ideas and to express them articulately. Even professional authors say that at times they suffer from 'writer's block', when absolutely no ideas will come into their head. But, just as happened for Tom in the story, they invariably find that something triggers the ideas to begin to flow again, and they feel 'inspired' to write with renewed energy and enthusiasm. Have you ever had a similar experience—in speaking, in writing, or maybe in some kind of activity, such as on the sports field?
- What did you write or do when you were 'inspired' like that?
- Where do you think such **inspiration** might come from?

OUR CHURCH TEACHES THAT THE BIBLE IS THE INSPIRED WORD OF GOD

The Catholic Church teaches that the **Bible** can influence us precisely because its sacred authors were inspired by God. As the Second Vatican Council summarized:

> Holy [M]other [C]hurch . . . accepts as sacred . . . the books of the Old and New Testaments, whole and entire, with all their parts, on the grounds that, written under the inspiration of the [H]oly Spirit, they have God as their author, and have been handed on as such to the [C]hurch itself.
> —*Constitution on Divine Revelation*, no. 11

In other words, the Church teaches that the words of the Bible are the words God wants us to hear. This means that God speaks to us in human language, and in order to hear accurately what God is saying we must strive to understand the language the sacred authors used. The next paragraph in the *Constitution on Divine Revelation* states that, because this is so, we must interpret the words of the Bible very carefully. The *Catechism of the Catholic Church* puts it thus:

What do we mean by the word 'inspired'?

The reader must be attentive to what the human authors truly wanted to affirm, and to what God wanted to reveal to us by their words.

—CCC, no. 109

To truly understand what God is trying to teach us, we need to be open to the guidance of the **Holy Spirit** and the guidance of the Church. The Church guides us through the **Magisterium**—the living teaching office of the Church—and through the living Tradition of the Church. The *Catechism* states:

The task of interpreting the **Word of God** authentically has been entrusted solely to the Magisterium of the Church, that is, to the Pope and to the bishops in communion with him.

—CCC, no. 100

(You will learn more about the Magisterium in chapter 7.)

Magisterium

The living teaching office, or teaching authority, of the Catholic Church, made up of the Pope and bishops, guided by the Holy Spirit, whose responsibility and task is to give authentic interpretation to the Word of God contained in both Sacred Scripture and Sacred Tradition. 'The Magisterium ensures the Church's fidelity to the teaching of the Apostles in matters of faith and morals' (CCC, Glossary).

PEOPLE THE WORLD OVER HAVE BEEN INFLUENCED BY THE BIBLE

The following account tells of how God, through the Bible, influenced prisoners in Vietnam to survive appalling conditions, even when they did not have a Bible on hand!

The Bible provides solace

American prisoners of war in Vietnam knew moments of fear and darkness. Post-war interviews reveal that faith played a big role in their ability to survive. One prisoner said, 'Without God, I would not have been able to survive.' When asked by the interviewer whether God had really helped him, the prisoner said, 'No, not merely helped. I mean it when I say I could not have made it without God pulling me through.' Other prisoners

AMERICAN SOLDIERS IN VIETNAM, 1966

described worship services in the prisons, composed of Bible readings put together by the collective memory of the prisoners.

WHAT ABOUT YOU PERSONALLY?

⊙ Have you ever read anything in the Bible that had a lasting impact on you or that influenced you to act in a particular way? If so, you might like to share your story.

In this chapter we will explore how the Bible is the inspired Word of God and how the sacred authors received their inspiration.

The Bible is the inspired Word of God

OPENING CONVERSATION

Our society takes oaths very seriously. To tell a lie under oath is 'perjury', which is both a serious crime and a sin contrary to the Second and Eighth Commandments. Hence, court witnesses swear on the Bible that their testimony is true. During a court case, a witness is called to the witness stand and told by the clerk to place a hand on the Bible and repeat the following words: 'I solemnly swear that I shall tell the truth, the whole truth and nothing but the truth, so help me God.'

- Why do you think people swear an oath upon the Bible and ask for the help of God in giving testimony?
- Do they feel any different, do you think, after they have sworn that their testimony will be true and asked for God's help? Why might this be the case?

WHAT MAKES THE BIBLE THE WORD OF GOD?

The Bible is a sacred and unique text. The Church teaches that the people who wrote the Bible were inspired by God and, therefore, that the Bible is the Word of God spoken through the words of human beings. This means that in matters of the truths of God's Revelation for our salvation, the Bible is without error because God is its author. This quality of the Bible is known as **inerrancy**.

Since, therefore, all that the inspired authors, or sacred writers, affirm should be regarded as affirmed by the [H]oly Spirit, we must acknowledge that the books of scripture, firmly, faithfully and without error, teach that truth which God, for the sake of our salvation, wished to see confided to the sacred scriptures.

—*Constitution on Divine Revelation*, no. 11

To say that the authors were inspired means that the Holy Spirit assisted them so that they wrote faithfully and without error the truth that God wanted them to write. This does not mean that the authors were simply secretaries, recording the words God dictated directly from Heaven; or were like robots, with no individual thoughts and feelings of their own. Of course, the authors' own ideas and the influences of their time and cultures came through in what they wrote. However, under the inspiration of the Holy Spirit, their words were also God's Word, conveying the truths we need to know for our salvation. The Bible could be said, therefore, to

The Bible is the Word of God spoken through the words of human beings

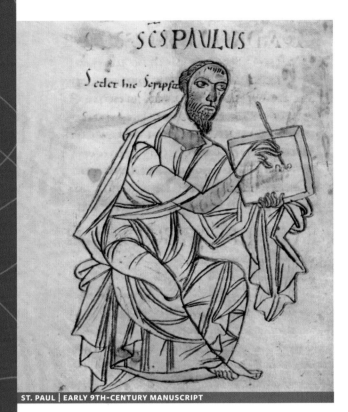

ST. PAUL | EARLY 9TH-CENTURY MANUSCRIPT

have two sets of authors: God and the human writers of the Bible. The Church states it this way:

> To compose the sacred books, God chose certain men who, all the while he employed them in this task, made full use of their powers and faculties so that, though he acted in them and by them, it was as true authors that they consigned to writing whatever he wanted written, and no more.
>
> —*Constitution on Divine Revelation*, no. 11

The biblical authors were people of their time and culture, with personal and social points of view, insights and limitations, expertise and ignorance. They probably struggled to compose their sentences and create their paragraphs, compile their stories and marshal their arguments, exactly as any other writer would do. The biblical authors may not have received any visions from God (though a few of them, like Isaiah, Ezekiel, St. John and St. Paul, did).

The human authors of the Bible were limited by the knowledge that was available to them in their time and in their culture to communicate God's Word. For example, the people who wrote the Book of Genesis, telling the story of Creation, did not have the benefit of the scientific instruments or experimentation that we have today. They did not know that Earth was a sphere turning on its axis around its sun, nor did they have the advantage of any of the scientific discoveries that have since been made about the universe. In fact, the writers of the Book of Genesis thought that the earth was flat. But their purpose in writing the Creation story was not to convey scientific truths. What they wanted people to know was that the world and everything in it came from the creative action of God, that nothing in existence came into being without God. They wrote from the point of view of faith in God and in the creative work of God. What they wrote was the great truths of faith that God wanted us to know about the divine origins of the earth and everything on it. If we remember that the Bible is meant to teach us great truths of faith, then we will find no conflict between science and religion, and between faith and reason.

REFLECT AND DISCUSS

- ⊙ In light of what you have learned so far, explain what it is that makes the Bible unique and so different from any other book.
- ⊙ How does the Bible differ from a scientific text in terms of the knowledge it seeks to impart?
- ⊙ What types of truth might you look for in the Bible that you would not find in a scientific or historical text, and vice versa?

WHERE DID THE BIBLICAL AUTHORS FIND THEIR INSPIRATION?

God is the author of the Bible. It is God's own Word to us. The Holy Spirit inspired the human biblical authors to write down accurately what God intended to reveal. All the sacred authors, whether they were Jewish or members of the early Church, were members of communities of faith, God's people. It was the Holy Spirit who guided them to reflect on the lived faith of their faith communities to come to know what God wished to reveal. In other words, the Holy Spirit inspired the sacred authors within the lived faith of the People of God.

While they could be mistaken about medicine and other forms of science, about the exact details of geography and historical events as we have come to understand these realities today, the sacred human authors of Sacred Scripture, through the grace of the Holy Spirit, accurately and without error passed on in their writings what God wanted to reveal for our salvation. This included the events that they had personally witnessed or that had been handed on to them by the community through the oral tradition of God's people.

The biblical authors had the spiritual wisdom that we need in order to live as the People of God. God the Holy Spirit filled them with this wisdom. The same Spirit is present today with and in the Church, whose Magisterium has the responsibility to interpret Revelation authentically. The same Spirit invites all the faithful to open their minds and hearts to hear and respond to the living Word of God.

TALK IT OVER

⊙ How do you think the fact that the biblical authors lived in communities of faith helped them to be inspired by the Holy Spirit?

WHAT ABOUT YOU PERSONALLY?

⊙ What do you understand by the phrase 'open to God's grace'? (You might like to look again at the definition of 'grace' in chapter 3.)
⊙ How 'open' are you to God's grace and Revelation? Explain.

FAITH WORDS

Inerrancy

Because the authors of Sacred Scripture were inspired by God, the saving meaning or truth found in the Scriptures cannot be wrong.

—*United States Catholic Catechism for Adults*, 516

Divine Inspiration

'Divine Inspiration' is the term the Catholic Church uses to describe the gift of the Holy Spirit given to the human writers of the Bible, so that, using their talents and abilities, they wrote the truth that God wanted people to know for their salvation. (See CCC, no. 137.)

EZEKIEL'S VISION | GUSTAVE DORÉ

The Bible speaks to us today just as it spoke to the generations of old

OPENING CONVERSATION

How would you go about reading the Bible? Where might you look for help in interpreting the sacred texts? Or do you think you could get through them on your own? What problems might you encounter?

UNDERSTANDING THE BIBLE TODAY

Today, we need help to understand what the Bible is actually saying to us about God, about his work in the world, and especially about how we are to live as the People of God, following the 'way' of Jesus Christ.

The best help we have for interpreting the Bible is the guidance of the whole faith community, the Church, guided by her teaching authority, the Magisterium. In other words, we must 'read the Scripture within "the living Tradition of the whole Church" ' (CCC, no. 112).

The *Catechism* reaffirms this traditional teaching of the Church by quoting the *Constitution on Divine Revelation:*

'The task of giving an authentic interpretation of the Word of God, whether in its written form or in the form of Tradition, has been entrusted to the living teaching office of the Church alone. Its authority in this matter is exercised in the name of Jesus Christ' [*Constitution on Divine Revelation*, no. 10]. This means that the task of interpretation has been entrusted to the bishops in communion with the successor of Peter, the Bishop of Rome.
—CCC, no. 85

The Church is guided by a long tradition of faith in how she interprets the Bible for us today. As the Second Vatican Council made clear: 'Tradition and scripture make up a single sacred deposit of the Word of God' (*Constitution on Divine Revelation*, no. 10). For this reason, 'both scripture and tradition must be accepted and honored with equal devotion and reverence' (*Constitution on Divine Revelation*, no. 9). And the

ST. PETER, BISHOP OF ROME | ÜBERWASSERKIRCHE, MÜNSTER, GERMANY

two should be interpreted within a Christian community. 'Sacred [T]radition, [S]acred [S]cripture and the [M]agisterium of the Church are so connected and associated that one of them cannot stand without the others. Working together, each in its own way under the action of the one [H]oly Spirit, they all contribute effectively to the salvation of souls' (*Constitution on Divine Revelation*, no. 10).

HOW DO SCHOLARS HELP IN THE TASK OF INTERPRETING THE BIBLE?

There are many biblical scholars who spend years studying the Bible and deciphering its words and meaning. This includes their study of the time and the place in which the different books of the Bible were written, taking into account the culture and customs that were in vogue back then. The various translations of the Bible are constantly being updated in light of new insights from such scholars. It is important to take all of these things into consideration when we are trying to discover the meaning of a particular story or passage in Scripture.

We must also consider the biblical author's intention if we are to interpret correctly a biblical text. This includes identifying who the biblical author was primarily addressing and what style of writing, or **literary genre**, the biblical author used. Biblical scholars help us to achieve these criteria. For example, Mark's account of the **Gospel**, which was the first account of the Gospel to be written, was primarily addressed to non-Jewish people who had become Christian. Because Mark's audience was not primarily Jewish, there are very few references to the Old Testament in his Gospel.

On the other hand, Matthew's Gospel, which was written about twenty years after Mark's, was addressed primarily to a Jewish audience. This would explain why his Gospel has many references to the Old Testament. It is important to know this detail about Matthew's Gospel. When trying to understand correctly what is being said in Scripture, we need to take into account who the writer was, the time in which he lived and the people for whom he was actually writing.

Matthew's extensive use of the Old Testament clearly shows the unity of the whole Scripture and passes on the **Apostolic Tradition** that Jesus

is the center and heart of Sacred Scripture and the fullness of Revelation. 'Through all the words of Sacred Scripture, God speaks only one single Word, his one Utterance in whom he expresses himself completely [see Hebrews 1:1–3]' (CCC, no. 102).

The biblical authors also used a variety of literary genres to pass on the truth of God's Revelation. The term 'literary genre' is used to describe different kinds of writing; for example, poetry, fiction, history, parables, hymns, sermons, letters and so on. Knowing the literary genre of a particular book or passage helps us both to discover the message the author intended to communicate and to interpret the meaning of God's Word, or Revelation, for us. Just as we would approach a novel with a different frame of mind than we would read a history or science book, so we read the biblical historical books in one way, and biblical poetry or parables or hymns or sermons or letters in another way. (We will discuss literary genres in greater detail in chapter 8.)

REFLECTIVE ACTIVITY

- Working in pairs, find and read the following biblical quotations: Psalm 9:9; Luke 25:27; Luke 9:48; John 15:5; Matthew 5:5.
- What does each one of these mean for people in today's world?

WHAT ABOUT YOU PERSONALLY?

- What do these quotations mean for you in your own life?

How should we honor our Sacred Scripture?

OPENING ACTIVITY

⊙ Form into groups of three. Each person in your group reads the information in one of the following boxes. (Make sure that each person reads a different one.) Study the text carefully and pick out the key points. When you have finished, put away your books and give each person a minute to 'teach' the main points they have learned to the other group members. Then take a look at your books again to check if anyone missed out on anything important or gave incorrect information.

The Qur'an

The Qur'an contains the sacred writings of Islam. Muslims have a deep reverence for the Qur'an. They show this reverence in a variety of ways. For example, the actual book of the Qur'an is generally not used in public worship as Muslims consider it to be too sacred. Muslims will never place the Qur'an on the floor, nor will they put another book on top of it. And because they believe that **Muhammad** received the Qur'an directly from God in Arabic, they believe that their sacred writings should not be translated. Muslims maintain that human beings need to learn Arabic to read the Qur'an and understand the sacred text. The word 'Qur'an', in fact, means 'recitation' and not 'writing'.

The Qur'an contains many stories from the Bible, from both the Old and New Testaments. Muslims honor and hold in high regard Jesus Christ and Mary, as well as Abraham and the patriarchs and prophets of Israel.

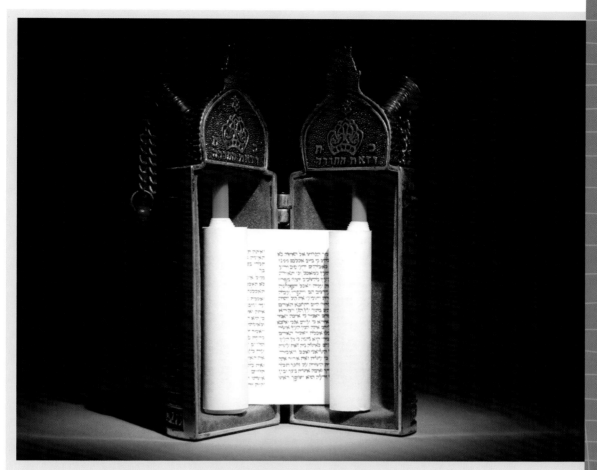

The Tanakh

The Tanakh contains the Scriptures the Jewish people believe and accept to be the inspired Word of God. For our Jewish brothers and sisters, their Sacred Scriptures are truly the Word of God that reveals God's purpose for them and how they are to live the Covenant that they and God have entered. These Scriptures, which are contained in the Old Testament of the Bible, are sacred to Jews as well as to Christians today, as they have been since apostolic times. The Bible, Old and New Testaments, is *one* expression of the Word of God. 'Christians venerate the Old Testament as true Word of God. The Church has always vigorously opposed the idea of rejecting the Old Testament under the pretext that the New has rendered it void' (CCC, no. 123), as the second-century Marcionism heresy taught.

Many Jews, especially when assembled in the synagogue for Sabbath worship, read their Scripture from scrolls (large rolls of paper) instead of from folios or books. They keep these scrolls in a sacred place and treat them with great care, reverence and respect, bringing them out to be read at their services. The scrolls are not printed but handwritten by a specially trained scribe known as a *sofer*. No mistakes are allowed. Any error in the writing means that the whole scroll must be started again. When a scroll gets old and tattered by age and use, it is burned, the ashes disposed of with dignity, and a new scroll is then commissioned.

Some Jews read their Scripture and pray only in the Hebrew language. They say that God spoke to them using the Hebrew language and that any translation would change the meaning of the Word of God.

The Bible

The Bible contains the Sacred Scriptures the Church accepts as the divinely inspired Word of God. The Church, since apostolic times, has taught that there is a unity between the Old Testament and the New Testament. 'All Sacred Scripture is but one book, and this one book is Christ, "because all divine Scripture speaks of Christ, and all divine Scripture is fulfilled in Christ" [Hugh of St. Victor, Sermon on Noah's Ark, 2, 8]' (CCC, no. 134). God is the author of all Sacred Scripture, the Old and New Testaments. He 'inspired its human authors; he acts in them and by means of them. He thus gives assurance that their writings teach without error his saving truth' (CCC, no. 136).

Catholics accept translations of the Bible that the Church has approved to be the divinely inspired written Word of God. Jesus, when he lived in Palestine more than two thousand years ago, spoke Aramaic. Since Greek was more widely understood and used than Aramaic in the early Church, Christians immediately saw the need for and accepted the translation of the Gospel into Greek. Such a translation could help the Church proclaim the Gospel more effectively and put Christians in touch with Jesus himself, the Eternal and Incarnate Word of God. (In chapter 6 we will explore in more detail both the development of the canon of Scripture, or the list of sacred writings accepted by the Catholic Church as divinely inspired, and the task of translating the Bible.)

All Sacred Scripture is but one book, and this one book is Christ, because all divine Scripture speaks of Christ, and all divine Scripture is fulfilled in Christ

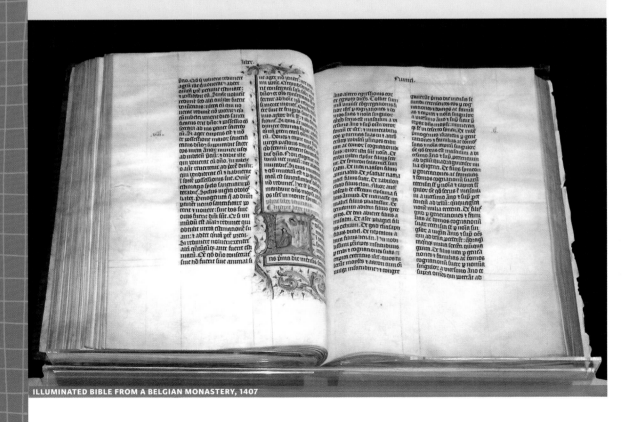

ILLUMINATED BIBLE FROM A BELGIAN MONASTERY, 1407

The Bible is the most read book in the world today

WHAT DO YOU THINK NOW?

⦿ What do you think of the way other religions respect the physical book of their sacred writings and the way many Catholics and other Christians treat theirs?

⦿ Do you think the Bible should be treated with respect? Why or why not?

⦿ How can you treat the actual book of the Bible with more care and respect?

⦿ How about your own Bible? Do you own one? If not, might you buy one?

THE MOST WIDELY READ BOOK IN THE WORLD

The Bible is the most read book in the world today, and not only among the two billion Christians. It was the first book to be printed using a printing press (by Johannes Gutenberg in the 1450s) and remains the most printed book of all time. An estimated 2.5 billion copies have been printed and distributed since 1815.

For Christians in the United States, the Bible plays a huge part in our lives and in our culture. Many of our social values are rooted in the Bible. Our respect for peace, our search for justice, our hope for universal neighborliness, our energy for human rights, our concern for the poor, our ambition for progress and continual improvement, our love of family, our interest in education, our delight in beauty, architecture, literature, music, art and drama, and many other aspects of our lives can be traced back to biblical values. Knowledge of the Bible helps us understand more completely our history and life in our country today—as well as the way we are called to take part in the global community. Continuing to integrate the teachings of the Bible, God's Word, into our lives will enrich our lives, now and for generations to come.

OVER TO YOU

⦿ The previous paragraph lists some of the values and aspects of life of Christians in the United States that have been directly influenced by the Bible. How many of your own beliefs and values are influenced by the Bible? Share some examples.

⦿ What difference do you think having these values makes to your life—to the type of person you are? To your relationships with other people? To your relationship with God?

SOME INTERESTING FACTS ABOUT THE BIBLE

⦿ The Bible is available, in all or in part, in 2,426 languages, accessible to 90 per cent of the world's population.

⦿ Over one hundred million copies of the Bible are sold or given away each year.

⦿ The first Bible written in the New World was not in English but in Algonquin (John Eliot's Indian Bible).

JUDGE AND ACT

REFLECT ON WHAT YOU HAVE LEARNED
- ⊙ Reflect on what you learned in this chapter about the Bible being the inspired Word of God. Think for a few moments about what it means to you to have access to such divinely inspired wisdom.

Sacred Scripture continues to influence people today, just as it influenced the prophets of old, Jews of Jesus' time, the early Church and Christians through the centuries. Let's read the story of one man who was influenced by the Bible to provide inspiring leadership.

LEARN BY EXAMPLE

An inspiring Christian of our time

On April 4, 1968, a thirty-nine-year-old man was shot in the neck on the balcony of the hotel in which he was staying. He died shortly afterward. This man had never held a gun himself, and, in 1964, was the youngest ever recipient of the Nobel Peace Prize. This man spoke with presidents and popes. He championed civil rights for his fellow men and women. His name was Dr. Martin Luther King, Jr. Dr. King delivered his most famous and inspiring speech, entitled 'I have a dream', on the steps of the Lincoln Memorial in Washington D.C. on August 28, 1963. Here is an excerpt from Dr. King's speech:

MARTIN LUTHER KING, JR: 'I HAVE A DREAM'; AUGUST 28, 1963

I have a dream today. I have a dream that one day every valley shall be exalted, every hill and mountain shall be made low, the rough places will be made plains, and the crooked places will be made straight, and the glory of the Lord shall be revealed, and all flesh shall see it together.

This will be the day when all of God's children will be able to sing with a new meaning 'My country, 'tis of thee, sweet land of liberty, of thee I sing. Land where my fathers died, land of the pilgrim's pride, from every mountainside, let freedom ring'.

Many Americans know Dr. King's speech very well, but not all are aware that it was inspired by the prophet Isaiah from the Old Testament:

Every valley shall be lifted up,
    and every mountain and hill be made low;
the uneven ground shall become level,
    and the rough places a plain.
Then the glory of the LORD shall be revealed,
    and all people shall see it together,
    for the mouth of the LORD has spoken.
—Isaiah 40:4–5

JUDGE AND DECIDE

⊙ Why do you think some people describe Dr. Martin Luther King, Jr. as a true prophet?

⊙ How did he influence people?

⊙ Where do you think he got much of his inspiration from and what evidence is there for this?

⊙ Can you think of any other famous people who were obviously influenced by the Bible? Share what you know about them with the rest of the group.

⊙ Why do you think the Bible has had such an influence on people through the ages?

WHAT ABOUT YOU PERSONALLY?

⊙ Will you open yourself to the inspiration that God is offering *you* through the Bible? How? (For example, you could listen more attentively to the readings from Scripture at next Sunday's Mass.)

⊙ Pause and decide on what is your own best dream for the world. Write it down.

TALK IT OVER

⊙ What most influences your dream?

⊙ What does it involve?

⊙ Is it realistic; that is, could it possibly happen some day?

⊙ Are the different dreams of individuals connected in some way? Explain.

⊙ Do you think that God has a dream for the world? What do think this is?

⊙ How could you participate in bringing about God's dream for all people and all creation?

RESPOND WITH YOUR FAMILY

⊙ Discuss what you understand as 'the American Dream' at this time. How closely does the American Dream correspond with what the Bible and the Church says is God's dream for the world?

JOURNAL EXERCISE

⊙ You have already reflected on what you think God's dream for the world might be. Now write what you think God's dream for *you* might be.

WHAT WILL YOU DO NOW?

⊙ Will you allow the Bible to be a special source of inspiration and revelation in your own life? How will you let this happen? Do you think you could make a decision to read a passage of the Bible every day? Most days?

⊙ Decide *now* how you will live into your dream for the world, into God's dream for the world, day by day. And where will you look for continued inspiration to sustain you?

LEARN BY HEART

The Bible is the Word of God expressed in human language.

BASED ON VATICAN II, *CONSTITUTION ON DIVINE REVELATION*, NO. 13

PRAYER REFLECTION

Pray the Sign of the Cross together.

READER
A reading from the holy Gospel according to Luke.

ALL
Glory to you, Lord.

READER
When he came to Nazareth, where he had been brought up, he went to the synagogue on the sabbath day, as was his custom. He stood up to read, and the scroll of the prophet Isaiah was given to him. He unrolled the scroll and found where it is written:
>'The Spirit of the Lord is upon me,
>>because he has anointed me
>>>to bring good news to the poor.
>>He has sent me to proclaim release to the captives
>>>and recovery of sight to the blind,
>>>>to let the oppressed go free,
>>to proclaim the year of the Lord's favor.'

And he rolled up the scroll, gave it back to the attendant, and sat down. The eyes of all in the synagogue were fixed upon him. Then he began to say to them, 'Today this scripture has been fulfilled in your hearing.'
>—Luke 4:16–21

This is the Gospel of the Lord.

ALL
Praise to you, Lord Jesus Christ.

LEADER
From Old Testament times, Jews and Christians have prayed in the words of the Psalms. Let us now pray together these verses from Psalm 9:

ALL
I will give thanks to the LORD with my whole heart;
>I will tell of all your wonderful deeds.

I will be glad and exult in you;
>I will sing praise to your name, O Most High. . . .

The LORD is a stronghold for the oppressed,
a stronghold in times of trouble.
And those who know your name put their trust in you,
>for you, O LORD, have not forsaken those who seek you. . . .

For the needy shall not always be forgotten,
>nor the hope of the poor perish forever.
>>—Psalm 9:1–2, 9–10, 18

All exchange a sign of peace with one another.
Pray the Sign of the Cross together.

> The Spirit of the Lord is upon me, because he has anointed me to bring good news to the poor.

CHAPTER 5

The Bible: God's Living Word for Our Lives

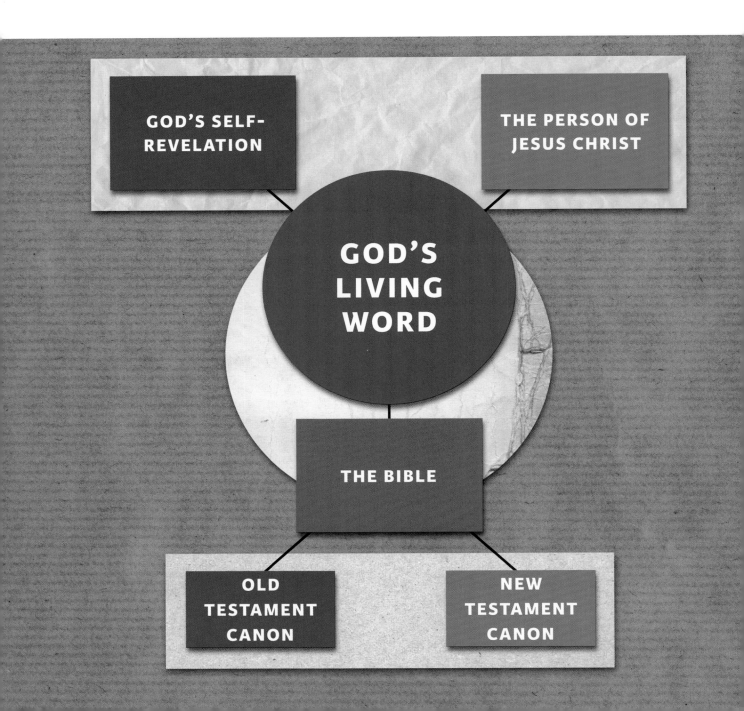

IN THIS CHAPTER WE LEARN HOW THE BIBLE GREW out of an oral tradition of recalling and reflecting upon God's Revelation through real events and experiences in the lives of the people of Israel, and later from the life and preaching of Jesus. Under the guidance of the Holy Spirit, this oral tradition was eventually committed to writing, to become our Sacred Scripture.

GOD'S SELF-REVELATION

THE PROPHETS

THE ORAL TRADITION OF THE ISRAELITES

THE LIFE AND PREACHING OF JESUS

THE ORAL TRADITION OF THE EARLY CHURCH

SACRED TRADITION

SACRED SCRIPTURE

Faith Focus: These teachings of the Catholic Church are the primary focus of the doctrinal content presented in this chapter:

- God's Revelation in Scripture first came to the people of ancient Israel.
- God's Revelation contained in Sacred Scripture was first passed on by word of mouth, or oral tradition, before it was written by the inspired sacred human authors.
- The Catholic Church accepts seventy-three books, found in the Old and New Testaments, to be the inspired Word of God.
- God has revealed himself fully by sending his own Son, Jesus Christ.
- Jesus Christ, the Son of God made man, is the Father's one, perfect and unsurpassable Word.
- The Son is the Father's definitive Word; there will be no further Revelation after him.
- Jesus entrusted his Revelation and his teachings to the Apostles.

Discipleship Formation: As a result of studying this chapter and discovering the meaning of the faith of the Catholic Church for your life, you should be better able to:

- be more aware of God's presence in particular times or events in your life;
- articulate what is the 'good news' for you at this time;
- reflect on the importance of words in life, leading toward an understanding of the Bible as the living Word of God;
- recognize what the life and teachings of Jesus, the Incarnate Word of God, say to you for your life right now;
- value more deeply the spiritual wisdom that God offers you in the Bible;
- select a passage of Scripture as a motto for your life.

Scripture References: These Scripture references are quoted or referred to in this chapter:
OLD TESTAMENT: Genesis 1:3; **Leviticus** 26:12; **Isaiah** 55:10–11; **Jeremiah** 1:4, 17
NEW TESTAMENT: Matthew 1:23, 28:19; **Mark** 1:15, 5:41, 14:36, 15:34; **Luke** 1:1–4, 10:29–37, 12:27–28; **John** 1:1 and 14, 4:14, 6:33, 48, 67; **Acts of the Apostles** 8:4–25, **1 Corinthians** 10:31, 11:23–26, 13:4–7; **Hebrews** 1:1–2

Faith Glossary: Familiarize yourself with the meaning of these key faith terms. Definitions are found in the Glossary: **apocrypha, Apostles, Apostolic Tradition, canon of Scripture, Evangelists, Gnostics/Gnosticism, New Testament, Old Testament, oral tradition, prophets, Sacred Scripture, Sacred Tradition, Septuagint, Word of God**

Faith Words: canon of Scripture; Apostolic Tradition
Learn by Heart: John 1:1, 14
Learn by Example: Desmond Tutu

How are major events communicated to us today?— a clue to how to read the Bible

Today we receive images and pictures almost instantaneously of any major event, whether good or bad, from any part of the world, and then live coverage round the clock as the story unfolds. No matter where it occurs, any major event will attract hordes of news reporters and radio and TV camera crews, all poised to present the story in the manner that will attract the widest audience.

REFLECT AND DISCUSS

⊙ Can you recall how you first heard about Hurricane Katrina, which happened at the end of August 2005? You may have seen a newsflash on the TV. You may have received a call from family or friends in the area. In some way or other, someone told you about Hurricane Katrina and you wanted to find out more, given the scale of the tragedy. Maybe you searched the internet, tuned to the news channels or read newspapers to find out what happened and why.

⊙ You might ask your parents the same question about 9/11 or the invasion of Iraq in 2003 or the Virginia Tech massacre in 2007. You might also ask your parents and grandparents and other older adults about their experience on hearing of the assassination of President John F. Kennedy in November 1963 or of Dr. Martin Luther King, Jr. in April 1968. Many people remember, to this day, exactly where they were when they heard the news of these events. And you will probably remember in years to come where you were when you watched the first African American president of the United States taking his oath of office. Why do you think this is? Share your stories.

⊙ Choose some major event in your area that affected your life deeply. Try to recall, not so much the details of the event but its effect upon you. How did you feel after hearing about it, seeing the recorded pictures, and talking it over with friends and family? Did you and your friends have different opinions and perspectives on what happened? Explain.

WHERE DOES GOD FIT INTO SUCH EVENTS?

God never causes tragedies to happen. Yet, people often use God's name in talking about the causes of such events. They pray for God's help and guidance, or thank God for being spared. Likewise, people often thank God for great positive events in their lives.

- ⊙ How do you think God is present in the events of our lives?
- ⊙ Recall an experience in your own life where you 'noticed' the presence of God. What was it? How was God present to you? What can you learn from this experience for your own faith now?

INFORMATION IS PRESENTED AND 'INTERPRETED' FOR US

The fact that we experience world events and even history much more immediately and instantaneously than our ancestors were able to do may not necessarily be a good thing. We are drawn closer to the events themselves by the graphic nature of the reporting, by sensationalism in the selection of pictures and perspectives, and by the motive of the news organizations to expand their audience of viewers or readers. We are not only presented with 'selected' pictures, but these are often interpreted for us, from the perspective or bias of those doing, or indeed paying for, the reporting.

Let's look at an extract from one person's blog giving a snapshot of life in New Orleans after Hurricane Katrina.

Homelessness in New Orleans

Posted by Paul at 13.00

Have you heard of Duncan Plaza? If you do not live in New Orleans, chances are you have not. Duncan Plaza is an open area downtown, surrounded by office buildings, one that used to house the Louisiana State Supreme Court. Since Hurricane Katrina, Duncan Plaza has become 'home' to hundreds of homeless people who live alternately in tents and other makeshift shelters. The media seems intent on using the number 150 to quantify the homeless population in Duncan Plaza, but I disagree. I drive by Duncan Plaza every day on my way to work, and if that is 150 people I am looking at, then my third grade math teacher did not do her job. I see hundreds of people and, more importantly, I see a community of disenfranchised citizens who are suddenly an inconvenience to a city that has decided to demolish a nine-storey former state office building that borders the plaza. The city announced last week that all of the homeless in Duncan Plaza have to leave.

 Comments (0)

 Forward this post

 RSS feed

WHAT DO YOU THINK?

- ⊙ How does this blogger's view of the situation in Duncan Plaza differ from the accounts he has read in the media? Which account would you feel is the most accurate one and why?

- ⊙ How might the coverage of a story be slanted in order to appeal to a wider, or particular, audience? Try to think of and name examples.
- ⊙ What might we learn from how we hear news of events today for how we read our Bible?

- Working in pairs, consider what factors we
  should take into account when evaluating a
  news story that has been presented to us by
  the media. Consider also how we might go
  about getting a wider perspective on a news
  story; that is, getting it from a number of
  different angles or points of view.
- Share your conclusions with the class.

READING AND INTERPRETING THE BIBLE

At the time when **Sacred Scripture** was being
written, mass media did not exist. **Oral tradition**
was the primary means by which stories were
preserved and passed on from one generation
to the next. As is the case today, the version of
the story that was handed on by any particular
person was influenced by their background, their
culture, their history and the way in which they
had been educated to understand the world
around them. This was also true of those who
wrote the books of the Bible.

The Second Vatican Council reminded us that,
though Sacred Scripture is the inspired **Word
of God**, its Revelation is 'expressed in human
language' (*Constitution on Divine Revelation*,
no. 13). When reading and interpreting Sacred
Scripture, we need to bear these factors in mind.
In later chapters we will explore the various aids
that are available to us as we strive to understand
and interpret God's Revelation as it is handed
down to us through the Bible.

TALK IT OVER

- What have you learned already about how to
  approach reading and interpreting the Bible?

The Second
Vatican Council
reminded us
that, though
Sacred Scripture
is the inspired
Word of God,
its Revelation
is 'expressed in
human language'

MONK AT WORK IN A SCRIPTORIUM | 15TH-CENTURY WOODCUT

The Bible's journey from oral tradition to the written word

OPENING CONVERSATION

⊙ Name one of your favorite Bible stories. Why is it a favorite? What is the truth and wisdom that it can teach today?

STORY AS A VEHICLE FOR TRUTH

Have you heard of Alex Haley and his famous historical novel *Roots*? *Roots* is a story about the family history of a black slave from the Gambia, called Kunte Kinte, reputed to be Haley's distant ancestor. The book was made into a television series that attracted a massive audience in the 1970s. In particular, it made people very aware of and inquisitive about their own personal 'roots'.

JOHN AMOS IN THE TV MINI-SERIES *ROOTS*

Some people dispute whether Haley's story is true at all, and others wonder whether he gullibly believed everything he was told when he visited Africa. Haley had learned much about his own history from a person known as a 'griot', a term used for a storyteller/historian in West Africa. Chiefs had their own griots, who were entrusted with the task of being their personal historians. These people could recall enormous amounts of information, especially genealogies, or lists of ancestors.

Similar storytellers are to be found in many cultures. For example, in Native American culture storytellers have an honored role and are revered. Storytellers in all cultures entertain their listeners with stories that are usually based on the facts but often embellished, as the story in Haley's *Roots* probably was. Even when not factual (literally true), such stories often convey great truths for people's lives. Indeed, stories that are totally made up can be 'true to life' and reflect much practical wisdom.

In our Bible we find stories that are factual, stories based on fact, and non-factual stories; in other words, we find a wide variety of literary genres. For example, the story of Jesus' Death is the account of his actual, historical death on the Cross. Whereas, the stories of the Good Samaritan and of the Prodigal Son are not accounts of historical events; they are parables, a form of storytelling used to teach great truths and spiritual wisdom for life. This points to the importance of knowing the literary genre of the biblical text or passage we are reading. 'The fact is that truth is differently presented and expressed in the various types of historical writing, in prophetical and poetical texts, and in other forms of literary expression' (*Constitution on Divine Revelation*, no. 12).

Every person, every family and every country have their own particular stories that bring together their history and confirm for them who they are and where they have come from. For example, when a family gathers at a wedding or a funeral, the stories of the family are told and retold. By listening to these stories, children learn who they are and why things are as they are in their particular family.

All good stories convey truths, though not all stories are historically factual. As one old proverb says: 'All stories are true, and some of them actually happened.'

OVER TO YOU

⊙ What are the stories in your family that are told and retold at family occasions, such as baptisms, weddings, funerals and so on? Share some of these stories.

ORAL TRADITION

The stories you have just shared are part of the oral tradition of your family—they have been passed on by word of mouth. As they are passed on, family stories help each new generation to learn about their family. Such stories usually tell of the things and the people that the family holds to be important. Sometimes these stories remain part of the oral tradition of a family. It often happens, however, that someone suggests recording these stories onto an electronic device, or writing them down for future generations—especially if there is a very good storyteller in a family. This is not unlike how Sacred Scripture came to be written and compiled.

THE DEVELOPMENT OF THE OLD TESTAMENT CANON

The Tanakh: The oral tradition contained in the **Old Testament**, which houses the Sacred Scriptures of ancient Israel, can be traced to God's chosen people, the Israelites, and their **prophets**, through whom God's Revelation first came to humankind. The books of the Old Testament evolved gradually, much like the stories of a large family, and were finally written down under divine guidance. As the *Catechism of the Catholic Church* teaches, 'God inspired the human authors of the sacred books' (CCC, no. 106). And Vatican II explains, 'Since, therefore,

As they are passed on, family stories help each new generation to learn about their family

During the reign of King David a collection was made of the written texts that existed

KING DAVID | NICOLAS CORDIER

all that the inspired authors, or sacred writers, affirm should be regarded as affirmed by the [H]oly Spirit, we must acknowledge that the books of scripture, firmly, faithfully and without error, teach that truth which God, for the sake of our salvation, wished to see confided to the sacred scriptures' (*Constitution on Divine Revelation*, no. 11).

The sacred writings that have been gathered in our Old Testament evolved over many hundreds of years. They are the written expression of the faith of the Israelites, which was first passed on in their oral traditions or stories. During the reign of King David (1000–926 BC), which was a time of great peace and prosperity for the Israelites, a collection was made of the written texts that existed. This was how the *canon* or official collection of the books of Sacred Scripture began to be formed, but it was not completed until centuries later. As the community tried to live as God's own people, in response to God's Revelation, they gradually discerned which books bore the character of divine inspiration and, therefore, could be called the Word of God.

Most modern books are written by a single author over a period of a few weeks, months or possibly years. Few of the biblical books, especially in the Old Testament, come to us from the pen of an individual author. Many of them were edited and re-edited over several generations, in much the same way as we retell and enlarge the stories of our families and peoples today.

Sometimes it was not easy to decide which of the writings of the Israelites should be included in their Sacred Scriptures, and sometimes there were disputes, just as families or groups will disagree about a story today. Among the criteria, or standards, for accepting a text as 'canonical' was the Jewish community's conviction and belief that it reflected the Revelation of God's presence and mighty deeds among his people and that the text was a true expression of their faith and of how they were to live the Covenant as God's chosen people.

The Old Testament canon: The sacred writings of the people of ancient Israel, found in the Old Testament, are 'an indispensable part' of the Christian Bible. The Old Testament books 'are divinely inspired and retain a permanent value, for the Old Covenant has never been revoked'

The Dead Sea Scrolls and the targums

In 1947 a young shepherd boy was searching for a stray goat among caves near the Dead Sea, thirteen miles east of Jerusalem. He picked up a stone and threw it through the opening of one of the caves to see if the goat was there. Instead, he heard the sound of breaking pottery. He was scared and ran away but returned the following day with his cousin. When they looked inside they found many old pottery jars. The jars were two inches long and just over nine inches wide and they contained what looked like rolls of wallpaper. These were very fragile scrolls that broke easily into tiny pieces. When experts began to examine the pieces they realized that they had found the oldest copies of parts of the Jewish Hebrew Scriptures. Other caves have since been explored and more pottery jars with scrolls inside have been discovered. These scrolls are known today as the Dead Sea Scrolls. They, as well as the targums and other authentic ancient texts, are extremely important for scholars who wish to study early versions of the Old Testament.

Targums are Aramaic oral translations or paraphrases of the Hebrew Scriptures. They have been part of the Jewish traditional literature and have played a significant role as explanations or expansions of the Hebrew Scriptures and in the celebration of the Sabbath liturgy of the synagogue. The use of targums arose among the Jewish people in the first century BC as Aramaic became the primary language spoken among Jews.

(CCC, no. 121). While the members of the early Church were beginning to write and compile their own Scriptures, which would become the **New Testament**, they continued also to cherish and revere the Jewish Scriptures as the revealed Word of God. Under the guidance of the Holy Spirit and 'relying on the faith of the apostolic age', the Church identified those texts that were to be included in the Old Testament.

During the first centuries of the Church, there were two listings of canonical writings accepted by the Jewish people, one shorter and one longer, before the official canon of the Old Testament was established. The longer list was based on a Greek translation of the Hebrew Scriptures, called the **Septuagint**. The early Church debated which Jewish 'canon' to accept. In the late fourth century the Synod of Hippo (393) and the Council of Carthage (419), both in North Africa, accepted a fixed longer number of Old Testament books, found in the Septuagint manuscripts.

Eventually, at the Council of Trent in 1546, the Catholic Church officially embraced the longer listing of Old Testament canonical books, while the Protestant Reformers favored the shorter listing. The teaching of Trent reaffirmed the canon recognized by the Council of Florence in 1442. We now count forty-six Old Testament books (forty-five if we count the Book of Jeremiah and the Book of Lamentations as one) in the Catholic Bible. However, many Protestant Bibles have only thirty-nine books in the Old Testament; other Protestant Bibles contain the additional seven disputed books, referring to them as 'deuterocanonical'.

THE DEVELOPMENT OF THE NEW TESTAMENT CANON

It is easier to follow the development of the New Testament canon. After Jesus' Resurrection and Ascension, his disciples remembered and continued to preach what he had proclaimed through his words and actions. The first time that Jesus appears in public in Mark, the earliest account of the Gospel, he announces, 'The time is fulfilled, and the kingdom of God has come near; repent, and believe in the good news' (Mark 1:15). Convinced that Jesus had risen from the dead, that he was the promised Messiah for all people, and empowered by the Holy Spirit at Pentecost, the **Apostles** began to fulfill the commission that the risen Jesus gave to them just prior to his Ascension: 'Go therefore and make disciples of all nations' (Matthew 28:19).

They first spread the Good News of the Kingdom of God throughout the Mediterranean countries, preaching in the same way as they had seen Jesus preach. They announced the coming of God's Kingdom in Jesus, calling people to do 'God's will on earth as it is done in heaven'. As people professed faith in Jesus Christ and were baptized, the Church took root throughout the Mediterranean. It was only when the Church was established in far-off places that the leaders began to write letters in which they continued to instruct and encourage Christians to live as disciples of Jesus. The letters of St. Paul and the other Apostles were the earliest writings of the New Testament.

For example, in one of his letters to the Christians in Corinth, St. Paul encouraged them to evaluate their behavior at the celebration of the Eucharist and to take part appropriately in its celebration. After admonishing them for their irreverent behavior, he wrote:

For I received from the Lord what I also handed on to you, that the Lord Jesus on the night when he was betrayed took a loaf of bread, and when he had given thanks, he broke it and said, 'This is my body that is for you. Do this in remembrance of me.' In the same way he took the cup also, after supper, saying, 'This cup is the new covenant in my blood. Do this, as often as you drink it, in remembrance of me.' For as often as you eat this bread and drink the cup, you proclaim the Lord's death until he comes.

—1 Corinthians 11:23–26

As the Apostles and the other disciples who were eyewitnesses to the life and mission and Death and Resurrection of Jesus began to grow old and die, the members of the early Church feared that the message of his life and teaching would be lost if it were not written down. Thus, beginning around the year AD 70, the Apostles and **Evangelists** (meaning 'Gospel writers') and their disciples began to write down what the Apostles and the other disciples of Jesus had been preaching. They gathered the oral traditions, memoirs and other writings that had been circulating within the early Church, and the formation of the four Gospels in the New Testament began. At the beginning of his account of the Gospel, for example, Luke, writing for both Jews and Gentiles (non-Jews), points out that what he is about to write has been drawn from a number of already existing sources. Addressing the opening lines to Theophilus, Luke writes:

ST. LUKE | TRINITY CHURCH, BOSTON, MASSACHUSETTS

Since many have undertaken to set down an orderly account of the events that have been fulfilled among us, just as they were handed on to us by those who from the beginning were eye-witnesses and servants of the word, I too decided, after investigating everything carefully from the very first, to write an orderly account for you, most excellent Theophilus, so that you may know the truth concerning the things about which you have been instructed.

—Luke 1:1–4

Over three decades, four different accounts of the Gospel were written, as well as the Acts of the Apostles, the Epistles and the Book of Revelation (also known as Apocalypse). All of the Evangelists wrote from their own perspective and according to the audience for whom they were writing. For example, Matthew was writing for a mainly Jewish audience, so he highlighted how Jesus fulfilled the promises and messianic prophecies of the Jewish Scriptures. Eventually, after a century of teaching, preaching, editing and writing, the New Testament books that are in the Bible were completed.

Along with the writings that eventually formed the New Testament, other writings, even several gospels, were written. The leaders of the early Church had a number of rules for deciding whether a book was 'inspired' and to be accepted as part of the official, or canonical, writings of the Church. Was it written by or closely connected to an Apostle or eyewitness of the life and mission of Jesus? Did it ring true to the person and teaching of Jesus, as we know him from other New Testament books? Did it help people to 'follow the way' of life modeled by Jesus and now expected of his disciples? Was the book accepted generally among Christians? Finally, the present list of twenty-seven New Testament books was agreed as canonical, and eventually became part of the canon of Sacred Scripture. The **canon of Scripture** refers to the list of Old and New Testament books that are accepted by the Catholic Church as the inspired Word of God.

WHAT ABOUT YOU PERSONALLY?

 Have you ever read a whole book of the Bible? If not, would you like to? You might begin with Luke's Gospel in the New Testament or the Psalms from the Old Testament; they can really hit home!

 What do you think are the best attitudes and expectations to bring to reading the Bible?

 The members of the early Church were very keen to share the Good News of Jesus Christ and his invitation to God's Kingdom, or reign, with one another and with others. What for you is the 'best news' from Jesus? How might you share it with others?

ILLUMINATED MANUSCRIPT OF PSALM 110

FAITH WORD

Canon of Scripture

The canon of Scripture refers to the list of Old Testament and New Testament books that are accepted by the Catholic Church as the inspired Word of God. The Catholic canon lists seventy-three books—forty-six in the Old Testament and twenty-seven in the New Testament. The Catholic canon of Scripture differs from the Protestant canon, which also includes writings that the Catholic Church has judged to be apocryphal.

The living Word of God through the ages

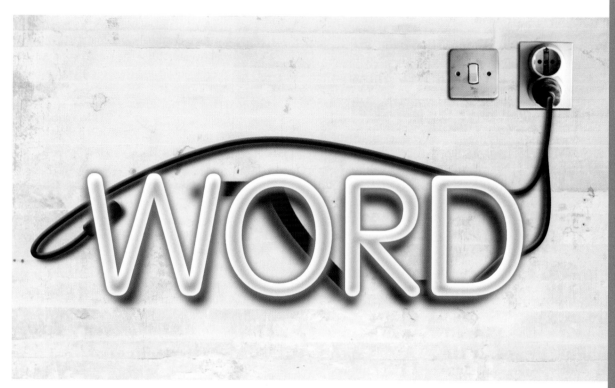

OPENING CONVERSATION

⊙ Have you ever heard the phrase 'She is a woman of her word' or 'He is a man of his word'? What do you think it means to be a person of your word? Do you know someone of whom you would say 'he or she is a person of their word'? On what basis? Are you a person of your word?

⊙ At Mass, after the reading of Scripture, the lector says, 'The word of the Lord'. What do you think this means?

THE WORD OF GOD

We are now going to explore what we mean when we talk about 'The Word of God'.

God spoke the Word of Creation in the beginning. The universe is the fruit of the Word of God, which is responsible for its order and arrangement.

In the Book of Genesis we read that the Word of God was not just spoken, it was active and effective. We read: 'Then God said, "Let there be light"; and there was light' (Genesis 1:3). What God said came to be! The Book of Isaiah also professes this deep faith in the power of God's Word active among humanity:

For as the rain and the snow come down from
    heaven,
      and do not return there until they have
      watered the earth,
making it bring forth and sprout. . . .
so shall my word be that goes out from my
    mouth;

JEREMIAH LAMENTING THE DESTRUCTION OF JERUSALEM | REMBRANDT

Now the word of the LORD came to me
    saying,
'Before I formed you in the womb I
    knew you,
and before you were born I consecrated
    you;
I appointed you a prophet to the
    nations.'

—Jeremiah 1:4

In verse 17, God says to Jeremiah:

Stand up and tell them everything that I
    command you.

THE INSPIRED WRITTEN WORD OF GOD

All Christians cherish the Word of God that comes to us through the Old Testament. However, at the beginning of the Letter to the Hebrews, a book of the New Testament, we read this amazing statement: 'Long ago God spoke to our ancestors in many and various ways by the prophets, but in these last days he has spoken to us by a Son' (Hebrews 1:1–2). Jesus Christ is the ultimate and final Revelation of God. There is no more Revelation after him. The *Catechism* summarizes this faith of the Church:

God has revealed himself fully by sending his own Son, in whom he established his covenant for ever. The Son is the Father's definitive Word; so there will be no further Revelation after him.

—CCC, no. 73

In the Prologue of St. John's Gospel, also called the Fourth Gospel, we read:

In the beginning was the Word, and the Word was with God, and the Word was God.... And the Word became flesh and lived among us, and we have seen his glory, the glory as of a father's only son, full of grace and truth.

—John 1:1, 14

What an amazing statement! What an extraordinary event! Surely this is the best news

it shall not return to me empty,
but it shall accomplish that which I purpose.

—Isaiah 55:10–11

God's Revelation continued throughout the history of Israel. God's people had a deep faith that he was always present to and with them, revealing to them how to live the Covenant. We read one expression of this faith in the Book of Leviticus: 'I will walk among you, and will be your God, and you shall be my people' (Leviticus 26:12).

Throughout the Old Testament we read over and over again that the Word of the Lord God comes to his people. In a special way God spoke through Abraham, Isaac, Jacob, Moses, David, Solomon, Ruth, Judith, Esther and the prophets. He also spoke through wisdom writers and historians and all the writers of Sacred Scripture who recorded what God said and had done for his people. For example, in the opening words of the Book of Jeremiah, God speaks to Jeremiah and calls him to do the work of a prophet:

ever made known to humanity! The Son of God came and lived among us. He became a man without giving up his divinity. Jesus is God's own Son. He is 'the Word made flesh'. No wonder John said that he was 'full of truth'. Later in John, Jesus says, 'The bread of God is that which comes down from heaven and gives life to the world.' Then he adds, 'I am the bread of life.' A little later, Simon Peter says to Jesus, 'You have the words of everlasting life.' (Read John 6.)

Jesus is the fullness of God's Revelation to us. He is the most effective word that God has ever spoken to us. According to the *Catechism of the Catholic Church*:

Christ, the Son of God made man, is the Father's one, perfect and unsurpassable Word. In him he has said everything; there will be no other word than this one.

—CCC, no. 65

Have you ever noticed how someone hard of hearing looks intently at the lips and face of a speaker to help him or her make out what is being said? When we can see the face of the person who is speaking to us, we understand the spoken word better. Jesus Christ, the Second Person of the Blessed Trinity, is the Incarnate Word of God. 'The Word of God dwelt in man and became the Son of man in order to accustom man to perceive God. . . .' (St. Irenaeus, quoted in CCC, no. 53). Jesus Christ, the Living Word of God, is Emmanuel, meaning 'God is with us' (Matthew 1:23). In him and in Sacred Scripture we encounter the living God.

Do you know the prayer called the *Angelus*? The tradition is that the *Angelus* is prayed daily at noon and at 6 p.m. We will pray the *Angelus* for our Prayer Reflection at the end of this chapter. This beautiful prayer includes the extraordinary words of St. John's Gospel, 'The Word was made flesh and dwelt among

us', and tells the story of the Incarnation; that is, the Son of God 'taking on flesh' (the word 'incarnation' means 'taking on flesh') in the one divine Person of Jesus, who lived among us as a human being.

TALK IT OVER

⊙ How did the Revelation of God in Jesus differ from all previous forms of Revelation?

⊙ In what ways do you think Jesus' coming among humanity helps us to understand and begin to know God and how to live better as a People of God?

LET'S PROBE DEEPER

⊙ What do you hear from the statement: 'The Word became flesh and lived among us . . . full of grace and truth'?

⊙ What grace (gift) or truth might Jesus have for your life now?

⊙ What words of Jesus do you think have the greatest influence on your life?

⊙ What important things has Jesus' teaching taught you about God? About yourself?

⊙ What important things has it taught you about how you should live?

THE ANGELUS | JEAN-FRANÇOIS MILLET

The challenge of remaining faithful to the Word of God

OPENING CONVERSATION

◉ Why do you think it is important to have the canon of Scripture, rather than have everything that has been written about Jesus over the ages presented for study?

ACCOUNTS OF JESUS THAT WERE NOT ACCEPTED INTO THE CANON OF SCRIPTURE

There were several other accounts of Jesus' life written in the early centuries of Christianity that were not accepted into the canon of Scripture. Some of these accounts were even called gospels, such as the Gospel of Thomas, which is mentioned in the modern novel the *Da Vinci Code*. Such gospels did not pass the criteria for authenticity that the Church had established. For example, some writings portrayed an image of Jesus that was not in keeping with the Jesus of the four accounts of the Gospel according to Matthew, Mark, Luke and John. While Matthew and John were Apostles and eyewitnesses to the events of Jesus' life, Death and Resurrection, and Mark and Luke recorded the testimony of eyewitnesses, all four Evangelists were deeply involved with the leaders and people of the early Church. Their writings were acknowledged by the whole community as accurately passing on the authentic **Apostolic Tradition**. The accounts of the Gospel that did not match these criteria were excluded.

There were numerous other 'gospels', called **apocrypha** gospels, being written and circulating during the first four centuries which were not included in the canon of Scripture. The judgment of the Church was that these erred in passing on the Apostolic Tradition and the teaching of the early Church. For example, some of the apocrypha did not make it clear that Jesus Christ was, at the same time, both God and man. They portrayed Jesus to be either a lesser kind of divinity or not truly a man. As both of these presentations of Jesus are not true to the Apostolic Tradition that Jesus was true God and true man, the union of a divine nature and a human nature in one divine Person, these writings were excluded from the canon.

These writings differed not only in content but also in overall narrative structure from the

Numerous other 'gospels' written and circulated during the first four centuries were not included in the canon of Scripture

four canonical accounts of the Gospel. The apocrypha gospels often focus on and develop at length a 'particular element of canonical Gospel tradition'; namely, (1) the infancy and childhood of Jesus (Infancy Gospel of Thomas and Gospel of Pseudo-Matthew), (2) sayings of Jesus (Gospel of Thomas), (3) the Passion and Resurrection of Jesus (Gospel of Peter and Gospel of Philip), and (4) dialogs of the risen Jesus with his Apostles (Gospel of Mary and Gospel of the Savior).

Some of the apocrypha were influenced by **Gnosticism**. Among those apocrypha is the Gospel of Thomas. The name 'Gnosticism' comes from the Greek word *gnosis*, meaning 'knowledge'. Gnosticism refers to the teachings of a variety of Christian 'sects' that arose in the first century AD and existed into the fifth century, and whose origins date back to Simon Magus, who is named in Acts of the Apostles 8:4–25. Gnostics, who considered themselves 'elitist', falsely claimed to have a special and secret spiritual knowledge; for example, secret teachings that the risen Jesus gave to one or the other of the Apostles. In their teaching, Gnostics also often used a mythology to teach erroneously that the physical world is evil, 'a product of the fall, and is thus to be rejected or left behind' (CCC, no. 285).

The Nag Hammadi manuscripts are a primary source for our understanding of the teachings of Gnosticism. Nag Hammadi is a city located in

Egypt where farmers in December 1945 found a sealed jar containing thirteen papyrus manuscripts dating back to the second century AD. A copy of the apocrypha gospel, the Gospel of Thomas, was found among the Nag Hammadi manuscripts.

TALK IT OVER
⊙ What were the apocrypha gospels?
⊙ Why did the Church not include the apocrypha gospels in the Church's canon of Scripture?

THE CHALLENGE OF TRANSLATING THE BIBLE
The Old Testament was originally written in Hebrew and the New Testament in Greek. There

were 'old Latin' translations of both Testaments by the end of the second century. For about a thousand years, only scholars who knew these ancient languages could read the Bible for themselves. Then, as part of his Reformation movement, and convinced that every Christian should read the Bible, Martin Luther (1483–1546) translated it into German. This was the first translation into a modern language. Since then, the Bible has been translated into more than two thousand languages and dialects.

Even among the English translations, there are many different versions. These versions represent scholars' attempts to bring us the word of God in an understandable form and in ways that engage us personally.

The various translations of the Bible are constantly being updated in light of new insights from biblical scholars. The best translations go back to the original languages of the Scriptures, Hebrew and Greek, to convey what the authors intended. This is not an easy task, as anybody who has tried to translate a piece of literature from one language to another will testify.

Probably the most difficult task for the translator is to make the new version read well in the second language while at the same time remaining faithful to the original message and content. The translator could translate the original text word for word, but this would result in very stilted language that would make the translation difficult to read and would probably be seriously inaccurate. The good translator balances accuracy and faithfulness to the original words on the one hand, with a sense of style and timeliness on the other.

Jesus himself spoke in Aramaic, a dialect related to Hebrew. There are only a few words or phrases of Aramaic as it was spoken by Jesus recorded in the Gospels. One is 'Abba', the word for 'Father' or, more informally, 'Papa' (Mark 14:36). Another is the command to the daughter of Jairus, the twelve-year-old who had died: "'Talitha cum", which means, "Little girl, get up"' (Mark 5:41). The last are Jesus' words from the Cross: "'Eloi, Eloi, lema sabachthani", which mean, "My God, my God, why have you forsaken me!"' (Mark 15:34).

Some Bible scholars have tried to translate some of the Greek of the Gospels into Aramaic in order to get a sense of the actual words that Jesus might have used and how they might have sounded. The challenge of translation points to a very important responsibility for every Christian generation today: God's Word through Sacred Scripture must always be a *living word* for us.

Jesus promised the Samaritan woman at the well, and Christians ever after, that his Gospel would always be like fresh water, springing up to eternal life (John 4:14). This means that we must always be bringing the living word of God in the Bible to our own lives and to the times in which we live. Above all, translators of Sacred Scripture must be attentive to what God wants revealed through the sacred authors for our salvation.

REFLECT AND DISCUSS
⊙ 'Every translation is an interpretation.' What do you think this means?

REFLECTIVE ACTIVITY
⊙ With a companion, take a favorite text of the Bible; for example, Jesus' parable of the Good Samaritan (Luke 10:29–37).
⊙ Decide how you would tell the story to a six-year-old, being faithful to the original story and yet in such a way that a child could understand its message.
⊙ Share your best suggestion.

St. Jerome (c. 340–420)—a great biblical scholar

St. Jerome, a Doctor and Father of the Church, was one of the earliest biblical scholars in the history of the Church. He was born around 340 in the town of Stridon in modern-day Albania. Though born into a Christian family, Jerome was not baptized until he was a student in Rome. At the age of thirty-three he had a mystical experience, after which he decided to give up the study of the classics and devote himself to studying the Bible. For a time Jerome lived the life of a hermit in order to study and write, and during that time he also began to learn Hebrew. After periods in Constantinople, Rome and Alexandria, he decided to spend the rest of his life living in a hermit's cell near Bethlehem, where he died.

Jerome was a student of the language, history and geography of Palestine as well as the theology of the Sacred Scripture. He translated the whole Bible into Latin, including a translation of the Old Testament from the Hebrew, a task he completed in 405. He also wrote a vast number of other works, including history, theology, commentaries on the Bible, sermons and letters. Jerome's translation, called the Vulgate, became the basis for many other translations into other languages. His advice to students was: 'Ignorance of the Scriptures is ignorance of Christ.' St. Jerome is the patron saint of librarians, students and, naturally enough, of Bible scholars and translators. His feast day is September 30.

ST. JEROME IN HIS STUDY | ALBRECHT DÜRER

OVER TO YOU
⊙ If you were to learn one lesson from St. Jerome, what might it be?

JUDGE AND ACT

REFLECT ON WHAT YOU HAVE LEARNED
⊙ Review what you have learned about the Bible's journey from oral tradition to the written word and the challenges that formed part of that journey.

LEARN BY EXAMPLE

The story of Desmond Tutu

Let us now look at the life and inspiration of Archbishop Tutu, a man who has always sought to live the spiritual wisdom he has learned from the Bible.

Desmond Tutu was born in Klerksdorp, near Johannesburg, South Africa, in 1931. He grew up in a house without electricity or sanitation. As a child he developed tuberculosis and had to spend two years in hospital. There he befriended Fr. Trevor Huddleston, an Anglican priest who visited him every day. This friendship inspired Desmond's lifelong devotion to Christianity and the Person of Jesus.

Desmond initially qualified as a teacher, like his father. In 1958 he decided to enter the seminary to study for the priesthood. He was ordained an Anglican priest in Johannesburg three years later. Then, following further theological studies at King's College in London, he held several teaching and theological positions in South Africa.

A turning point in his life came in 1978 when he was persuaded to become the new general secretary of the South African Council of Churches (SACC). By now he was Bishop Tutu and in his new role he became a national and international figure.

The SACC was committed to social justice in South Africa. As general secretary, Bishop Tutu worked tirelessly and courageously to bring about justice and peace between the different races in this bitterly divided country. He became a formidable opponent of apartheid—a system that separated the black majority from the ruling white class, to the latter's advantage and privilege.

In 1984 Bishop Tutu's efforts were recognized when he was awarded the Nobel Peace Prize. In 1985 he was appointed Bishop of Johannesburg and in 1986 he became the Archbishop of Cape Town, the most senior position in the South African Anglican Communion. He held this position until his retirement in 1996.

Since then, Archbishop Tutu has traveled the world in his efforts to end poverty and human rights abuses. He has become a 'moral voice' of tolerance and inclusivity and respect for the rights of others. His whole life and his writings are about how Christians must make Sacred Scripture a living and lived word in their lives, something which demands that we work for justice and equality, for peace and freedom for all people.

- What is the best wisdom you have learned from Archbishop Tutu?

RESPOND WITH YOUR FAMILY

- Choose a passage of Scripture that could become a motto for your family. For example, you might choose from the following:

Love is patient; love is kind; love is not envious or boastful or arrogant or rude. It does not insist on its own way; it is not irritable or resentful; it does not rejoice in wrongdoing, but rejoices in the truth. It bears all things, believes all things, hopes all things, endures all things.

—1 Corinthians 13:4–7

Consider the lilies, how they grow: they neither toil nor spin; yet I tell you, even Solomon in all his glory was not clothed like one of these. But if God so clothes the grass of the field, which is alive today, and tomorrow is thrown into the oven, how much more will he clothe you—you of little faith!

—Luke 12:27–28

Whatever you do, do everything for the glory of God.

—1 Corinthians 10:31

- Discuss with your family how, together, you can make your chosen piece of Scripture come alive in your home.

LEARN BY HEART

In the beginning was the Word, and the Word was with God, and the Word was God. . . . And the Word became flesh and lived among us.

JOHN 1:1, 14

PRAYER REFLECTION

Pray the Sign of the Cross together.

LEADER
Today we will pray the *Angelus*.

The Angel of the Lord declared unto Mary,
and she conceived of the Holy Spirit.

ALL
Hail Mary, full of grace,
the Lord is with thee.
Blessed art thou among women,
and blessed is the fruit of thy womb, Jesus.
Holy Mary, Mother of God,
pray for us sinners,
now and at the hour of our death. Amen.

LEADER
Behold the handmaid of the Lord,
be it done unto me according to your Word.

ALL
Hail Mary. . . .

LEADER
And the Word was made flesh,
and dwelt among us.

ALL
Hail Mary. . . .

LEADER
Pray for us, O holy Mother of God,
that we may be made worthy of the promises of
Christ.

Pour forth, we beseech you, O Lord,
your grace into our hearts: that we, to whom
the Incarnation of Christ your Son was made
known by the message of an Angel, may by his
Passion and Cross be brought to the glory of his
Resurrection. Through the same Christ our Lord.

ALL
Amen.

Pray the Sign of the Cross together.

> Pray for us, O holy
> Mother of God,
> that we may be
> made worthy of the
> promises of Christ

THE ANNUNCIATION | ANTONELLO DA MESSINA

CHAPTER 6

The Bible:
A Blueprint for Living

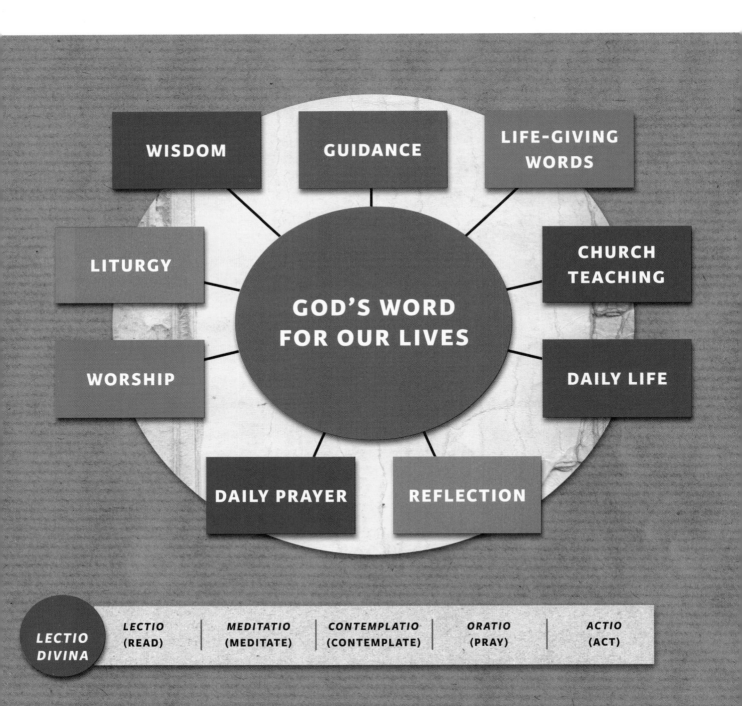

WISDOM

GUIDANCE

LIFE-GIVING WORDS

LITURGY

CHURCH TEACHING

GOD'S WORD FOR OUR LIVES

WORSHIP

DAILY LIFE

DAILY PRAYER

REFLECTION

| LECTIO DIVINA | LECTIO (READ) | MEDITATIO (MEDITATE) | CONTEMPLATIO (CONTEMPLATE) | ORATIO (PRAY) | ACTIO (ACT) |

IN THIS CHAPTER WE EXPLORE HOW THE BIBLE helps us live as Christian people of God today. We learn how the Catholic Church uses the Bible in its worship and Liturgy, and how we can turn to the Bible for God's Revelation to live our lives each day and for personal and communal prayer.

PRAYING WITH THE BIBLE

PSALMS

PLAINCHANT

TAIZÉ MUSIC AND PRAYER

THE LORD'S PRAYER

LECTIO DIVINA

Faith Focus: These teachings of the Catholic Church are the primary focus of the doctrinal content presented in this chapter:

- God is the author of Sacred Scripture because he inspired its human authors.
- The Christian faith is not a 'religion of the book'. Christianity is the religion of the 'Word' of God.
- The Church has always venerated the divine Scriptures as she has venerated the Body of the Lord.
- The Church has always regarded Sacred Scripture, taken together with Sacred Tradition, as the supreme rule of her faith.
- The Catholic Church's celebration of the Liturgy and the Sacraments always includes the proclamation of the Word of God.
- The Church has its own calendar year, known as the liturgical year.
- The Lord's Prayer is the summary of the whole Gospel.

Discipleship Formation: As a result of studying this chapter and discovering the meaning of the faith of the Catholic Church for your life, you should be better able to:

- value the Bible as a source for living your life;
- give reading the Bible a central place in your life;
- be more conscious of how you use words and realize how your words can affect others;
- be able to identify times when you have heard a 'Word of God' for you from the Bible;
- make a greater effort to hear the Word of God in the readings at Mass;
- value the Our Father more deeply;
- be open to receiving wisdom for your life from the Bible.

Scripture References: These Scripture references are quoted or referred to in this chapter:
OLD TESTAMENT: Psalms 23:1–2, 27:1, 77:1, 138:3; **Isaiah** 61:1
NEW TESTAMENT: Matthew 6:9–13; **Luke** 24:45; **Acts of the Apostles** 2:42; **Hebrews** 4:12

Faith Glossary: Familiarize yourself with the meaning of these key faith terms. Definitions are found in the Glossary: *lectio divina*, Lectionary, liturgical year, Liturgy, Liturgy of the Hours, Liturgy of the Word, Lord's Prayer, Magisterium, Mass, prayer, Psalms

Faith Words: *lectio divina*; Liturgy
Learn by Heart: Hebrews 4:12
Learn by Example: Jean Donovan

How can words make a difference to our lives?

BRAINSTORM
- Make a list of all the words or phrases you can think of that represent healing, encouragement or love.
- Then make another list of words that can damage, hurt or bring us down.

DISCUSS
- Someone once said, 'The word is mightier than the sword.' Do you think this is true? Why or why not?

REFLECT
- What difference would it make to you and to others if you were to use more words of healing, encouragement and love?

Words can change our lives

Mitch Albom's bestselling book *Tuesdays with Morrie* is the story of his conversations and relationship with his former college professor Morrie Schwartz. In *Tuesday's with Morrie* Mitch shares how these conversations led him to change his life and outlook. Here are some examples of what Mitch learned from his conversations about what is important in life:

When you learn how to die, you learn how to live.

You cannot substitute material things for love.

Death ends a life, not a relationship.

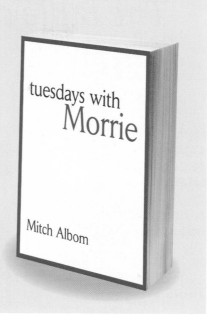

OVER TO YOU
- Do you think God's 'Word' seeks us out in our conversations with people? How? Why?

REFLECT AND DISCUSS
- Who do you know who speaks words of wisdom? Tell the group about this person.
- Who do you know who would say that words changed their life? Tell their story.

LET'S PROBE DEEPER
- Think of a time when words you heard or read made a big difference in your life. What kind of words were they? What difference did they make?
- What are some words that you have used that made a difference in someone else's life? What kind of words were they and what difference did they make?

The story of Mitch Albom is but one example of how words can change lives. Morrie's words of wisdom led Mitch to change his whole outlook on life and his way of living. Through his bestselling book, Mitch in turn brought this wisdom to millions of others, touching and helping them. In this chapter we will learn that the words of the Bible, the Word of God, are the most life-changing words of all. God's Word revealed through Scripture and its spiritual wisdom can put us on the path to true happiness—if we listen and are open to its message.

The Bible can be a powerful influence

God is the author of Sacred Scripture. 'The divinely revealed realities, which are contained and presented in the text of Sacred Scripture, have been written down under the inspiration of the Holy Spirit' [Vatican II, *Constitution on Divine Revelation*, no. 11].

—CCC, no. 105

OPENING RELECTION

⊙ Sacred Scripture is the revealed Word of God. Give an example of a Scripture verse you have heard from the Bible. Why was it significant for you?

PEOPLE RESPOND TO THE BIBLE IN DIFFERENT WAYS

Have you ever witnessed a Pentecostal or Evangelical **prayer** meeting, or a black Baptist service, or been present at a gospel choir service? Have you ever participated in a charismatic prayer meeting in a Catholic church? Such Christians enthusiastically express their faith in the Bible and its message. Just from looking at how they worship and praise God, you would know that they believe that the words of Scripture are spoken for them and apply to them in their daily lives. They respond to readings from the Bible with fervor and enthusiasm. They sing the hymns and psalms with joy. They are animated and excited about the whole experience.

Other people read the Bible on their own or listen quietly to the readings in church and then try to apply its wisdom and teaching to their daily lives and to their relationships with others and with God.

For some, of course, the Bible readings they hear in church may simply glide over their heads and have no effect on them whatsoever. Some people may feel that the Bible has no relevance for their lives because it was written such a long time ago and therefore it belongs to a different time and a different world.

WHAT ABOUT YOU PERSONALLY?

⊙ What is your own attitude toward the Bible?
⊙ What has shaped your attitude?
⊙ What relevance does the Bible have in your life?
⊙ When have the Scripture readings at Mass spoken to you personally?
⊙ Can you think of any situations that might lead you to turn to the Bible for help and guidance? Give examples.

The Church has always venerated the divine scriptures as she has venerated the Body of the Lord

READING THE BIBLE HAS A CENTRAL PLACE IN THE DAILY LIFE OF CATHOLICS

The Church, from her beginning, has revered the Sacred Scriptures as the revealed Word of God. The Acts of the Apostles, which describes life in the early Church, tells us, 'They devoted themselves to the apostles' teaching and fellowship, to the breaking of bread and the prayers' (Acts 2:42). (The reference to 'the breaking of bread' is to the celebration and sharing of Eucharist.) As those teachings of the Apostles developed and were written down with the inspiration of the Holy Spirit, they became the New Testament. We know that Jesus' disciples, the Church, also cherished the Hebrew Scriptures—which are contained in the Christian Old Testament—as Jesus himself did. From the life and teachings of Jesus and the preaching and teachings of the Apostles, new sacred texts began to emerge that would be recognized by the whole Church as the inspired Word of God, and these have been passed down to us in the Bible.

Vatican II summarized the role of the Bible in the life of the Church: 'The Church has always venerated the divine scriptures as it has venerated the Body of the Lord, in that it never ceases, above all in the sacred liturgy, to partake of the bread of life and to offer it to the faithful from the one table of the word of God and the Body of Christ' (*Constitution on Divine Revelation,* no. 21).

While Sacred Scripture has always played a vital role in the life of the Church, this was not always the case in the faith life of Catholics, for many reasons. One historical reason was the Protestant Reformation and the teachings of Martin Luther, John Calvin and other Protestant Reformers who insisted that 'Scripture alone' is the guide to Christian faith and living. They also taught that each person should read Sacred Scripture for themselves and make up their own minds about its meaning for them individually. Behind this teaching was the desire of the Protestant Reformers to downplay the role of Sacred Tradition in the life of the Church, especially the role of the Pope and other clergy. The Catholic Church responded to the Protestant Reformers by emphasizing that Sacred Scripture was truly understood within the living Sacred Tradition of the Church as well. Vatican II restated this teaching of the Church: 'The Church has always regarded and continues to regard the scriptures, taken together with sacred tradition, as the supreme rule of its faith' (*Constitution on Divine Revelation,* no. 21). The Catholic Church also saw a danger in everyone making up their own mind about the Bible's teachings.

In summary, the Catholic teaching was and is that every Catholic should read the Bible but do so in the context of Sacred Tradition, within the context of the whole Church and with the guidance of the Church's **Magisterium**, whose responsibility it is to interpret authentically the Word of God handed down to us through Sacred Scripture and Sacred Tradition. While the teachings of the Protestant Reformation put greater emphasis on the Bible alone, the Catholic Church emphasizes the Bible *and* Tradition, which includes the Sacraments and the official teachings of the Church.

Today the Catholic Church strongly encourages all Catholics to read the Bible prayerfully and give it a central place in daily life. As Vatican II insisted, 'Access to sacred scripture ought to be widely available to the Christian faithful' (*Constitution on Divine Revelation,* no. 22). Today, more and more Catholics are reading and studying the Bible, praying with its texts and sharing the Faith in Bible-study groups.

It is important that we do not see the Bible as a 'dead letter'—a document of the past. The Bible, the living Word of God, speaks to us today in our place and time. The Bible is the source of the living Word of God that we are called to live in our daily lives. The Bible is for living—not just for reading or studying. Here the *Catechism* gives us good advice:

[T]he Christian faith is not a 'religion of the book'. Christianity is the religion of the 'Word' of God, 'not a written and mute word, but incarnate and living' [St. Bernard of Clairvaux, *Sermon on the Incarnation,* 4, 11]. If the Scriptures are not to remain a dead letter, Christ, the eternal Word of the living God, must, through the Holy Spirit, 'open [our] our minds to understand the Scriptures'.

—CCC, no. 108

TALK IT OVER

⊙ When have you been helped, encouraged or motivated by what you read in the Bible? You might like to share your experience.

JOURNAL EXERCISE

⊙ Write about how you might open yourself to God's Word revealed through the Bible.

The Bible has some of the best stories in world literature inside its covers. Indeed, the whole Bible is itself a wonderful story. It covers the full spectrum of human experience. Comedy, tragedy, promise, disappointment, success and suffering are emotionally and factually described, enacted and resolved in its pages. It contains the human story from God's perspective.

BOB DYLAN IN 1979

Bob Dylan was once given the following advice: 'If you want to write songs, read your Bible.' This was life-changing advice for Dylan

THE BIBLE—A POWERFUL INFLUENCE

Those who take the time to read and reflect on the Bible have the opportunity to really come to appreciate the power of its words and the message that lies behind them. For such people, the words are no longer those of an ancient language (translated into their own language), which were addressed to a far-off people, a relic of an age now past. Rather, the words and message of the Bible are alive, vibrant, powerful and relevant to their lives today.

The Bible teaches us how we are to live and act—how we have been created to live and act as images of God and as the People of God. If we are willing to read the Bible and be open to God's Word, we can receive the gift of great spiritual wisdom for our everyday lives. The words of the Bible encourage endurance in the face of suffering, and perseverance in the pursuit of justice, goodness and truth. Most especially, they reveal the love and care of God for each of us individually and for all humanity.

If you feel you have never had a meaningful experience during prayer or after listening to Scripture, consider why this might be the case.

It is a good idea to try different approaches to prayer that are centered on the Bible to see what might be the more meaningful for you. One popular approach that you will get to try during this week's Prayer Reflection is *lectio divina*.

LECTIO DIVINA

Lectio divina (meaning 'divine reading' or 'holy reading') is an ancient method of paying attention to God's Word in Scripture in order to achieve a fuller understanding of the message and thus be better able to take it to heart in daily life. It was first practiced in the early Christian monasteries. (We use the Latin words first used to name its various stages.) Pope Benedict XVI said: 'I would like in particular to recall and recommend the ancient tradition of *lectio divina*: the diligent reading of Sacred Scripture accompanied by prayer brings about that

FAITH WORD

Lectio divina

A manner of praying with Scripture; the person praying either reflectively reads a passage from Scripture or listens attentively to its being read, and then meditates on words or phrases that resonate.

—*United States Catholic Catechism for Adults* [USCCA], 518

intimate dialogue in which the person reading hears God who is speaking, and, in praying, responds with trusting openness of heart.'

Lectio divina is a particularly simple approach to prayer. It can be used individually or in groups. Ideally, you should choose the same time each day for this exercise and in a place free of distraction so that a daily habit will be learned. (This week's Prayer Reflection will offer suggestions for using *lectio divina* as a group.)

So, choose a text of Scripture, something fairly brief and engaging. Then:

- ⊙ *Lectio* (read): Slowly read the text, being alert for God's Word to your life; notice what stands out for you or seems significant.
- ⊙ *Meditatio* (meditate): Read the text again. Pause and talk to God about what you are hearing. Meditation is like *talking* to God.
- ⊙ *Contemplatio* (contemplate): Read it again. Now listen to and receive what God may be saying to you. Contemplation is like *listening* to God.

- ⊙ *Oratio* (pray): Recognize and pray whatever may be the deep desire of your heart.

Then some traditions add:

- ⊙ *Actio* (action): What does this study and prayer reflection call you to do? How will you take it to heart in your life now?

People from all walks of life are realizing the benefits of this type of spiritual exercise. *Lectio divina* allows the pray-er to explore the deep wisdom of Scripture and to experience God in a very personal way.

OVER TO YOU
- ⊙ After you have tried *lectio divina*, share with a partner or small group how you found the experience. For example, did it help you feel closer to God? Did it help you to find greater meaning in the Bible?

The place of the Bible in Church life, teaching, Liturgy and worship

OPENING CONVERSATION

In the Letter to the Hebrews, we read:

Indeed, the word of God is living and active, sharper than any two-edged sword, piercing until it divides soul from spirit, joints from marrow; it is able to judge the thoughts and intentions of the heart.   —Hebrews 4:12

◉ What do you hear the Word of God saying in this New Testament letter?

◉ The Bible has wonderful teachings not only for our minds, but, even more so perhaps, for our hearts. How do you think the Bible can 'judge the thoughts and intentions of the heart'?

THE LITURGY OF THE WORD

The Church's official public worship is called the **Liturgy**. The Catholic Church's celebration of the Liturgy and the Sacraments always includes proclaiming and listening to the Word of God. This sometimes includes readings from both the Old Testament and the New Testament, responding to the readings with a psalm or canticle drawn from the Bible, followed by an explanation of the Scripture passages and the wisdom they have for people's lives today (in the homily).

The **Liturgy of the Word** is an integral part of the celebration [of **Mass**]. The meaning of the celebration is expressed by the Word of God which is proclaimed and by the response of faith to it.
—CCC, no. 1190

The *Catechism* explains the importance of the proclamation of the Scriptures in this way:

The Holy Spirit gives a spiritual understanding of the Word of God to those who read or hear it, according to the dispositions of their hearts. By means of the words, actions and symbols that form the structure of a celebration, the Spirit puts both the faithful and the ministers into a living relationship with Christ, the Word and Image of the Father, so that they can live out the meaning of what they hear, contemplate and do in the celebration.
—CCC, no. 1101

The **Lectionary** is the book from which the Scripture readings are proclaimed during the Liturgy. The Lectionary contains the readings assigned by the Church for the celebration of Mass

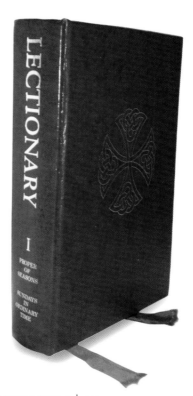

on Sundays, weekdays and feast days throughout the year. There is a three-year cycle of Scripture readings (Year A, Year B and Year C) for the Sundays, so that the principal passages relating to the deeds of God, the words of the prophets, the life, mission and teachings of Jesus and the teachings of the Apostles are proclaimed and heard by all over a three-year cycle. Weekday Mass readings follow a two-year cycle (Year 1 and Year 2).

Through the proclamation of Sacred Scripture during the Liturgy, the Church gives us the opportunity to hear the Word of God at Mass. Through the homily, we are helped to discern how the Word of God connects with our lives today, and we are challenged to respond to God's Word and change our ways of living by acting in the light of God's Revelation that we have heard.

The Church has its own calendar or year, known as the **liturgical year**. The Church's

liturgical year is the 'celebration throughout the year of the mysteries of the Lord's birth, life, death and Resurrection in such a way that the entire year becomes a "year of the Lord's grace". Thus the cycle of the liturgical year and the great feasts constitute the basic rhythm of the Christian's life of prayer, with its focal point at Easter' (CCC, Glossary). The liturgical year marks important seasons, feasts and events, as outlined in the following diagram. As you study the diagram, you will see that all the times of special significance have their origins in the Bible.

REFLECT AND DISCUSS

◉ Which is your favorite season of the liturgical year and what do you know of its origins?

◉ Why is it a favorite and what does it mean for your own faith?

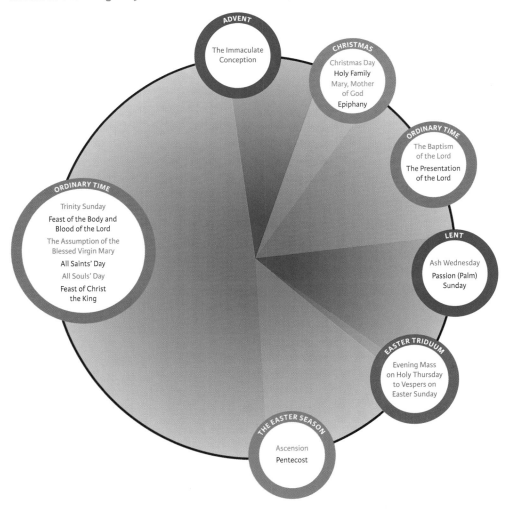

ADVENT
The Immaculate Conception

CHRISTMAS
Christmas Day
Holy Family
Mary, Mother of God
Epiphany

ORDINARY TIME
The Baptism of the Lord
The Presentation of the Lord

LENT
Ash Wednesday
Passion (Palm) Sunday

EASTER TRIDUUM
Evening Mass on Holy Thursday to Vespers on Easter Sunday

THE EASTER SEASON
Ascension
Pentecost

ORDINARY TIME
Trinity Sunday
Feast of the Body and Blood of the Lord
The Assumption of the Blessed Virgin Mary
All Saints' Day
All Souls' Day
Feast of Christ the King

THE PSALMS

The Word of God in the Bible, particularly in the **Psalms**, is also the basis for other forms of prayer, including sacred music. The Psalms from the Old Testament, sung or recited, are a tremendous reservoir for our spirit in the rushed and crowded lives we live today. The Psalms have an amazing power to bring us consolation when we need it, and confrontation when we need that as well. No book of the Bible is more likely to 'comfort the disturbed and disturb the comfortable' than the Psalms. Here are some examples:

The LORD is my shepherd, I shall not want.
    He makes me lie down in green pastures;
he leads me beside still waters;
    he restores my soul.

—Psalm 23:1–2

The LORD is my light and my salvation:
    whom shall I fear?
The LORD is the stronghold of my life;
    of whom shall I be afraid?

—Psalm 27:1

I cry aloud to God,
    aloud to God, that he may hear me.

—Psalm 77:1

The spirit of the Lord GOD is upon me,
    because the LORD has anointed me;
he has sent me to bring good news to the oppressed,
    to bind up the brokenhearted,
to proclaim liberty to the captives,
    and release to the prisoners.

—Isaiah 61:1

On the day I called, you answered me,
    you increased by strength of soul.

—Psalm 138:3

REFLECTIVE ACTIVITY

- ⊙ Open your Bible to the Psalms and choose a verse or verses that speak to your life right now.
- ⊙ Share your choice with a partner, and then listen to what she or he has chosen.
- ⊙ Then discuss why you chose those particular verses and how they spoke—as the Letter to the Hebrews promised—to your 'heart'.

PLAINCHANT

Plainchant, also called plainsong, is a type of church music developed in the Middle Ages. Plainchant does not use any instrumental accompaniment; instead, words are simply sung or 'chanted'. In Christian tradition it was believed that music should make a listener receptive to spiritual thoughts and reflections. This was why the melody was kept pure and unaccompanied.

Plainchant is usually used to sing the Psalms. It has become very popular in recent times and is another way in which people respond to the Bible and its spiritual wisdom.

GROUP ACTIVITY

- ⊙ With your group, listen to some plainchant on CD or DVD. Afterward, discuss your thoughts and feelings about your experience. What might we learn from this tradition of the Church for our own lives?

THE DIVINE OFFICE—A PRAYERFUL APPROACH TO SCRIPTURE

The Church has a very old tradition of praying the **Liturgy of the Hours**, more commonly known as the Divine Office. While, in the past, this form of

FAITH WORD

Liturgy

Liturgy refers especially to the public worship of the Church, including the Mass and the Liturgy of the Hours.

—USCCA, 518

The word 'liturgy' originally meant a 'public work' or a 'service in the name of/on behalf of the people'. In Christian tradition it means the participation of the People of God in 'the work of God'.

—CCC, no. 1069

In the liturgy of the Church, God the Father is blessed and adored as the source of all the blessings of creation and salvation with which he has blessed us in his Son, in order to give us the Spirit of filial adoption.

—CCC, no. 1110

daily prayer was prayed almost exclusively by the clergy and members of religious communities as a responsibility of their state of life within the Church, today praying the Liturgy of the Hours is also becoming popular with laypeople. The prayers and readings for the Liturgy of the Hours are found in a book known as the Breviary. Sometimes the praying of the Liturgy of the Hours is done communally, combining the recitation of prayers and readings with singing of hymns or chanting.

The Liturgy of the Hours is the official daily prayer of the whole Church, which laypeople often do not have the opportunity to share. It is a wonderful experience to participate in the Liturgy of the Hours being recited or sung. The Church encourages priests to schedule times to pray the Liturgy of the Hours with laypeople.

TALK IT OVER

◉ Why do you think the clergy and members of religious communities pray the Liturgy of the Hours each day?

◉ Have you ever attended a sung Liturgy of the Hours or heard any chant recordings of the Liturgy of the Hours? If you have, what was your reaction?

Taizé music and prayer

Taizé is a small village in the south of France. It is home to the Taizé community of over a hundred monks who come from the Catholic, Orthodox and Protestant traditions. Over 100,000 young people from around the world make pilgrimages to Taizé every year to take part in prayer and Bible study. They share their reflections on Bible passages and take part in communal work.

The community was founded by Brother Roger Schutz in 1940. In the years that followed, many other young men joined and committed themselves to live lives of simplicity, celibacy and community. In the 1960s young people began to visit Taizé. The community welcomes people of many different nationalities and religious traditions from across the globe. This diversity is reflected in the music and prayers. Taizé prayer includes chants that are sung in many languages. The chants usually consist of lines or phrases from the Psalms or other

parts of Sacred Scripture, which are repeated many times. The repetition is intended to aid meditation and prayer.

Today, in many places around the world, ecumenical prayers using music from Taizé are organized by people young and old who have visited Taizé.

Brother Roger, the founder of Taizé, was murdered on August 17, 2005. Pope Benedict XVI said on hearing of his tragic death, 'Brother Roger is in the hands of eternal goodness and eternal love, and has arrived at eternal joy.'

GROUP ACTIVITY

◉ With your group, listen to some Taizé music on CD or DVD. Afterward, discuss your response.

◉ Why do you think so many people find Taizé music conducive to prayer and reflection?

Applying the Word of God in Scripture to daily prayer and daily life

OPENING CONVERSATION

⊙ How does God's Word in the Bible help you in your day-to-day life?

GOD'S WORD FOR OUR LIVES

The Bible is the Word of God for our lives. It is readily available to guide us on life's path. Its wisdom can be taken to heart in all of life's situations. Reading the Bible, combined with prayer and reflection, helps us grow in both our understanding and our love of God.

It is important to have your own personal copy of the Bible. This way you can have it in your room, to read any time you like.

A great way to approach reading and praying from the Bible is first to 'bring your life to the Bible' and then to 'bring the Bible to your life'. In other words, before you start reading, stop and think about what is 'going on' in your life; name your hopes and fears, joys and sorrows, questions and issues. Then, bring your own 'life' to the Bible. Read it slowly and carefully, until you find the words that speak to your life and heart. Then pause and talk with God and try to understand what his Word says to you. Finally, try to imagine how you will bring the truth and wisdom you have found in the Bible back to your own life and put it into practice.

Another way to take the Bible to heart is by praying from it. For example, place yourself in the presence of God, open your Bible to the Book of Psalms, and slowly read a psalm, one verse at a time—now you are praying to God.

GROUP ACTIVITY

⊙ Take a few lines from last Sunday's Gospel reading or any favorite passage of Sacred

Scripture. Either individually or together, try bringing your life to these words, and these words to your life.

THE LORD'S PRAYER

Many of our favorite prayers, such as the Hail Mary, the *Angelus* and the Our Father (or **Lord's Prayer**), have their origins in the Bible. When Jesus' disciples asked him to teach them to pray, he gave them (and his disciples of all times) the Our Father. The version of this prayer that is closest to the words you will have learned can be found in Matthew's Gospel:

Our Father who art in heaven,
hallowed be thy name.
Thy kingdom come.
Thy will be done on earth, as it is in heaven.
Give us this day our daily bread,
and forgive us our trespasses,
as we forgive those who trespass against us,
and lead us not into temptation,
but deliver us from evil.

—Based on Matthew 6:9–13

Read these words carefully, as if they are new to you. What is Jesus suggesting for our prayer?

Notice that there are eight prayer movements, going line by line. Someone described them as two ladders, the first going up to God in praise and worship, the second as petitions for the blessings we need to 'come down' from God to our lives.

Why do you think Jesus tells us to address God as 'Father'?

Surely he was inviting us to acknowledge that we live in a close relationship with God, his Father, and that praying to our Father should develop in us the will to become like him. Through Baptism, we have become adopted daughters or sons begotten of one and the same Father. Surely, as children of God and his adopted sons and daughters, we are brothers and sisters of one and the same Father; sons and daughters in one large family—the family of God.

Surely this is the heart of the Church's message. Thus, the *Catechism of the Catholic Church* states: 'The Lord's Prayer is truly the summary of the whole gospel' (CCC, no. 2774). The Lord's Prayer is the quintessential prayer of the Church. It is a summary of the Good News announced and revealed in Jesus.

TALK IT OVER

⊙ Why do you think the *Catechism* describes the Our Father as 'the summary of the whole gospel'?
⊙ How would you summarize the message of the Our Father?
⊙ How different do you think the world would be if everyone were truly to live by the Lord's Prayer?

WHAT IS YOUR PERSONAL RESPONSE?

⊙ Which lines of the Our Father carry the most meaning for you?
⊙ In what sort of situations might you need to take the message of the Our Father to heart?
⊙ Can you pray it 'by heart'? If not, be sure to learn it.

JUDGE AND ACT

WHAT HAVE YOU LEARNED?

⊙ What is the best thing you have learned about the Bible in this chapter?

⊙ How has your own understanding of the Bible and opinion about it changed?

⊙ What difference might this make in your daily life?

⊙ Will you try to read the Bible more often? When?

RESPONDING TO THE CHALLENGE OF GOD'S WORD IN SCRIPTURE

The Bible calls us to live as 'people of God'. As Catholics, we are called to do so as disciples of Jesus, following 'the way' that he revealed and made possible by his Paschal Mystery—his life, Death, Resurrection and Ascension. While God always gives us his grace (loving help) to respond to his Revelation, we must accept his grace and freely respond and follow the way of Jesus. We know, however, that it is not always easy to respond and to live as a Christian; but there is no better way to live.

LEARN BY EXAMPLE

The story of Jean Donovan

This is a story of how one remarkable woman made the ultimate sacrifice in order to respond to God and live out the message of the Gospel in her life.

Jean Donovan was born in Westport, Connecticut in 1953 into an upper-middle-class family. After college, she worked as a management consultant in Cleveland and was engaged to a doctor. Though she felt a strong call to motherhood, she also felt that God was calling her to do mission work. As she herself said: 'I sit there and talk to God and say, why are you doing this to me? Why can't I just be your little suburban housewife?'

Jean responded to God's calling and traveled to El Salvador in July 1977, where she worked as a lay missionary along with Dorothy Kazel, an Ursuline nun. The pair provided help to refugees of the Salvadoran civil war and to the poor. They provided shelter, food and transportation to medical-care centers, and buried the bodies of the dead left behind by death squads.

Jean admired and was encouraged by the zeal and work of Archbishop Oscar Romero, and she often went to the cathedral to hear him preach. Romero was eventually assassinated, on March 24, 1980, for standing up for the Gospel and the poor against the Government. Jean and Sister Kazel stood beside his coffin during the night-long vigil of his wake.

In December 1980 Jean and three nuns joined the more than seventy-five thousand people who were killed in the Salvadoran civil war. On the afternoon of December 2, Donovan and Kazel, unaware that they were under surveillance by a National Guardsman, traveled to the airport in San Salvador to pick up two Maryknoll missionary sisters who were returning from a conference in New York. Acting on orders from their commander, five National Guard members changed into plain clothes and stopped the vehicle they were driving after they left the airport. Jean Donovan and the three sisters were taken to a relatively isolated spot, where the soldiers beat, raped and murdered them.

Early the next morning, local peasants found the bodies of the four women, and were told by local authorities to bury them in a common grave in a nearby field. Four of the local men did so; but they informed their parish priest, and the news reached the local bishop and the US Ambassador to El Salvador the same day. The shallow grave was opened the next day and the bodies exhumed. In the weeks before she died, Jean Donovan wrote to a friend:

> The Peace Corps left today and my heart sank low. The danger is extreme and they were right to leave. . . . Now I must assess my own position, because I am not up for suicide. Several times I have decided to leave El Salvador. I almost could, except for the children, the poor, bruised victims of this insanity. Who would care for them? Whose heart could be so staunch as to favor the reasonable thing in a sea of their tears and loneliness? Not mine, dear friend, not mine.

TALK IT OVER
- Which aspects of the message of the Our Father (of the Gospel) do you think most influenced Jean Donovan's decision to become a missionary?
- Where would you say she got the courage and the strength to continue with this work?

DECIDE FOR YOURSELF
- What can you learn from Jean's story for your own life?
- Give some examples of situations in your everyday life that might call you to make sacrifices in order to live according to the teachings of the Our Father and the values of the Gospel. Would you be prepared to make such sacrifices? Why?

RESPOND WITH YOUR FAMILY OR FRIENDS
- You might invite your family to read a passage from Sacred Scripture this week and reflect on it together. Perhaps take a few minutes to do so before an evening meal. Take a favorite parable, read it, and then ask people what they hear from it for their lives. End with 'Grace before Meals', weaving in the wisdom that you have heard through the parable.
- Try to find some Gregorian chant (a form of plainchant) on a DVD or CD and listen to it with your family or friends.

WHAT WILL YOU DO NOW?
- What do you think God is calling you to do in your world to build up his Kingdom? How will you answer God's call?

A PRACTICAL SUGGESTION
- Spend some time thinking about how you can put a Bible value into action in your life—right here, right now! For example, you might call on an elderly neighbor and enquire if they need help with anything, or perhaps just drop by for a chat; you might help with a fundraising or awareness campaign for a needy cause; you might join a local community action group aimed at helping those in need or simply designed to make your community a better place to live in.

LEARN BY HEART

The word of God is living and active, sharper than any two-edged sword.

HEBREWS 4:12

With the help of a teacher or spiritual guide, practice the following group method for *lectio divina*.

Begin by becoming quiet and calm within yourself. You might achieve this by taking some deep breaths, listening to some calming music or saying a short prayer.

The leader slowly reads aloud a passage from Sacred Scripture (maybe the Our Father or Psalm 139) as all listen for what God is saying to them through it.

The leader reads the text aloud again. Pause and talk to God in your own heart about what you are hearing.

The leader reads the text aloud yet again. Now listen and receive what God may be saying to you.

Recognize and pray whatever may be the deep desire of your heart.

CHAPTER 7

The Bible Is the Book of the Church

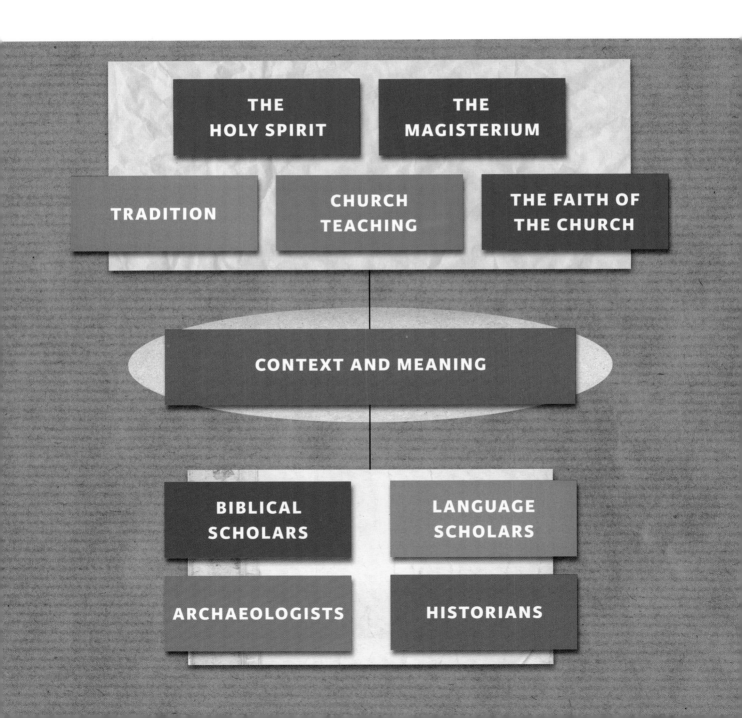

THE HOLY SPIRIT

THE MAGISTERIUM

TRADITION

CHURCH TEACHING

THE FAITH OF THE CHURCH

CONTEXT AND MEANING

BIBLICAL SCHOLARS

LANGUAGE SCHOLARS

ARCHAEOLOGISTS

HISTORIANS

IN THIS CHAPTER WE BEGIN TO LEARN HOW TO approach our reading of the Bible so that we can come to know its meaning for our lives. The key is that the Catholic Church provides the guidance we need to understand what the Bible means for our lives and what our lives mean before God.

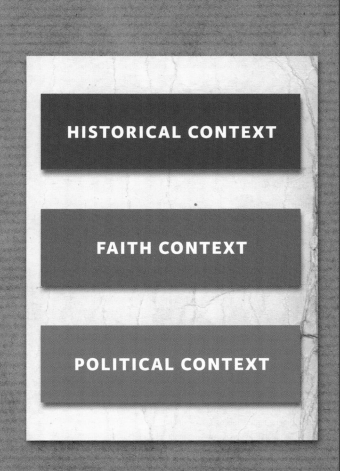

HISTORICAL CONTEXT

FAITH CONTEXT

POLITICAL CONTEXT

Faith Focus: These teachings of the Catholic Church are the primary focus of the doctrinal content presented in this chapter:

⊙ Scripture must be read and interpreted, keeping its divine authorship in mind, because Scripture is, first and foremost, the inspired Word of God.

⊙ Read and interpret Sacred Scripture within the Tradition and teaching of the Church.

⊙ Give attention both to what the human authors intended to say and to what God reveals to us by their words.

⊙ Read and interpret Sacred Scripture in the light of the same Holy Spirit by whom it was written.

⊙ There is a unity of content and teaching within the Bible; that unity is founded in the unity of God's plan, of which Jesus Christ is the center and heart.

⊙ The task of giving authentic interpretation to the Word of God, whether in its written form or in the form of Tradition, has been entrusted to the living teaching office of the Church, the Magisterium.

Discipleship Formation: As a result of studying this chapter and discovering the meaning of the faith of the Catholic Church for your life, you should be able to:

⊙ have a greater awareness of how you interpret and, at times, misinterpret, information and situations, and how this tendency can affect your interpretation of the Sacred Scripture;

⊙ realize that you need the guidance of the Church to interpret what the Bible means for your life;

⊙ value the role of Sacred Tradition and of the Magisterium in helping you to interpret the Bible for your life;

⊙ understand the meaning of the parable of the Good Samaritan for your life;

⊙ be more likely to value the Bible as a primary source of wisdom for living your life.

Scripture References: These Scripture references are quoted or referred to in this chapter:
OLD TESTAMENT: Psalms 119:105
NEW TESTAMENT: Matthew 5—7, 10:7–10, 16:16–19; **Luke** 10:25–37, 15:11–32

Faith Glossary: Familiarize yourself with the meaning of these key faith terms. Definitions are found in the Glossary: **Apostles, Church, Deposit of Faith, doctrine/dogma, Magisterium, Pentecost, Petrine ministry (office), Tradition**

Faith Words: Deposit of Faith; Tradition
Learn by Heart: Luke 10:27
Learn by Example: St. Francis of Assisi

How can we know what the Bible means?

All human beings want to make sense out of their lives, to find meaning and purpose. In the day-to-day events, activities and relationships we engage in, we are constantly trying to make sense out of things, to interpret what they mean and how to respond. Our Catholic faith teaches that our lives are meaningful and worthwhile because we are made in the image and likeness of God.

REFLECT AND DISCUSS

Someone once said, 'Your standpoint is your viewpoint.' In other words, where you stand determines what you see. Let's see if this is true!

Read this ancient legend of the people of India and then discuss how it shows the importance of seeing things from different perspectives.

The Elephant and the Blind Man

One day, a rajah's son asked, 'Father, what is reality?' 'An excellent question, my son. Come, everyone, we will go to the marketplace.' So the rajah and his son went outside and mounted their royal elephant. The rest of the entourage followed on foot. When they got to the marketplace, the rajah commanded, 'Bring me three blind men.' When the blind men arrived, the rajah commanded, 'Place one blind man at the elephant's tusk, one at the elephant's leg and one at the elephant's tail.' When that was done, the rajah said, 'Describe the elephant to me, blind men.' The man at the tusk said, 'It's like a spear.' The man at the leg said, 'It's like a tree.' The man at the tail said, 'It's like a rope.' As the men started to argue, the rajah said to his son, 'Reality, my son, is the elephant. And we are all blind men.'

BLIND MEN EXAMINING AN ELEPHANT | 19TH-CENTURY WOODCUT

WE ARE ALL INTERPRETERS

A thousand times a day we need to interpret the meaning of events, actions, relationships and so on. Even to stop at a traffic light requires us to 'interpret' the meaning of a red light, and then of a green light when it's time to go. The big name for interpretation is 'hermeneutics'. So, when scholars study and try to figure out the meaning of a Bible passage, they are engaged in hermeneutics. We get this word from the ancient Greek god, Hermes. Hermes was the messenger of the gods to the people. However, while Hermes could bring the people truth and meaning, he could also be a trickster and bring falsehood and delusion. It is still true when interpreting life that we should not 'jump to conclusions'; they could be wrong. This also applies to interpreting and understanding the Bible.

In our daily life we can be very quick to form impressions or jump to conclusions before we have checked out the full facts of a story or situation. Have a look at the following examples.

Mary, Mother of God slaughters Christ the King

St. Mary clobbers Child Jesus

These are the type of headlines you could expect to find in your morning newspaper after the previous day's Catholic high school football or basketball games. If you didn't know that these were the names of schools, and you knew nothing of the schools' games season, how might you falsely interpret these headlines?

OVER TO YOU

⊙ When might you have misinterpreted a situation or message? What consequences resulted from this?
⊙ What could you have done that might have prevented the misinterpretation?
⊙ How might you avoid misinterpreting a situation or message in the future?
⊙ How do you imagine people might misinterpret the meaning of a Bible story or passage?

WHAT CAUSES MISINTERPRETATION AND MISUNDERSTANDING?

Words and stories can be misinterpreted when we do not know the wider situation or circumstances to which they relate. To know 'the wider situation or circumstances' is to know the *context*. Knowing the context of a Scripture passage is very important when we come to interpret the meaning of Sacred Scripture.

Let's explore the importance of considering the *context* by taking some words 'out of context'.

If you heard someone say the word 'bear', what would you think of? How would you know whether they were referring to a furry animal, a naked object or person, or asking you to carry something, and so on?

If you heard someone say the word 'tip', what would you think of? How would you know whether they were referring to a point, talking about something toppling over, referring to money given for services, or talking about a light tap, and so on?

How would knowing the context help in each case?

Similarly, it is important to know the context of a Bible passage or a book of the Bible.

THE BIBLE—CONTEXT AND MEANING

The Bible is the greatest resource for enabling us to discover the meaning of our life. The Bible, because it is God's own Word to us, assures us that our life has great meaning, helps us to know what life is all about and guides us to live our life in meaningful ways. In order for the Bible to do this, so much depends on how we authentically interpret its meaning—and not misinterpret God's Word to us.

One key element in avoiding misinterpretation and in correctly interpreting and understanding the meaning of the words and stories in the Bible for our lives is to be aware of the context in which they were written. The context of a Bible story, teaching or passage—and even a book of the Bible—encompasses several different dimensions. We will explore some of these dimensions in this chapter. The *Catechism of the Catholic Church* emphasizes this point when it teaches:

In order to discover the sacred authors' intention, the reader must take into account the conditions of their time and culture, the literary genres in use at that time, and the modes of feeling, speaking and narrating then current.
—CCC, no. 110

For the remainder of this chapter we will discuss the meaning and importance of the 'context' of the Bible in reading and interpreting it accurately. (We will explore literary genres in the Bible in chapter 8.)

The contexts in which each of the books of the Bible was written

OPENING CONVERSATION

- Recall what you already know about the contexts in which different parts or books of the Bible were written—from your own reading of the Bible alone or in theology class or from listening to the Bible being proclaimed at Mass.
- What difference might these contextual circumstances make to how we read and understand the meaning of the Bible for us today?

UNDERSTANDING THE CONTEXT OF THE BIBLE

The world in which we live is very different from the world in which the Bible was written. If one of the authors of the Gospels were to pick up a newspaper today, how much of what they read would they understand? What kinds of information would they need in order to understand even the headlines and main stories? You have similar needs when you try to read and understand the Bible, which was written thousands of years ago. In order to understand correctly what the authors of the Bible intended to write, you will need pertinent information about the context; that is, the culture and customs, politics and religious practices and so on of the time. We will now explore some of the elements that make up the context in which the Bible was originally written.

First, we need to consider the **historical context**, which would have influenced how and what the biblical authors wrote. Understanding the historical context means taking into account

THE ANDROMEDA GALAXY, PHOTOGRAPHED THROUGH THE GALEX TELESCOPE

the views and beliefs that people held at the time. We need to understand, as best we can, the culture that was prevalent. The authors of the Book of Genesis, for example, did not write the accounts of Creation with the benefit of scientific knowledge that we have today. Science as we know it today only emerged at a much later time. Hence we cannot read the accounts of Creation with the mind of a twenty-first-century scientist. The writers of the biblical accounts of Creation wrote from a faith perspective. They wrote to communicate the central truth that our loving God created the world and everything in it. While science might argue about how and in what order the universe came into being, this 'faith' truth remains unchanged; namely, God created all that

THE GOOD SAMARITAN | VINCENT VAN GOGH

would have been amazed (perhaps even insulted) when they heard this because the priest and the Levite who passed by would have been expected to do the right thing; namely, live the demands of the Covenant. Instead, it was the Samaritan who stopped and helped. Anyone reading this story who does not know this context—that the Samaritans were despised by Jews of the time—would not get the point that Jesus was making. To interpret the parable correctly, one has to be aware of the political context in which it was written.

Third, we need to consider the **faith context** that permeated the life of the biblical authors. The inspired writers of the Bible were telling the story of the People of God; they were telling the story of their relationship with God and God's relationship with them as they came to know it, in faith, in the story of their lives as the People of God. In other words, the Bible is a book of faith written by people of faith who were deeply convinced of its Divine Revelation and meaning for people's lives. The one true God, the God of Abraham, had himself been revealed to them and continued to reveal himself to them in their experience. The writers of the Bible and the community of the People of God of whom they were a part, truly believed that God loved and cared for them and was part of their lives. When they wrote, their main concern was to share that faith with others. They were not seeking to write a 'history' of the time, as we understand history today. They were writing the story of God's relationship with his people, the story of God's merciful and saving love. They sought to awaken in the listeners a deep faith in God's goodness, love and mercy. When we remember that the overall context of the Bible is faith, we can better interpret, understand and apply its meaning to our lives.

exists and he continues to hold it in existence. God is the author of all life, seen and unseen.

Second, we need to consider the **political context**. For example, to help us understand the depth of meaning behind the parable of the Good Samaritan we need to appreciate that, at the time of Jesus, the Samaritans were the group most looked down upon by the Jews; the Jews considered the Samaritans to have been unfaithful to the Covenant. When Jesus told the parable of the Good Samaritan, he was addressing Jewish people, and the sharpness of his message would have been clearly understood; namely, the Samaritan in the parable was far more faithful to the Covenant than the priest and the Levite. Jews would have considered the priest and the Levite to be living embodiments of the Covenant. The parable tells of a traveler who had fallen among thieves and was left to die on the side of the road. The injured traveler was first ignored by a priest and then by a Levite (clergyman), both of whom avoided the injured traveler by passing him on the other side of the road. Then a Samaritan came along and crossed over to help him. Those listening to the parable

REFLECTIVE ACTIVITY

Take a favorite passage of Scripture (for example, the parable of the Prodigal Son in Luke 15:11–32) and try to figure out its historical, political and faith contexts. (The footnotes in the *Catholic Study Bible* will be a big help.)

WE CANNOT INTERPRET ALONE

Before his Death, Jesus promised to send the Holy Spirit upon the **Church** to continue his teaching ministry. The Holy Spirit came upon the disciples and the early Church at the celebration of the Jewish feast of **Pentecost** that immediately followed Jesus' Death, Resurrection and Ascension. The Holy Spirit, who inspired the writers of Sacred Scripture to write faithfully and without error the saving truth that God wished to reveal, continues to guide the Church to understand that Revelation. That is why Catholics turn to the Church for help in interpreting and understanding God's Word to us. In faith, we turn to and draw upon the wisdom and faith of the Church, not just our own opinion. Our Catholic faith encourages us to understand the Bible *for ourselves*, but not to do so *by ourselves*.

PENTECOST | CHURCH OF THE ASSUMPTION, CO. WEXFORD, IRELAND

TALK IT OVER

The following are some of the reasons why we need both our own insights and the guidance of the faith of the whole Church to read and understand the Bible. Read these on your own or with a partner and then discuss which one you think is the most important.

⊙ The Bible was written in different languages, and what we are reading is a translation. Knowledge of the original language is helpful to interpret a passage from Scripture correctly. Because most of us do not have this knowledge, we depend on others to provide us with such information.

⊙ The Bible was written a long time ago, in quite different life conditions and in radically different social and political situations. We need to be aware of these differences in order to understand what the Bible is saying to us. We need biblical scholars to provide us with this information.

⊙ Through the Church, the Bible has been at the center of a two-thousand-year-old tradition of religious thought, worship, activity and culture; it has been studied, celebrated, prayed with, meditated upon and commented about for millennia. Within itself and through the tradition that has grown up around it, the Bible reflects the great spiritual

wisdom of our foreparents in faith. We must always consider and be guided by this—the accumulated spiritual wisdom of the ages—when discerning the Bible's meaning and the meaning it lends to our lives now.

Hence, we need to approach the Bible humbly and with faith. In order to understand the Bible's message we must seek the assistance of the Church and of others. We need to learn from language scholars, archeologists and historians. We need to listen to the faith of the Church, to her teachings and **Tradition**, and to the way the Bible has been used in the Church. Without such help, we are in real danger of making mistakes, misinterpreting its meaning and misleading ourselves and others. With such help and guidance, the Bible can help us to understand the meaning of our lives and how to make meaning out of our lives from day to day.

WHAT ABOUT YOU PERSONALLY?

⊙ What is the most important thing you have learned from this chapter so far?

⊙ In what way do you think this will influence how you read the Bible in the future?

We know now why it is necessary, when reading the Bible, to be guided by the Church and to respect the accumulated wisdom and scholarship that has accompanied the Bible down through the centuries. In the following section we will look at where these teachings come from and who decides on what are the accepted teachings of the Church.

The teaching authority of the Catholic Church

OPENING CONVERSATION

⊙ What do you know about how the Catholic Church is structured in terms of her leadership roles and positions of authority?

QUICK QUIZ

⊙ Who is the current Pope?
⊙ Who was the previous Pope?
⊙ Who is the bishop of your diocese or the archbishop of your archdiocese?
⊙ Who is the pastor of your parish?
⊙ How are Catholic Church teachings formulated and agreed upon?
⊙ How are these teachings communicated to the Catholic people, and by whom?

READ AND RECORD

⊙ Read the following texts; that is, 'The Magisterium', 'Sacred Tradition' and 'The Unity of the Teaching of the Church'. As you read, underline or note down in your journal three key points from each one. Later you can check to see if you have the same points as your classmates.

THE MAGISTERIUM

The New Testament makes clear that Jesus commissioned the **Apostles** to be the proclaimers and guardians of his teachings, and made St. Peter the first among the Apostles and their leader (see Matthew 16:16–19). This was the origins of what we now call the **Petrine office**, or the ministry of Peter that has been passed on to the Pope since the time of St. Peter. The Pope is the successor of St. Peter and is the Bishop of Rome and pastor of the universal Church. Ever since then, this ministry and its responsibilities have been handed on and exercised by the Pope and the bishops.

As we learned in chapter 3, this living teaching office of the Church is called the **Magisterium**. *Magisterium* is a Latin word meaning 'teacher'. The Magisterium is made up of the Pope, together with the bishops of the whole Catholic Church, whose responsibility it is to give an authentic interpretation to the Word of God, whether contained in Sacred Scripture or in Sacred Tradition. It is the responsibility of the Magisterium, guided by the Holy Spirit, to 'ensure the Church's fidelity to the teaching of the Apostles in matters of faith and morals' by listening to and discerning the faith of the whole Catholic community. In other words, the Magisterium is the final judge of how

> The Magisterium is made up of the Pope, together with the bishops of the whole Catholic Church

we Catholics should interpret Scripture. The *Catechism of the Catholic Church* states:

> The task of giving an authentic interpretation of the Word of God, whether in its written form or in the form of Tradition, has been entrusted to the living teaching office of the Church alone. Its authority in this matter is exercised in the name of Jesus Christ. This means that the task of interpretation has been entrusted to the bishops in communion with the successor of Peter, the Bishop of Rome.
> —CCC, no. 85

SACRED TRADITION

The Magisterium gets its authority from Jesus, who promised and sent the Holy Spirit upon the Church to inspire and guide it down through the ages. Over our history, the Tradition of the Church emerged, helping to maintain the unity of the teaching of the Church. The Tradition of the Catholic Church 'is the living transmission of the message of the Gospel in the Church . . . conserved and handed on as the deposit of faith through the apostolic succession in the Church'. It refers to the body of teaching of the Church, made up of beliefs, doctrines, rituals and Scripture, that has been handed down from the Apostles to their successors, the Pope, the Bishop of Rome, and the other bishops. As the Second Vatican Council summarized so well:

> The tradition that comes from the apostles makes progress in the [C]hurch, with the help of the [H]oly Spirit. There is a growth in insight into the realities and words that are being passed on. This comes about through the contemplation and study of believers who ponder these things in their hearts [see Lk 2:19 and 51]. It comes from the intimate sense of spiritual realities which they experience. And it comes from the preaching of those who, on succeeding to the office of bishop, have received the sure charism of truth. Thus, as the centuries go by, the [C]hurch is always advancing towards the plenitude of divine truth, until eventually the words of God are fulfilled in it.
> —*Constitution on Divine Revelation*, no. 8

When an article of Catholic teaching on faith or morals is taught and tested over time, authentically reflects the teachings of the Apostles, and is officially proclaimed by the Magisterium, we name it Tradition—with a capital 'T' because it identifies it as part of the **'Deposit of Faith'** entrusted to the whole Church by the Apostles. Tradition is expressed in the Church's official teachings, in the holy lives of her faithful members and in her prayer and worship. The Magisterium is the final authority on Divine Revelation, whether in the Sacred Scripture or in Sacred Tradition.

THE UNITY OF THE TEACHING OF THE CHURCH

We need to distinguish between this Apostolic Tradition and the traditions (with a small 't') within the Church. These traditions are expressions of Tradition that have developed over time in different places and are part of the particular heritage of local churches in different places or within groups of Christians, such as religious orders.

The ministry and responsibility of the Magisterium includes guiding the authenticity of these traditions to ensure and maintain a unity in matters that are essential to Catholic faith and morals. There is lots of room for diversity of opinions and practices in non-essential matters or where different perspectives and practices can enrich our faith. However, in matters that define our faith, there is and must be an integral unity. The need for such unity, and efforts to ensure and maintain it, has been recognized from the days of the early Church. The Fathers of the Church, such as St. Athanasius, and the Doctors of the Church, such as St. Teresa of Ávila, have played a major role in helping the Church fulfill this responsibility. Their authority came from their standing in the community, their learning and wisdom and, in particular, their lived witness as disciples of Jesus Christ.

St. Irenaeus, a bishop of Lyons and a Father of the Church, was one of the earliest Christian theologians. Irenaeus was born about AD 125 in

ST. IRENAEUS | CARL ROHL SMITH

modern-day Turkey, was a student of St. Polycarp, who was martyred in AD 155, and was, in turn, a disciple of St. John the Apostle. Irenaeus is also famous for his work in helping to establish the official canon of Scripture, in particular by identifying the four Gospels as inspired books and recognizing how they maintained the unity of the early Church. Irenaeus also recognized and worked to maintain unity within the Church in matters of faith and doctrine. The only way to remain unified, he wrote, was by having one teaching authority, the bishops with the Bishop of Rome, whose mandate and authority was securely based on their succession from the Apostles. This has been the practice of our Catholic Church ever since—to be guided and united in faith by the teachings of the Magisterium.

TALK IT OVER

⊙ What might be dangers in interpreting the Bible in isolation, without reference to Catholic Church teaching and Tradition?

FAITH WORDS

Deposit of Faith

The heritage of faith contained in Sacred Scripture and Tradition, handed on in the Church from the time of the Apostles, from which the Magisterium draws all that it proposes for belief as divinely revealed.
—*United States Catholic Catechism for Adults*, 509

Tradition

The Tradition of the Catholic Church refers to the body of teaching of the Church, expressed in her beliefs, doctrines, rituals and Scripture, that has been handed down from the Apostles to their successors, the Pope and the bishops, through the ages, in an unbroken line of succession.

We must approach the Bible with an open mind and heart

The Bible is the inspired, written Word of God. It has sold more copies than any other book down through history. Sacred Scripture has been and is so central to human life and has influenced society so deeply that we cannot really fully understand the masterpieces of literature, art and music without some knowledge of the Bible. When we read the Bible with an open mind and heart and are guided by the Holy Spirit and the Church, our life is nourished. The Bible truly helps us to 'make meaning' out of our lives. The Word of God 'is a lamp to [our] feet / and a light to [our] path' (Psalm 119:105 adapted).

OPENING CONVERSATION

⊙ Talk about something from the Bible that has influenced your life. Why and how has it done so?

THINGS TO REMEMBER WHEN READING THE BIBLE

The Church teaches: 'Sacred Scripture must be read and interpreted with its divine authorship in mind' *(Constitution on Divine Revelation*, no. 12*)*

This statement reminds us that all of us can call upon the guidance of the Holy Spirit when reading the Bible. However, we must remember that the Holy Spirit also 'works' through the rules and guidelines that the Church has developed and acknowledged through the centuries to guide our reading to a true, authentic and reliable interpretation. These guidelines include:

⊙ Read the Bible within the Tradition and teachings of the Catholic Church. This means that we must be aware of how the Catholic Church has traditionally interpreted any book or passage of Scripture, including what it has meant to our foreparents in faith.

⊙ Pay attention to what the human authors meant in the original context of the text.

⊙ Know the history and conditions and culture of the time in which the book was written.

⊙ Read each part of the Bible in light of the unity of content and teaching of the whole Bible. No one passage of Scripture can contradict the overall message. For example, Jesus' saying 'I have not come to bring peace but a sword' (Matthew 10:34) cannot be taken out of context to mean that Jesus favored war; the rest of the Gospels make very clear that he was totally committed to peace-making.

⊙ Read the Bible for its spiritual wisdom and witness to faith, looking for how it can help you to live a wise and meaningful life as a disciple of Jesus. So, do not read it simply for the historical data it contains. Instead, read it

to come to understand the Word of God for your life in faith.

- Seek to learn its spiritual wisdom for life. This helps bring your own current issues and questions—your life—to its texts. Deliberately search out the truths and meaning you can bring back to your everyday life again.

Some consequences of these principles are:

- Different books or parts of the Scriptures cannot contradict one another because they all come from the same Holy Spirit. Our interpretation of one part of the Bible cannot be in conflict with the interpretation of another. Sounds simple, but this can easily be ignored!
- Revelation is God's own Word to us. Scripture and Tradition are two distinct modes of transmitting Revelation. Together they are a single Deposit of Faith of the Church. Scripture and Tradition are the one source of what the Church believes to be revealed by God. Both Sacred Scripture and Sacred Tradition are to be equally accepted and honored with reverence.
- There is a unity to our faith that we must always preserve. Any new interpretation must be measured against this unity.
- It is true to say that our understanding of our faith and our knowledge of the Scriptures continues to evolve and deepen in the Church. But there can never be contradiction or conflict about the central tenets of what we believe. They all fit in. They hang together. They are coherent. If there is an apparent contradiction, it is a sign that our interpretation of Scripture or Tradition is mistaken or not yet complete—and with the guidance of the Holy Spirit this work does and will continue.

GROUP WORK/DISCUSSION
- We already referred to the parable of the Good Samaritan and to the context in which it was told. Now read the whole story.

The Good Samaritan

Just then a lawyer stood up to test Jesus. 'Teacher,' he said, 'what must I do to inherit eternal life?' [Jesus] said to him, 'What is written in the law? What do you read there?' He answered, 'You shall love the Lord your God with all your heart, and with all your soul, and with all your strength, and with all your mind; and your neighbor as yourself.' And [Jesus] said to him, 'You have given the right answer; do this, and you will live.' But wanting to justify himself, he asked Jesus, 'And who is my neighbor?' Jesus replied. 'A man was going down from Jerusalem to Jericho, and fell into the hands of robbers, who stripped him, beat him, and went away, leaving him half dead. Now by chance a priest was going down that road; and when he saw him, he passed by on the other side. So likewise a Levite, when he came to the place and saw him, passed by on the other side. But a Samaritan while traveling came near him; and when he saw him he was moved with pity. He went to him and bandaged his wounds, having poured oil and wine on them. Then he put him on his own animal, brought him to an inn, and took care of him. The next day he took out two denarii, gave them to the innkeeper, and said, "Take care of him; and when I come back, I will repay you whatever more you spend." Which of these three, do you think, was a neighbor to the man who fell into the hands of the robbers?' He said, 'The one who showed him mercy.' Jesus said to him, 'Go and do likewise.'

—Luke 10:25–37

THE GOOD SAMARITAN | JAN LUKEN

REFLECT AND DISCUSS

- What do you think was the lawyer's way of making meaning out of his life? (Hint: Something about eternal life.)
- What do you think of how he asked the question 'What must I do?'?
- Why did the lawyer quote the Great Commandment of love when queried by Jesus?
- What did Jesus mean by 'Do this and you will live'?
- Sounds as if the priest and Levite went out of their way to avoid the wounded person. Why?
- Sounds as if the Samaritan 'crossed over' to the wounded one? Why?
- Why do you think the lawyer cannot answer 'the Samaritan' in response to Jesus' closing question?

LET'S PROBE DEEPER

- Imagine that you were there when Jesus told this parable for the first time. How do you think you would have felt upon hearing it? What would have surprised you? What might have caused you to question some of your prejudices?
- In this parable Jesus challenges our worldview, whereby we separate the world into friends and enemies. Through this parable Jesus asks us to expand and deepen our understanding of 'Who is my neighbor?'.

REFLECTIVE ACTIVITY

- Having heard this parable told by Jesus, how do you think you would have answered the question 'Who is my neighbor?'?
- With a partner, have the conversation that you think you would have had on that day.

JOURNAL EXERCISE

- Reflect on those people or groups whom many would not value or consider to be 'neighbors'; for example, people who are despised or marginalized in society today. Explain how the parable of the Good Samaritan challenges you to revisit your definition of those whom Jesus calls you to value and treat as your neighbor.
- Now write a modern version of the parable of the Good Samaritan, taking the characters and questions from our world today.

The parable of the Good Samaritan challenges you to revisit your definition of those whom Jesus calls you to value and treat as your neighbor

JUDGE AND ACT

WHAT HAVE YOU LEARNED?

◉ How can the Bible help you find meaning and purpose in your life?

◉ What are the best lessons you have learned from this chapter about how to read and interpret the Bible? How will you follow them in your life ahead?

LEARN BY EXAMPLE

The story of St. Francis of Assisi

How well do you know the life journey of St. Francis of Assisi and how that journey led him to the Bible to find the direction and meaning for his life?

ST. FRANCIS | GLORIA DEI EPISCOPAL CHURCH, NEW YORK

Francesco (Giovanni) Bernardone's birth date is uncertain; but it was some time during 1181 or 1182 in the city of Assisi in Umbria, Italy. His father, Pietro, was a very successful cloth merchant who traveled frequently between Assisi and France. Because of his love for France, Pietro renamed his son Francesco soon after Giovanni's Baptism. From this he was nicknamed 'Francis'.

The Bernardones were, by today's standards, an affluent upper-middle-class family. Francis' parents easily gave in to his every whim for fine clothes and the money he needed to entertain his friends. Francis was a good-looking teenager with a quick wit, who loved music and whose companionship his friends and others thoroughly enjoyed.

All this, however, lost meaning for Francis as he entered his twenties. He now longed for and began a very short-lived military career—in those days called 'gallant knight'. On his first expedition he was captured and imprisoned, during which he became seriously ill and began to question his newest quest. After recuperating, Francis soon forgot his doubts and he went off in battle again, and once more he became seriously ill. During this illness Francis dreamed that he was a prince dressed in armor marked with a

cross. When he returned to Assisi, his friends noticed that he was a changed young man; he was no longer the party-throwing center of Assisi's youth scene.

Francis was now on another journey. After several radical decisions that changed his relationship with his family and the opinions of the townspeople of Assisi, he went off alone into the rolling hills surrounding Assisi, dressed no longer in the fine clothes of his younger days but in the simple clothes worn by the poorest of the poor in and around Assisi; and living in a simple hut that he had built for himself.

In 1205, while Francis was praying before the crucifix in the ancient chapel at San

Damiano (St. Damien), he asked the Lord to give him further direction to his life. While in prayer, the answer came: 'Go Francis and rebuild my house, for it is about to fall into ruins.' The 'house', Francis would come to understand years later, was not the chapel at San Damiano, which was literally falling into ruins, but the Church.

Three years later, in February 1208, the living Word of God gave final and clear direction to his life. While at Mass in the chapel of Our Lady of the Angels, Francis listened attentively as the Gospel was proclaimed, 'As you go, proclaim the good news, "The kingdom of heaven has come near." Cure the sick, raise the dead, cleanse the lepers, cast out demons. You received without payment; give without payment.

Take no gold, or silver, or copper in your belts, no bag for your journey, or two tunics, or sandals, or a staff' (Matthew 10:7–10). Francis interpreted these words as God's word to him. From that day on he lived what he heard to the letter. These words would be his rule of life.

Francis and his Gospel way of life soon drew companions who joined him. St. Clare of Assisi, the founder of the Poor Clares, and her sister, St. Agnes, were among his earliest followers. Through Francis' way of life, his followers have seen God's Word interpreted for them and come alive and give direction to their lives. Today the followers of St. Francis of Assisi are known as Franciscans. The Franciscan way of living the Gospel is followed by members of the consecrated life, both men and women, and by laypeople.

OVER TO YOU
What do you find inspiring about Francis' life?

RESPOND WITH YOUR FAMILY
- Take some time to share what you have learned from the Gospel with your family. Talk about how what you have learned might influence the attitude of your whole family toward others in the future.

RESPOND WITH YOUR FRIENDS
The Sermon on the Mount is a collection of Jesus' teachings on what it means to be and live as his disciple.

- Choose a passage from the Sermon on the Mount (Matthew 5—7).
- With some friends, decide on one thing that you already do in your daily lives that is in line with the message of the passage you have chosen.
- Now decide upon something that you believe you should begin to do differently. Discuss how you will go about taking the first steps.

LEARN BY HEART

You shall love the Lord your God with all your heart, and with all your soul, and with all your strength, and with all your mind; and your neighbor as yourself.

LUKE 10:27

PRAYER REFLECTION

Pray the Sign of the Cross together.

LEADER
Today let us ask the Holy Spirit, who inspired the authors of Sacred Scripture to write what God wanted to reveal, to guide us too so that we will hear in the Bible what God wants us to hear.

We pray together:

ALL
Holy Spirit, our teacher and our guide. . . .

Open our minds so that we may better understand God's Word in the Bible.

Open our ears so that we may listen intently whenever God's Word is spoken.

Open our imagination to recognize what the Bible means for our own lives and for the life of the world.

Open our hearts so that our whole lives, all that we think, say and do, are lived in response to God's Word, as disciples of Jesus Christ.

We ask this through Jesus Christ our Lord. Amen.

LEADER
Let us spend some time quietly reflecting on how we can find meaning for our lives in the inspired words of Sacred Scripture.

All reflect in silence.
Pray the Sign of the Cross together.

CHAPTER 8

Interpreting the Word of God in the Bible

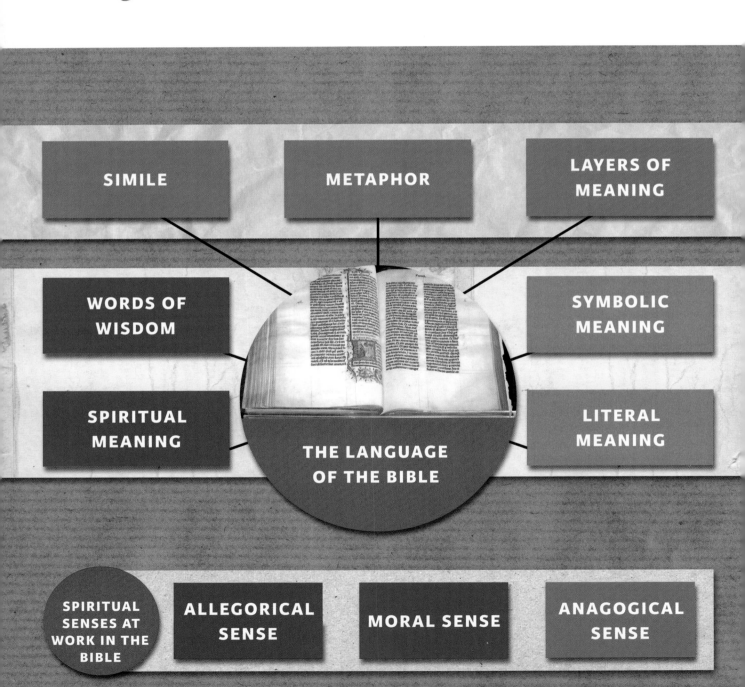

SIMILE

METAPHOR

LAYERS OF MEANING

WORDS OF WISDOM

SYMBOLIC MEANING

SPIRITUAL MEANING

THE LANGUAGE OF THE BIBLE

LITERAL MEANING

SPIRITUAL SENSES AT WORK IN THE BIBLE

ALLEGORICAL SENSE

MORAL SENSE

ANAGOGICAL SENSE

IN THIS CHAPTER WE EXPLORE THE DIFFERENT literary genres, or kinds of writing, found in the Bible and how to approach them in order to make our own the great spiritual wisdom of the Word of God for our lives

LITERARY GENRES IN THE BIBLE

HISTORICAL ACCOUNTS

HYMNS

STORIES

PSALMS

POETRY

PRAYERS

MYTHS

LETTERS

PARABLES

PROVERBS

PROPHETICAL TEXTS

LAW CODES

Faith Focus: These teachings of the Catholic Church are the primary focus of the doctrinal content presented in this chapter:
- All truth comes from God, who is Truth.
- One truth cannot contradict another truth. There is no conflict between religious truths and scientific and historical truth.
- The Church teaches us how to relate truths of faith to science.
- Truth is presented and expressed in the Bible through various forms of writing, or literary genres.
- Research by biblical scholars and the discoveries of biblical archaeology support our understanding of the biblical texts.
- There is a spiritual meaning to the Scriptures as well as a literal meaning.

Discipleship Formation: As a result of studying this chapter and discovering the meaning of the faith of the Catholic Church for your life, you should be able to:
- grow in confidence in your ability to read the Bible;
- appreciate that the Bible contains wisdom for your life;
- come to a deeper appreciation of the layers of meaning in the biblical texts;
- come to a fuller understanding of how Catholics should approach reading the Bible;
- reflect on your life in light of the parable of the Sower;
- select a biblical passage that has special significance in your life and consider how your life would change if you were to live its message.

Scripture References: These Scripture references are quoted or referred to in this chapter:
OLD TESTAMENT: **Genesis** 1:1—2:25; **Exodus** 1, 3:1–12, 4:19, 20:1–6; **Joshua** 10:12–14; **1 Kings** 3:17–27; **Psalms** 23:1, 37:30, 145:8–9, 13–16; **Proverbs** 10:12, 22:24 and 25, 26:20, 27:19, 28:15 and 18, 29:11; **Song of Songs**, 5:10–16; **Wisdom** 13:1–9; **Isaiah** 11:1–3, 6–9
NEW TESTAMENT: **Matthew** 2:13 and 20, 5:9, 14–16, 7:12, 13:31; **Luke** 4:4, 6:49, 8:5–15, 11:28; **John** 1:14, 3:16; **1 Corinthians** 1:18–25; **Ephesians** 3:18–19

Faith Glossary: Familiarize yourself with the meaning of these key faith terms. Definitions are found in the Glossary: **compassion, exegesis, Exodus (the), fundamentalism, literary genre, oral tradition, parable, People of God, proverb, senses of Scripture, wisdom**

Faith Word: exegesis
Learn by Heart: Luke 4:4; Luke 11:28
Learn by Example: Oscar Romero

How does the Bible offer wisdom for life?

Solomon was the son of King David, whom he succeeded as King of Israel. After he succeeded his father, Solomon asked God for the **wisdom** to govern the people wisely. He prayed: 'Give your servant therefore an understanding mind to govern your people, able to discern between good and evil; for who can govern this your great people?' (1 Kings 3:9). The Bible tells us that God was pleased with Solomon's prayer and granted him his request. Here is a story that the sacred author included in the First Book of Kings to show Solomon's wisdom in making judgments.

The Wisdom of Solomon

[One day two women came before Solomon.] One woman said, 'Please, my lord, this woman and I live in the same house; and I gave birth while she was in the house. Then on the third day after I gave birth, this woman also gave birth. We were together; there was no one else with us in the house. . . . Then this woman's son died in the night, because she lay on him. She got up in the middle of the night and took my son from beside me while your servant slept. She laid him at her breast, and laid her dead son at my breast. When I rose in the morning to nurse my son, I saw that he was dead; but when I looked at him closely in the morning, clearly it was not the son I had borne.' But the other woman said, 'No, the living son is mine, and the dead son is yours.' The first said, 'No, the dead son is yours, and the living son is mine.' So they argued before the king. . . .

So the king said, 'Bring me a sword', and they brought a sword before the king. The

THE JUDGEMENT OF SOLOMON | 18TH-CENTURY ITALIAN PLAQUE

king said, 'Divide the living boy in two; then give the half to the one, and half to the other.' But the woman whose son was alive said to the king—because **compassion** for her son burned within her—'Please, my lord, give her the living boy; certainly do not kill him!' The other said, 'It shall be neither mine nor yours; divide it.' Then the king responded: 'Give the first woman the living boy; do not kill him. She is his mother.'

—1 Kings 3:17–27

REFLECT AND DISCUSS

⊙ Who is a wisdom figure in your life?
⊙ Why do you consider this person as wise?
⊙ What wisdom have you learned from her or him?
⊙ Why is the Bible a great source of spiritual wisdom, truth and guidance for your life now? Give a specific example.

WORDS AND THEIR MEANINGS

A **proverb** is a succinct statement that is used to make a point or state a well-accepted truth. If we limit our understanding of the words in a proverb, we will surely miss the point or meaning of the proverb. Here are two well-known proverbs:

Don't count your chickens until they're hatched.

What do you think this means? If a person were to interpret this saying using only the dictionary meanings of the words, what are the chances that he or she would truly understand the meaning of the saying?

A bird in the hand is worth two in the bush.

What do you think the person who came up with this proverb intended for it to communicate? Is it literally about 'birds', 'hands' and 'bushes'? There is obviously a deeper meaning to the saying.

It would probably be impossible to trace the origins of these well-known and well-used proverbs, whose simple words convey pieces of wisdom that have withstood the test of time. Taken literally, the words have little meaning—except perhaps to someone in the business of rearing chickens or hunting wild fowl! It is the deeper or symbolic meaning of the words that gives each of these proverbs its power. To gain wisdom from them, the reader or listener must be aware of and understand their symbolic meaning, as intended by the writer or creator. The writer intended to pass on 'wisdom', not science.

WORDS OF WISDOM IN THE BIBLE
The Bible is full of words of wisdom, often couched in simple language—a wisdom far beyond any human wisdom, the Wisdom who is God. 'God's truth is his wisdom, which commands the whole created order and governs the world [see Wisdom 13:1–9]' (*Catechism of the Catholic Church* [CCC], no. 216). The Bible has its origins in an oral tradition of stories, poems and wise sayings. These were handed down from one generation to the next primarily by word of mouth, using simple language and examples from people's own life experiences. The stories, poems and sayings were the vehicles used to pass on the wisdom God wished to share with us for our life. (Read Psalm 37:30, 1 Corinthians 1:18–25.)

For example, for nomadic farmers, fishing folk, shepherds or merchants, the stories were fashioned to suit their situation. While stories of lost sheep might seem irrelevant to people today who live in a highly industrial, technological age, they spoke clearly to nomads, farmers and shepherds of biblical times. Readers of the Bible today need to take this into consideration. Once we understand that such biblical stories are a vehicle for meaning, and we peel back the layers and discover that meaning, we find that their wisdom is as relevant for us today as it was for the audiences of old. This is how we must approach the Bible if we are to learn from its infinite wisdom for our lives now.

OVER TO YOU
⊙ Read the following words of wisdom from the Book of Proverbs. What do these mean for your life today?
Proverbs 10:12; 22:24, 25; 26:20; 27:19; 28:15; 28:18; 29:11.

REFLECTIVE ACTIVITY
⊙ Have a go at composing your own wise saying using images that speak to people today.

In this chapter we will learn how to approach the Bible so as to uncover the Word of God for our lives—words of great wisdom for the best way to live. We will explore the different types of literature, or writings, in the Bible. Knowing the kind of writing, or **literary genre**, used by the sacred authors to communicate God's Word is vital to interpreting its meaning correctly and making our own its great spiritual wisdom.

Approaching the different literary genres and writing styles in the Bible

THE USE OF SIMILE AND METAPHOR IN THE BIBLE

You already know that a simile is a form of comparison that uses such words as 'like' or 'as' to compare one thing to another; for example, 'My love is like a red red rose'. You probably also know that a metaphor is another form of comparison but without the use of such words as 'like' or 'as'. Instead, in a metaphor, one thing is said to *be* another thing; for example, 'You are a lighthouse, showing me the way through troubled waters'. The writers of the Bible often used similes and metaphors to communicate God's Word. It is important to recognize when the sacred author is using simile or metaphor because the words used convey, deliberately, more than the literal meaning.

The Song of Solomon is an example of a biblical author's use of simile and metaphor. Here is an extract from it:

My beloved is all radiant and ruddy,
　　distinguished among ten thousand.
His head is the finest gold;
　　his locks are wavy,
　　black as a raven.
His eyes are like doves
　　beside springs of water,
bathed in milk,
　　fitly set.
His cheeks are like beds of spices,
　　yielding fragrance.
His lips are lilies,
　　distilling liquid myrrh.
His arms are rounded gold,
　　set with jewels.
His body is ivory work,
　　encrusted with sapphires.
　　His legs are alabaster columns,
　set upon bases of gold.
His appearance is like Lebanon,
　choice as the cedars.
His speech is most sweet,
　and he is altogether desirable.
This is my beloved and this is my friend.
　　　　　　　　　　　　—Song 5:10–16

OVER TO YOU

⊙ How many similes and metaphors can you identify in these verses?

Let's look at two more examples, this time from the Gospels:

The kingdom of heaven is like a mustard seed that someone took and sowed in his field; it is the smallest of all the seeds, but when it has grown it is the greatest of shrubs and becomes a tree, so that the birds of the air come and make nests in its branches.　　　　—Matthew 13:31

You are the light of the world. . . . No one after lighting a lamp puts it under the bushel basket, but on the lampstand, and it gives light to all in the house. In the same way, let your light shine before others, so that they may see your good works and give glory to your Father in heaven.

—Matthew 5:14–16

TALK IT OVER

⊙ First, what do *you* hear from each of these Scripture passages? What wisdom might they have for your life?
Then, review together:

⊙ What is the writer saying about the Kingdom of God in comparing it to a mustard seed?

⊙ What makes the mustard seed such an effective symbol?

⊙ Where is the metaphor in Matthew 5:14–16?

⊙ Why might the symbol of light have been especially effective and powerful some two thousand years ago, when the Gospels were written? (Hint: Think about how technology has developed since then.)

⊙ What have you already learned about how to read and discern the wisdom of the Bible?

REFLECTIVE ACTIVITY

⊙ Think of your own contemporary metaphor or simile for the Kingdom of God.

LITERARY GENRES IN THE BIBLE

The research of biblical scholars has concluded that the biblical authors used many different forms and styles of writing to convey what God intended to reveal to us through their words. It is necessary for us to recognize these different literary genres in order to get an accurate sense of what they were trying to communicate to us. 'The fact is that truth is differently presented and expressed in the various types of historical writing, in prophetical and poetical texts, and in other forms of literary expression' (Vatican II, *Constitution on Divine Revelation*, no. 12). For example, in the Old Testament we read the Books of Kings as historical accounts of the reigns of kings, while we

read the Books of Jonah and Job as short stories, not as factual accounts of actual happenings. We read the Song of Songs as a love poem, and the Books of Wisdom and Proverbs and Sirach (Ecclesiasticus) as books that offer guidance and advice on how to live the Covenant faithfully. In the New Testament we read the Gospels as witness to the faith of the Apostles and the early Church in Jesus, the Acts of the Apostles as a faith account of the missionary endeavors of the early Church, and the Epistles as circular letters of faith to the early Christians. To understand these genres, we must keep both the kind of text and its cultural context in mind.

LET'S SEE WHAT HAPPENS WHEN WE MISINTERPRET A LITERARY GENRE

In the Book of Joshua, chapter 9, we read the story of Joshua and the Israelites defeating the Amalekites. We are told that Joshua was winning the battle but that darkness was falling and night would allow the enemy to escape. So Joshua prayed that the sun would stand still, and the text seems to claim that it did. The sun stopped and the Israelites under Joshua finished the victory. We read:

On the day when the LORD gave the Amorites over to the Israelites, Joshua spoke to the LORD;

VICTORY OF JOSHUA OVER THE AMALEKITES | NICOLAS POUSSIN

and he said in the sight of Israel,
> 'Sun stand still at Gibeon,
> > and moon, in the valley of Aijalon.'
> And the sun stood still, and the moon
> > stopped,
> > until the nation took vengeance on their
> > enemies.

Is this not written in the Book of Jashar? The sun stopped in midheaven, and did not hurry to set for about a whole day. There has been no day like it before or since, when the LORD needed a human voice; for the LORD fought for Israel.

—Joshua 10:12–14

In former centuries, readers understood that the sun actually stood still for Joshua that day. Following on, they believed that the sun orbited the earth; it had to, if, according to the Bible, the sun could stand still! This interpretation caused great problems later when, for example, Galileo (1564–1642) discovered that Earth orbits the sun rather than the other way round. Galileo made this claim as a result of his astronomical observations. Opponents of Galileo argued that his discoveries had to be false because the Bible said that the sun orbits Earth. The difficulty was, of course, that the Book of Joshua was being read

(at least at that point) as a book of history, and so the expectation was that it contained historical facts.

More recently, Bible scholars realized that the Book of Joshua itself signals that it is quoting from an epic poem: 'Is this not written in the Book of Jashar?' Once you notice this, then you will read the phrase 'the sun stood still' in a different context. It is now clear that the writer is not speaking of astronomy; rather, the phrase is used simply as a figure of speech, just as we might say in describing a wonderful party or a historic sports victory that 'time stood still'. It conveys a feeling, the impact that something has made, rather than an actual occurrence. It was also the Israelites' way of expressing their faith that God had given them victory in battle.

REFLECTIVE ACTIVITY

- Think of other everyday examples of situations where we speak figuratively or metaphorically.
- Working in pairs or small groups, imagine the sort of misunderstandings that could arise if such types of speech were taken literally.

TALK IT OVER

- The Catholic Church now makes clear that there is no conflict between the truths of faith and the discoveries of science. Why do you think the Church takes this position?

SCRIPTURE READING ACTIVITY

- Read and discuss the following biblical passages from Exodus and Isaiah which represent different forms and styles of writing. Before you begin this activity, recall and remember that, to interpret the Bible, we must keep a number of questions—or 'rules'—in mind:
  - What kind of writing is the author using in this particular piece and for what purpose?
  - What does the text mean in the context of the lives of the people at the time when it was written?
  - What does the text say to us about God's action in the events being described?
  - What great truths of wisdom does the text suggest for our own lives in today's world?

GALILEO GALILEI | JUSTUS SUSTERMANS

EXTRACT 1: EXODUS 3:1–12

Background note: This is an extract from one of the greatest stories of the Bible—God's liberation of the Israelites from slavery in Egypt. The word 'Exodus' means 'departure' and the Book of Exodus is the story of this most important event in the history of Israel. It reminds us that God favors justice for all and helps to liberate people from slavery. Moses is the key figure in the Book of Exodus, as he leads his people to freedom.

Moses at the Burning Bush

Moses was keeping the flock of his father-in-law Jethro, the priest of Midian; he led his flock beyond the wilderness, and came to Horeb, the mountain of God. There the angel of the LORD appeared to him in a flame of fire out of a bush; he looked, and the bush was blazing, yet it was not consumed. Then Moses said, 'I must turn aside and look at this great sight, and see why the bush is not burned up.' When the LORD saw that he had turned aside to see, God called to him out of the bush, 'Moses, Moses!' And he said, 'Here I am.' Then he said, 'Come no closer! Remove the sandals from your feet, for the place on which you are standing is holy ground.' He said further, 'I am the God of your father, the God of Abraham, the God of Isaac, and the God of Jacob.' And Moses hid his face, for he was afraid to look at God.

Then the LORD said, 'I have observed the misery of my people who are in Egypt; I have heard their cry on account of their taskmasters. Indeed, I know their sufferings, and I have come down to deliver them from the Egyptians, and to bring them up out of that land to a good and broad land, a land flowing with milk and honey. . . . The cry of the Israelites has now come to me; I have also seen how the Egyptians oppress them. So come, I will send you to Pharaoh to bring my people, the Israelites, out of Egypt.' But Moses said to God, 'Who am I that I should go to Pharaoh, and bring the Israelites out of Egypt?' He said, 'I will be with you; and this shall be the sign for you that it is I who sent you: when you have brought the people out of Egypt, you shall worship God on this mountain.'

TALK IT OVER

- What do you think was the aim of the person who wrote this passage?
- What would this text have taught the people of Israel who first read it about God?
- What did they learn about Moses from this story?
- Now, as you bring your own life to this sacred text, think about the truths *you* hear, the wisdom it holds for *you*.

THE TREE OF JESSE | BAVARIA, C. 1200 AD

EXTRACT 2: ISAIAH 11:1–3, 6–9

Background note: Isaiah was a great prophet. The task of the prophets was to help the people to live the Covenant that they and God had entered into, especially at times when they were doing otherwise. Isaiah lived during the second half of the eighth century before the birth of Jesus. In this extract Isaiah foretells the coming of a time of worldwide peace, when a descendant of King David will be the ideal king.

The Peaceful Kingdom

A shoot shall come out from the stump of
   Jesse,
   and a branch shall grow out of his roots.
The spirit of the LORD shall rest on him,
   the spirit of wisdom and understanding,
   the spirit of counsel and might,
   the spirit of knowledge and the fear of the
   LORD.

His delight shall be in the fear of the
   LORD. . . .

The wolf shall live with the lamb,
   the leopard shall lie down with the kid,
the calf and the lion and the fatling together,
   and a little child shall lead them.

REFLECT AND DISCUSS

⊙ With a partner, pick out some of the symbolic language in the passage and explain its purpose.
   Then discuss:
⊙ What do you think Isaiah wanted to achieve through this passage?

⊙ What images speak to you of peace?
⊙ Now, as you bring your own life to this sacred text, think about the truths *you* hear, the wisdom it holds for *you*.

The literal meaning is a basis for the broader interpretation of Scripture

Do you know Texas Tyler's song 'The Deck of Cards'? It tells the story of a young soldier in the Second World War when, one Sunday, his company attended church. As the other soldiers produced their prayer books, this young man got out a deck of cards. The sergeant was angry, arrested him and brought him before the provost marshal.

When asked what he was doing, the young soldier replied, 'Sir, I have been on the march for about six months. I have neither a Bible nor a prayer book, but I hope to satisfy you, Sir, with the purity of my intentions. You see, Sir, when I look at the ace, it reminds me that there is but one God. And the deuce reminds me that the Bible is divided into two parts: the Old and the New Testaments. . . .'

Can you imagine what the young soldier thought of when he looked at each of the other cards?

The deck of cards was a 'coded text' for the young soldier. In other words, the cards had another meaning beyond the 'literal meaning' for him. The same is true of the Bible; the text often has much more meaning than the literal meanings of the words used.

REFLECT AND DISCUSS

⊙ From what you have learned already, how would you explain the young soldier's use of the cards?

⊙ What words and images in your own life have a spiritual meaning—a meaning beyond their literal meaning—for you?

THE WRITTEN WORD OF GOD HAS MANY LAYERS OF MEANING

To us, many parts of the Bible are like a coded text. It is not that the biblical authors were trying to hide or obscure their message; rather, they wrote in language suitable to their audience and culture, which may seem 'coded' to us. The Catholic Church recognizes and teaches that there is a 'spiritual meaning' to the Scriptures as well as a 'literal meaning'. We refer to these two aspects of Scripture as the **Senses of Scripture**.

For example, Genesis chapter 1 states that God created the world in six days, and rested

on the seventh day. But Catholics see this great poetical account as presenting truths of faith that God is the Creator and Sustainer of everything that exists. Genesis teaches great truths but NOT a scientific description of what actually occurred.

In other words, the biblical author intended to teach the great truths of faith that God created the world, that human beings are made in God's image and have the duty of acting as God's stewards of creation, that God loves human beings and wants them to be close to him, that the universe's order and design is God-given, that God sustains the world in being, and that the Sabbath day (the Lord's Day for Christians) is a day of rest, a day set aside to worship and honor God, the Loving Creator and Sustainer of all that is. This deeper spiritual reading of the text allows the reader to explore the layers of meaning buried beneath the written word, something that is not possible with a literal interpretation.

OVER TO YOU

- ◉ What examples of passages from Scripture can you think of where people might take the literal interpretation of the words too far?
- ◉ How would you help them to avoid doing so?

The *Catechism of the Catholic Church* states that the unity of Sacred Scripture is founded in 'the unity of God's plan, of which Christ Jesus is the center and heart' (CCC, no. 112). We need to keep in mind that the biblical authors of the later books of the Bible were members of the **People of God** who, by and large, were very familiar with the earlier books of the Bible. Many of their references, stories, symbols, metaphors and so on were influenced by the accounts and stories in the earlier books. For example, Matthew wrote his account of the Gospel primarily for Jewish converts. One point that Matthew was making in his Gospel was that Jesus is the new Moses. His readers' knowledge of the Scriptures of ancient Israel helped him accomplish this.

The story of **the Exodus**, of God saving his people from slavery in Egypt and from Pharaoh's actions, was the key saving event in the history of the Israelites, and it was celebrated yearly. Matthew's account of Herod's slaughter of the innocent children mirrors Pharaoh's role in the events of the Exodus. Similarly, the angel's leading the Holy Family to, and calling them from, exile in Egypt mirrors that of Moses. The saving events recorded in the Book of Exodus prefigured the saving of the infant Jesus, the new Moses. Both stories point to the faith of God's people in the saving love of God.

In Exodus we read:

The LORD said to Moses in Midian, 'Go back to Egypt; for all those who were seeking your life are dead.'

—Exodus 4:19

In Matthew we read:

Get up, take the child and his mother, and flee to Egypt and remain there until I tell you; for Herod is about to search for the child, to destroy him.

—Matthew 2:13

Get up, take the child and his mother, and go to the land of Israel, for those who were seeking the child's life are dead.

—Matthew 2:20

Yet, there is another level of significance to consider here. Since God is truly the author of the biblical text, the text not only speaks to the past but to the future as well. That is, an earlier incident in the Old Testament can prefigure its fulfillment in Jesus Christ and in other New Testament events. Such a prefiguring of what is to come is called a 'type' or 'sign'—the word Bible scholars use to refer to a spiritual promise/fulfillment of this kind.

In summary, there are three 'spiritual senses' at work in the Bible:

- The *allegorical* sense: This is when a particular story or detail stands for something in the life of Christ or of the Church. For example, the miracle at the Red Sea foreshadows Christ's victory over death and the Christian's new life through the waters of Baptism.
- The *moral* sense: This is when the spiritual meaning suggests things that we ought to do. For example, the love of God for Israel, and then for the Church, suggests that married love should be similarly supportive and forgiving.
- The *anagogical* sense: This is when the biblical events are a sign of something eternal. For example, the feeding of the Israelites with manna, and the multiplication of the loaves and fishes by Jesus, and the Last Supper in the Upper Room, all foreshadow the heavenly banquet in the Kingdom of God.

Catholic readers of the Bible read all of these meanings in prayerful study, guided by the faith of the whole Church and her teaching authority, the Magisterium.

Meanwhile, Scripture scholars discern the literal and spiritual meanings of the Bible in a process called **exegesis**—from a Greek word meaning both 'to interpret' and 'to explain'. Of course, just as the texts of the Bible were shaped by the time, events and culture of their authors, so even the most scholarly of readings by the best 'exegetes' today are influenced by their time and culture. This is why we need the guidance of the faith of the whole Church in discerning, interpreting and explaining the truths and wisdom of the Bible for our lives. This being said, all of us are called to be exegetes. We are constantly to bring our lives to

FAITH WORD

Exegesis

Exegesis is the process used by Scripture scholars to determine the literal and spiritual meanings of the biblical text.
—*United States Catholic Catechism for Adults*, 512

the texts of the Bible in order to figure out how to bring its wisdom and truths to our lives today.

As we interpret the Bible together, we find that its truth and wisdom can never be exhausted. The Bible is indeed the Greatest Book ever written with the Greatest Story ever told. Its overall story is of God's unconditional love for us. St. Paul summed it up this way: 'The breadth and length and height and depth' of God's love in Christ 'surpasses knowledge' (Ephesians 3:18–19). In other words, we can never fully comprehend the fullness of meaning of the biblical texts for our lives. The Bible, the written Word of God, will always have more to teach and reveal to us. As one great scholar noted, the Bible has 'a surplus of meaning'. We can read it one day and recognize some truth or wisdom for life, but then read the same text a week later, perhaps after experiencing a joy or sorrow, and find a new level of meaning. Guided by the Holy Spirit and the teachings of our Church, we are constantly to bring our lives to the Bible and the Bible to our lives in order to live as the People of God in Jesus Christ.

WHAT ABOUT YOU PERSONALLY?
- Do you feel more confident now in reading the Bible? Why or why not?

GROUP EXERCISE
- Read Matthew 2:13: 'An angel of the Lord appeared to Joseph in a dream and said, "Get up, take the child and his mother, and flee to Egypt, and remain there until I tell you; for Herod is about to search for the child, to destroy him." '
- Then read Exodus chapter 1 to find the passage that influenced the author of Matthew's Gospel in relation to this piece.
- Compare the two passages.

How, then, should we read the Bible?

WHAT IS THE CATHOLIC TEACHING ON READING AND INTERPRETING SCRIPTURE?

The Catholic Church clearly teaches that the Bible is the 'Word of God in human language', which passes on God's Revelation of himself and his divine plan of Creation and Salvation to our lives today as it has throughout history. Because that Revelation has been passed on 'in human language', Catholics also see the need to be very open to exploring the meaning of the Bible using scientific methods, history, archaeology, knowledge of ancient literature and language, genre study and so on. The Catholic Church teaches that all truth comes from God; God created the universe; God reveals God's own self, his own nature, in the Bible; and one truth cannot contradict another truth. All truths have the same Author, God who is Truth!

Accordingly, Catholics look behind the literal, or dictionary, meaning of the words and phrases used by the sacred authors. In our interpretation of the Bible we, as Catholics, take into account 'the sacred authors' intention . . . the conditions of their time and culture, literary genres in use at that time, and the modes of feeling, speaking and narrating then current' (CCC, no. 110). An interpretation that understands the biblical text only at its most obvious level of meaning, and does not take into account the criteria used by the Catholic Church, is sometimes referred to as fundamentalist.

THE CREATION OF THE SUN, MOON AND PLANETS | MICHELANGELO

> Catholics look behind the literal, or dictionary, meaning of the words and phrases used by the sacred authors

A . . . characteristic of biblical **fundamentalism** is that it tends to interpret the Bible as being always without error or as literally true in a way quite different from the Catholic Church's teaching on the inerrancy of the Bible. For some biblical fundamentalists, inerrancy extends even to scientific and historical matters.

The Bible is presented without regard for its historical context and development.
—*Pastoral Statement for Catholics on Biblical Fundamentalism*, National Conference of Catholic Bishops Ad Hoc Committee on Biblical Fundamentalism

The Scopes Trial

In 1925, an unusual court trial took place in Dayton, Tennessee. A high school biology teacher, John T. Scopes, had been charged with teaching about evolution in contradiction to the literal meaning of the Book of Genesis, chapters 1 and 2, and its accounts of Creation; namely, God created the world in six days (six 24-hour periods of time) and so on. This teaching was also seen as an act of disobedience to the Statutes of the State of Tennessee. As a result, the Scopes Trial became a major media event.

The prosecution was conducted by a famous conservative politician, William Jennings Bryan, who had at one time been a candidate for president of the United States. The defense attorney was Clarence Darrow, a noted liberal lawyer.

At issue was the way to read the Bible. Darrow argued that the account in Genesis of God creating the world in six days and of Adam and Eve was a fairytale, and that the random-chance evolution of Charles Darwin was what really happened. Bryan and his team argued that the biblical story of Creation

JOHN T. SCOPES, PHOTOGRAPHED IN 1925

was factual in every detail, that God created the universe in the space of a week and that species did not change over millions of years by the process known as evolution.

John T. Scopes was found guilty by the Tennessee Court (he had broken the law of Tennessee); but he was fined only one dollar!

OVER TO YOU

⊙ Imagine you were at the Scopes Trial. How would you explain your position to someone who takes the opposite position?

CLASS PROJECT

⊙ Read Genesis chapters 1 and 2. Then divide into two groups, one group to formulate reasons why evolutionary theory contradicts the Bible, and the other to produce reasons why it does not. Discuss your findings and/or use them as the basis for a class debate.

JUDGE AND ACT

THE SOWER | VINCENT VAN GOGH

REVIEW ACTIVITY

⊙ Working together as a class group, make a list of the best guidelines the Church teaches for how to read and discern the meaning of the Bible.

READ AND JUDGE

⊙ Read the following story from the Gospel according to Luke:

When a great crowd gathered and people from town after town came to him, he [Jesus] said in a **parable**: 'A sower went out to sow his seed; and as he sowed, some fell on the path and was trampled on, and the birds of the air ate it up. Some fell on the rock; and as it grew up, it withered for lack of moisture. Some fell among thorns, and the thorns grew with it and choked it. Some fell into good soil, and when it grew, it produced a hundredfold.' As he said this, he called out, 'Let anyone with ears to hear listen!'

When the disciples asked Jesus what this parable meant, he explained it to them:

'Now the parable is this: The seed is the word of God. The ones on the path are those who have heard; then the devil comes and takes away the word from their hearts, so that they may not believe and be saved. The ones on the rock are those who, when they hear the word, receive it with joy. But these have no root; they believe only for a while and in a time of testing fall away. As for what fell among the thorns, these are the ones who hear; but as they go on their way, they are choked by the cares and riches and pleasures of life, and their fruit does not mature. But as for that in the good soil, these are the ones who, when they hear the word, hold it fast in an honest and good heart, and bear fruit with patient endurance.'

—Luke 8:5–15

The parable of the sower sowing his seed is a very simple tale when it is read in a literal way.

However, when the deeper symbolic meaning is uncovered, it is quite a different story. In this instance, Jesus uncovers the deeper meaning for us. But this doesn't always happen in the Bible. Sometimes we have to discover the hidden meaning for ourselves. This we do guided by our Church, by the research of Bible scholars and by the good rules we are learning in these chapters. Remember, too, that the Holy Spirit works through the Church, the scholars and our own good faith to guide us to realize and make our own the truths and wisdom of the Bible.

WHAT IS YOUR RESPONSE TO THE PARABLE OF THE SOWER?

- Where do you think you fit into this story? What kind of soil does the Word of God find in your life?
- Which type of person would you like to be?
- What might be the 'thorns' that choke the seeds in our world today?

LEARN BY EXAMPLE

The story of Archbishop Oscar Romero

The story of Oscar Romero shows us what happens when someone takes the Word of God seriously in how they respond to what is happening in the world around them and how they live their lives.

Archbishop Oscar Romero is one of the best known witnesses of the Gospel in recent history. Born in 1917 into the privileged class of El Salvador in Central America, he increasingly realized that living the Gospel message and advocating for the rights of the oppressed and suffering people of society were inseparable for a Christian.

For most of the twentieth century, El Salvador had been ruled by a series of hard-line military governments. During this time, Salvadoran society became greatly divided by economic inequalities and classism, which left the majority of people living in poverty. This eventually led to social and political unrest. Tensions in the country increased in the 1970s and soon gave way to murder and acts of terrorism by guerrilla groups and right-wing 'death squads'.

In 1979 a junta government toppled the ruling right-wing government, which they accused of widespread human rights violations, and set about establishing a reforming civilian government. However, this junta government also perpetrated abuses and soon became another form of oppressive power. Paramilitary right-wing groups supported by the government, left-wing guerrilla groups and street violence sent the country into a civil war that lasted from 1980 to 1992. Millions of innocent Salvadorans were caught in this situation, and thousands of them lost their lives during the war.

On February 17, 1980, Oscar Romero, then Archbishop of San Salvador, the country's capital city, sent an open letter to President Jimmy Carter of the United States. In it, he accused the military in El Salvador of oppressing the people, particularly the poor, and of engaging in violent action on behalf of a small group of families who had become very wealthy through the sale of

Archbishop Romero condemned institutional violence in El Salvador; that is, violence directed against the poor by the State

THE 30TH ANNIVERSARY OF ARCHBISHOP ROMERO'S DEATH WAS COMMEMORATED IN 2010

coffee. He appealed to President Carter not to send any further military aid to the country. Scandalized by the unjust suffering of his people and reading the Bible for wisdom, Archbishop Romero condemned institutional violence in El Salvador; that is, violence directed against the poor by the State. He urged others to do likewise. With another bishop he issued a pastoral letter in which he condemned institutional violence, often quoting the Scriptures. He began the practice of using the Sunday readings from Scripture to preach about human rights abuses that had occurred the previous week. These sermons attracted a huge following to his cathedral and were also broadcast on the radio. This gave Romero a national and international profile. In another pastoral letter, again based on Scripture, Archbishop Romero condemned three idolatries: worship of wealth, worship of private property and worship of political power. (Read Exodus 20:1-6 for the condemnation of idolatry.)

Shortly after his letter to President Carter, in one of his famous Sunday sermons, Archbishop Romero appealed directly to soldiers to obey their conscience rather than an immoral command. This was the last straw for his enemies. On the day after this sermon, on March 24, 1980, while he was celebrating Mass in the chapel of the hospital where he lived, four men entered the building. One of them shot Archbishop Romero and he died at the altar.

OVER TO YOU

- What can you learn for your own life today from Oscar Romero?
- When have you ever heard a prophetic voice that challenged you to change your ways? Share your story with the group.
- When have you ever been a prophetic voice for anyone? Explain.

REFLECTIVE EXERCISE

- Reflect a little more on the 'thorns' that choke our reception of the Word of God or 'seed' of faith today. Is it more difficult for the seed of faith to take root and grow in our twenty-first-century society? Why do you think this is so? What can you do to counteract these thorns in your own life?

RESPOND WITH YOUR FAMILY, FRIENDS, NEIGHBORS

⊙ Find a Scripture passage that you would like to take root and bloom in your life, in the life of your family, in your neighborhood. Here are some you might consider:

For God so loved the world that he gave his only Son, so that everyone who believes in him may not perish but may have eternal life.

—John 3:16

The LORD is my shepherd, I shall not want.

—Psalm 23:1

The one who hears and does not act is like a house without a foundation. When the river burst against it, immediately it fell, and great was the ruin of that house.

—Luke 6:49

And the Word became flesh and lived among us.

—John 1:14

Blessed are the peacemakers, for they will be called children of God.

—Matthew 5:9

Do to others as you would have them do to you.

—[The Golden Rule] Matthew 7:12

⊙ Find ways of displaying this quotation in your home or in your parish.
⊙ What would you and the people who live around you be doing if you were truly to believe in and live according to the words you have chosen?
⊙ What would help you to do this?
⊙ Ask the Holy Spirit to help you live the Scripture you have chosen.

WHAT WILL YOU DO NOW?

⊙ What will you do to make the Word of God revealed through the Bible more relevant to your life from here on?

LEARN BY HEART

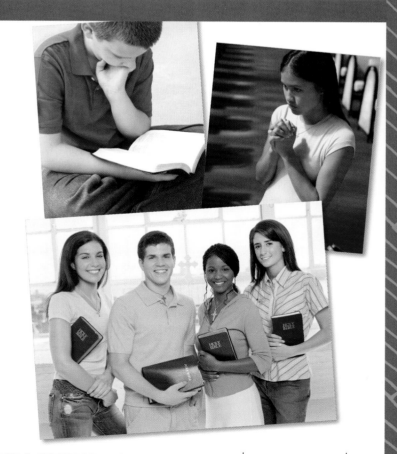

One does not live by bread alone, but by every word that comes from the mouth of the Lord.

DEUTERONOMY 8:3; ALSO QUOTED BY JESUS IN LUKE 4:4

Blessed are those who hear the word of God and obey it.

LUKE 11:28

Some background material before today's Prayer Reflection:

READING THE BIBLE IN SMALL ECCLESIAL COMMUNITIES

Thousands of Christians around the world meet in small groups to read the Scriptures and reflect on how God speaks to us here and now. In Latin America many of these communities have been really successful in affirming the deep bond between Christian faith and everyday life. By reading the Scriptures in small ecclesial communities, people have the opportunity to share their thoughts and questions, identify common concerns affecting the life of the neighborhood, and be empowered to engage their leaders in conversation. For many of the people in these communities, reading the Bible together in the context of their own lives is truly a transforming experience.

Sometimes people feel intimidated before the Bible because of the many books and stories and symbols it contains. However, when people read the Bible in small ecclesial communities, they read it with the Church. Many of the small ecclesial communities in Latin America are formed by people with very little education. But this is the least of their concerns. They are open to the guidance of the Holy Spirit through God's Word in Sacred Scripture and they know that when they have questions they can always consult with teachers, catechists or one of the church leaders in the local community.

PRAYER REFLECTION

Pray the Sign of the Cross together.

LEADER
Today we will read a Bible text as if in a small ecclesial community.

As we prepare to hear the Word of God, we ask the Holy Spirit to open our ears so that we will hear what God is saying to us, *(Pause)*
to open our minds so that we will understand what the Word of God means for our lives, *(Pause)*
and to open our hearts so that we will be able to respond. *(Pause)*

READER
Read Psalm 145:8–9 and 13–16 very slowly as all listen attentively.

The L ORD is gracious and merciful,
    slow to anger and abounding in steadfast
        love.
The L ORD is good to all,
    and his compassion is over all that he has
        made.

The L ORD is faithful in all his words,
    and gracious in all his deeds.
The L ORD upholds all who are falling,
    and raises up all who are bowed
        down.
The eyes of all look to you,
    and you give them their food in due
        season.
You open your hand,
    satisfying the desire of every living
        thing.

LEADER
What part of this reading got your attention, and why?

How does this text connect with your life? What does it mean for you?
(Students respond)

READER
Read the text again.
All listen in light of the foregoing conversation.

LEADER
How will we take this text to heart? What practical commitments does it invite in our lives?
(Students respond)

LEADER
Let us pray for the grace to hear what God is saying to us at this moment and for the courage to take God's Word to heart.

God our Creator, inspire us with wisdom to hear and understand your Word for our lives. Be with us as we try to live according to your will. Lord, hear us.

ALL
Lord, graciously hear us.

Pray the Sign of the Cross together.

CHAPTER 9

The Old and New Testaments

—God's Faithfulness over Time

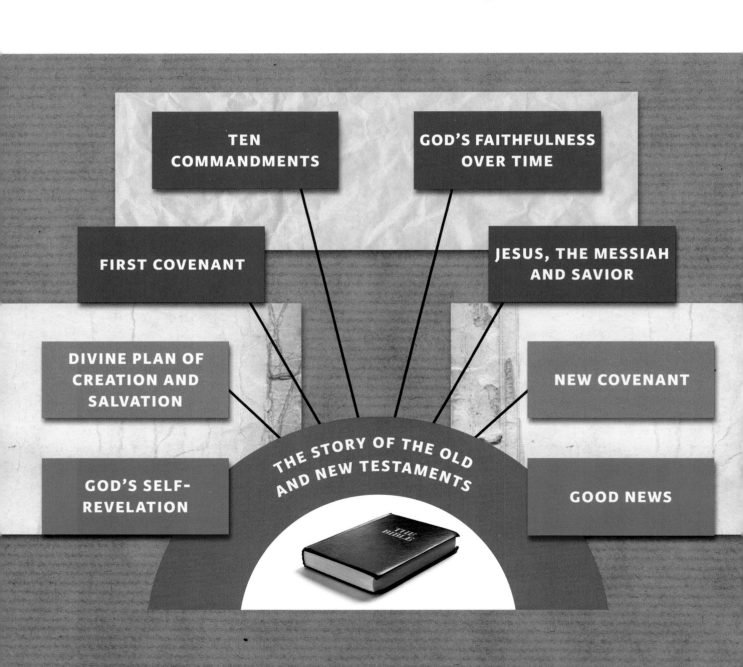

IN THIS CHAPTER WE STUDY THE UNITY OF THE Old and New Testaments; together they tell the story of God's Revelation of himself and the divine plan of Creation and Salvation, and the partnership, or Covenant, with humankind.

GOD'S PROMISE OF SALVATION

FAITHFULNESS TO THE COVENANT

THE GOOD NEWS: NEW HOPE FOR GOD'S PEOPLE

FULFILLMENT OF GOD'S PROMISES IN JESUS, THE CHRIST

Faith Focus: These teachings of the Catholic Church are the primary focus of the doctrinal content presented in this chapter:

⊙ The Old Testament is the inspired Word of God, which passes on God's fidelity to and dealings with humankind and, in particular, with his Chosen People, who lived prior to the coming of Jesus Christ, who is the fullness of Revelation.

⊙ The Old Testament focuses on the covenant God made with the Jewish people, which is called the 'Old Covenant' to distinguish it from the New Covenant made by Jesus Christ.

⊙ Catholics rely on the Greek version of the Old Testament for their Bible, while Protestants tend to rely on a Hebrew version.

⊙ The New Testament is the name given to those twenty-seven books that compose the second part of the Bible and that focus on the life and teachings of Jesus Christ and some writings of the early Church.

⊙ The heart of the four accounts of the Gospel and the other New Testament writings, and of the preaching of the Apostles, is the historical events of the suffering, Death, Resurrection and Ascension of Jesus Christ.

Discipleship Formation: As a result of studying this chapter and discovering the meaning of the faith of the Catholic Church for your life, you should be better able to:

⊙ reflect on your experience of faithfulness and of being faithful;

⊙ be more aware of God's faithfulness in your life;

⊙ allow your growing knowledge of who Jesus is to enhance your personal relationship with him;

⊙ be aware of the implications of God's promises in Scripture for the world today;

⊙ reflect on how God's promises have been fulfilled in your life.

Scripture References: These Scripture references are quoted or referred to in this chapter:
OLD TESTAMENT: Genesis 8, 9:1–17, 12:1–5 and 7, 17:5, 7 and 21, 22:17 and 18; **Exodus** 3:12 and 15, 6:6–7, 13:14; **2 Samuel** 7:12–14; **Psalms** 17:8, 23:4; **Isaiah** 2:4, 11:1–2, 29:18–19, 35:5–6, 61:1–3; **Ezekiel** 11:14–21, 37:1–6
NEW TESTAMENT: Matthew 1:23, 3:13–17, 10:21–22, 11:2–19, 16:16, 18:20, 28:16–20; **Luke** 1:1–4, 7:18–22, 22:20, 24:21, 25–27 and 44; **John** 1:14, 14:18, 17:2–24, 21:24–25; **Acts of the Apostles** 1:8, 6:13–15, 7:60, 11:26; **Hebrews** 1:1–2

Faith Glossary: Familiarize yourself with the meaning of these key faith terms. Definitions are found in the Glossary: **Bible, Covenant (The), Exile (The), faithfulness/fidelity (divine), Fourth Gospel, hope, Kingdom of God, Messiah, Old Testament, New Testament**

Faith Words: hope; Covenant
Learn by Heart: Luke 24:44
Learn by Example: St. Stephen

Why be trustworthy and faithful?

Stop and think about it: all of life operates on the trust we have in one another. We just have to presume that things and people will function as we hope—at least most of the time. Imagine if you could not trust the school bus to come in the morning? Or the school to be open when you arrive? Or your teacher to be there, ready to teach? The examples are a thousand a day. Daily life depends on being able to trust one another.

Life not only calls us to trust but to be trustworthy as well. One of the highest values we have as human beings is to be trustworthy, to be faithful to what we promise and to what is reasonably expected of us.

REFLECT AND DISCUSS

- ◉ Think of someone whom you consider to be trustworthy and faithful. What makes them so?
- ◉ Recognize the many ways that you are trustworthy and faithful. Why is this so?
- ◉ Do you want others to consider you trustworthy—for example, a faithful friend? Why? What does this require of you?
- ◉ Examine the word 'faithful'. What do you think 'faith' has to do with being trustworthy?
- ◉ Now, think about God's relationship with you and with all of humankind. Do you think of God as faithful and trustworthy? In what ways?

KEEPING PROMISES

Being faithful and trustworthy involves every aspect of our lives; indeed, it concerns every minute of our day. Let's delve a little deeper and look at one aspect of being faithful and trustworthy, namely, keeping promises.

All of us make promises, some of which may be very significant, others less so. We probably make most of our promises out of a personal choice to please, help, support, surprise or offer hope to another person. But we may also feel coerced or pressurized into making certain promises. For example, someone might be asked to make a promise not to tell anyone that a friend is using drugs.

GOD'S COVENANT WITH ABRAHAM | WENCESLAUS HOLLAR

TALK IT OVER

⊙ Name some promises—explicit or implicit—that you keep every day.

⊙ Talk about a particular and important promise you made and kept. Why did you keep it?

⊙ Have you ever broken a promise? Why did you not keep it? How did not keeping the promise make you feel? How did it make the other person feel?

⊙ Talk about an important promise that someone made to you. Did anyone ever break a promise that they had made to you? How did that make you feel?

⊙ In what kind of situations might it sometimes be best to break a promise?

⊙ What do you think are the most important promises we make in life?

⊙ What do all promises depend on—from the point of view of the person making the promise as well as the person to whom the promise is made?

⊙ A foundation of Christian faith is that God is always trustworthy and faithful. God continuously affirms—and God's people have always experienced and passed on, over and over again, in Sacred Scripture, that he is always faithful and always keeps promises. What do you know about some of the promises that God has made to humankind? How is God faithful to them?

REFLECT

⊙ How do you experience God's faithfulness in your own life?

GOD'S PROMISE AND FAITHFULNESS TO ABRAHAM

The **Old Testament** is the faith story of God's dealings with humankind and, in particular, with his chosen people, the Israelites. The story begins in the Book of Genesis, the first book of the Old Testament, with the accounts of Creation and the Fall. Beyond giving witness to himself in people and created things, God revealed himself, after the Fall, to be the Faithful One and the Keeper of Promises. He entered a **Covenant**—a great formal promise— with his people and promised them salvation. That promise and covenant is reaffirmed in the story of Noah and the Great Flood. God made a Covenant with Noah and all human beings that will remain in place for all time. (Read Genesis 8; 9:1–17.)

We next read about the great promise that God made to Abram, whom he later named Abraham. God chose Abram and made a Covenant with him and, in turn, with the descendants of himself and his wife Sarai, whose name God later changed to Sarah. God offered to be their God, to give them numerous descendants and a special land to live in, and to bring blessings upon all peoples through them and their offspring. In return, God asked them to believe in his promises and to be obedient to the commands of the Covenant. It is important to remember that Abram, Sarai and their family were part of a people who believed in 'many gods'. The challenge for Abram and Sarai to trust in God was made greater by the fact that they were very advanced in years and well past child-bearing age. Yet, Abram and Sarai trusted in God and agreed to enter into the Covenant with him. Abram had faith that God was trustworthy and would be faithful to all his promises. We read:

Now the LORD said to Abram, 'Go from your country and your kindred and your father's house to the land that I will show you. I will make of you a great nation, and I will bless you, and make your name great, so that you will be a blessing. I will bless those who bless you, and the one who curses you I will curse; and in you all the families of the earth shall be blessed.'

So Abram went, as the LORD had told him . . . and they set forth to go to the land of Canaan. . . .

Then the LORD appeared to Abram, and said, 'To your offspring I will give this land.' So he built there an altar to the LORD, who had appeared to him.

—Genesis 12:1–3, 4–5, 7

God changed Abram's name to Abraham. (Read Genesis 17:5.) In Old Testament times, the changing of a person's name often signified that God had chosen the person for a special task.

Because of his great faith and trust in God and in his promises, Abraham is known as the Father of all believers. Jews, Christians and Muslims all look to Abraham as their common ancestor in faith.

ABRAHAM | EMMAUSKIRKEN, COPENHAGEN

WHAT ABOUT YOU PERSONALLY?

⊙ God's promise called for a response from Abraham. What can you learn from Abraham's story for your own life and how to place your trust in God?

⊙ For what special purpose in life might God be calling you? How does this make you feel?

⊙ How and why can you trust in God?

GOD'S SPECIALLY CHOSEN PEOPLE

The descendants of Abraham and Sarah became the Hebrew people, also known as the Israelites (a name indicating that they were descendants of Israel, grandson of Abraham and son of Isaac), and later known as the Jews. The Old Testament traces their story through good times and bad, through their captivity in Egypt and their eventual freedom, through their **Exile** and return to their homeland. It tells of times when they turned their backs on God, of how the prophets admonished them for the folly of what they were doing, and how God was always faithful to the Covenant and to them and had mercy on them, as God does on us.

In this chapter we will learn that God promised a **Messiah**, a Savior for all peoples, who would rise from the descendants of Abraham and Sarah. This promise was fulfilled in Jesus, whose story is told in the **New Testament**. In Jesus we have the definitive Revelation and proof that God is forever faithful and trustworthy, the greatest keeper of promises.

The story of the Old and New Testaments

THE FAITH STORY BEHIND THE OLD TESTAMENT—GOD KEEPS PROMISES

In the Old Testament we read that God chose a people through whom his divine plan for humankind would be told. In reality they were, at first, hardly a 'people' at all—just wandering nomads, passing shepherds, vagrant tribes, on the fringes of civilized society. They were harassed and exploited by the cities and towns near which they passed. Yet, God chose them, saying to Abraham,

I will establish my covenant between me and you, and your offspring after you throughout their generations, for an everlasting covenant, to be God to you and to your offspring after you. . . . And by your offspring shall all the nations of the earth gain blessing for themselves, because you have obeyed my voice.

—Genesis 17:7; 22:18

OPENING CONVERSATION

- ⊙ Place yourself in the sandals of Abraham, Sarah and their tribespeople.
- ⊙ Could you believe such a promise? Trust in the God who made it?
- ⊙ When is your own trust in God most tested?
- ⊙ What helps you to 'trust on'?

God said to Abraham, 'But my covenant I will establish with Isaac, whom Sarah shall bear to you at this season next year' (Genesis 17:21). Abraham and Sarah had a son, Isaac, as God promised. Isaac and his wife Rebekah later had a son named Jacob (also called Israel). Over hundreds of years, Abraham and Sarah indeed had descendants 'as numerous as the stars of heaven and as the sand that is on the

seashore'—as God had promised. (Read Genesis 22:17.)

Each generation of the descendants of Abraham and Isaac told the succeeding generation how they had come to be God's chosen people. They recounted the events that marked their beginnings from Abraham and Sarah. They told of God's special concern for them by recalling the marvelous things God had done on their behalf, with the high point being the Exodus, their liberation from slavery in Egypt. They were concerned that their children would know the details of their history, of God's fidelity to his promises to them, inviting them to live, in return, as a people faithful to God.

When in future your child asks you, 'What does this mean?', you shall answer, 'By strength of hand the LORD brought us out of Egypt, from the house of slavery.'

—Exodus 13:14

After Abraham, God selected various leaders to guide the chosen people. When the Israelites were enslaved in Egypt, God called Moses to lead them out from oppression under the power of Pharaoh. Later, after wandering for forty years in the desert, Joshua led the Israelites in the conquest of the land of Canaan, the Promised Land. During their journey through the desert, at Mount Sinai, God gave the Israelites the Ten Commandments to keep faithfully as their part of the Covenant. Like ourselves, the Israelites did not always keep these commandments. However, God always had mercy on them—remaining faithful to the Covenant—and when they strayed away from God and from living the Covenant, God raised up prophets to remind them of the Covenant, admonish them and call them back to living as God's own people.

Having settled in the Promised Land, the Israelites, after a period of rule by Judges, eventually desired to have a king, much like their neighbors. The first three kings, and the most significant in the story of salvation, were Saul, David and David's son, Solomon (who ruled the Israelites from about 1020 BC through to 922 BC), after which the united Israelite kingdom split into northern and southern parts. The Northern Kingdom (still known as Israel) fell to the rule of the Assyrians in 721 BC (Fall of Samaria), and the Southern Kingdom (Judah, around Jerusalem) was conquered by the Babylonians in 587 BC (Fall of Jerusalem).

From that point in the history of God's people, the Israelites did not rule the land that God had given to them. From the time of the Exile (586–539 BC) until the middle of the twentieth century, about 2500 years, they were a subjugated and scattered people, as Palestine was ruled, in turn, by Persians, Greeks, Romans, Byzantines, Persians again (now Muslims), Crusaders, Mamaluke Muslims, Ottoman Turks and Britain. Only in AD 1948 was Israel established again as an independent country.

The Old Testament tells that throughout the history of God's people, when they were unfaithful to him and to the Covenant, God raised up and sent the prophets to remind his people that he was and would always be their God and would cherish them as his people. The prophets constantly spoke of God's special promise of a Messiah. 'Messiah' in Hebrew means 'Anointed One'; in Greek the word is 'Christos', meaning Christ. Through the prophets, God promised to send a Messiah who would be the Savior of all peoples. This Messiah–Savior would establish the New Covenant; he would be God's catalyst for the coming of God's reign, to have God's will done on earth as it is done in Heaven. Throughout the history of God's people, one message comes through loudly and clearly; namely, that God is trustworthy and keeps promises—even when we do not.

EARLY CHRISTIAN MOSAIC IN CHORA CHURCH, ISTANBUL

REFLECT AND DISCUSS

⊙ The story of God's chosen people in the Old Testament is one of trust in God's promises, lending **hope** in the face of adversity. What was the source of their trust? Of their hope?

LET'S PROBE DEEPER

⊙ The prophets kept hope alive in the hearts of God's chosen people in Old Testament times. Who keeps hope alive in the world today?

⊙ What messages of hope does God give to you in your life today?

GROUP WORK

⊙ The Exodus of Moses and the Israelites from Egypt to the Promised Land was a milestone in their history. Break up into groups and retrace their forty-year journey with the aid of a map. Mark out the significant stages of the journey for the Israelites, culminating in their arrival in the Promised Land. The story of the Exodus begins in Exodus, chapter 12, with the account of the Passover; you might like to check it out.

FAITH WORD

Hope

'Hope' is the desire and expectation of the salvation God promised. It is based on God's unwavering fidelity to keeping and fulfilling his promises.

THE FAITH STORY BEHIND THE NEW TESTAMENT—NEW HOPE FOR GOD'S PEOPLE

God's Great Promise—the promise of a Messiah—was fulfilled in Jesus, the Christ. What an amazing fulfillment: God the Son, the Second Person of the Blessed Trinity, freely became one of us without giving up his divinity. He came and lived among us as our Savior and accomplished God's definitive act of salvation for all humankind, for Jews and Gentiles alike.

After years of preaching and proclaiming Christ and his work of salvation, the Apostles and other disciples of Jesus began to put into writing his teachings and the accounts of his saving deeds. These writings make up the New Testament of the **Bible**. The New Testament tells us that Jesus chose and appointed the Twelve Apostles to continue his work and to be the leaders among his disciples, both men and women. (See Matthew 28:16–20; Acts of the Apostles 1:8). The New Testament is based on the testimony of the Apostles who were 'chosen and sent on mission by Christ himself; . . .' (*Catechism of the Catholic Church* [CCC], no. 857) and of other disciples who were also eyewitnesses to the life, Death and Resurrection of Jesus.

Luke begins his account of the Gospel:

Since many have undertaken to set down an orderly account of the events that have been fulfilled among us, just as they were handed

ST. JOHN THE EVANGELIST | GERMAN CHURCH, STOCKHOLM, SWEDEN

on to us by those who from the beginning were eyewitnesses and servants of the word, I too decided, after investigating everything carefully from the very first, to write an orderly account for you, most excellent Theophilus, so that you may know the truth concerning the things about which you have been instructed.

—Luke 1:1–4

And John the Apostle and Evangelist concludes the **Fourth Gospel**:

This is the disciple who is testifying to these things and has written them, and we know that his testimony is true. But there are also many other things that Jesus did; if every one of them were written down, I suppose that the world itself could not contain the books that would be written.

—John 21:24–25

THE WRITING OF THE GOSPEL

The heart of the Gospels and the other New Testament writings, and of the preaching of the Apostles, is the historical events of the suffering, Death, Resurrection and Ascension of Jesus and the meaning of those events for humanity. Some biblical scholars have concluded that the Crucifixion of Jesus occurred, most likely, during the Passover of AD 28 or 29. So Jesus' own preaching and other works and deeds would have happened during the previous couple of years. This was *the period of the public ministry of Jesus*, which the Apostles, other disciples and numerous others witnessed.

These eyewitnesses were the men and women who heard the words of Jesus from his own lips, witnessed his miraculous deeds and his care for the sick and hungry, spent time with him in prayer, became convinced that he was indeed the promised Messiah, and witnessed the events of his Paschal Mystery—his Death, Resurrection and Ascension. It was these women and men who would first carry on his ministry and mission to the world, after his return to his Father. This was the first stage of the formation of the four written accounts of the Gospel.

For the next forty years, from about AD 30 to 70, the Apostles and other disciples crisscrossed the ancient world spreading the Good News of Jesus. They traveled by foot, by horseback and by ship, primarily to places around the Mediterranean, such as Rome and Ephesus, Corinth and Colossae, Antioch and Galatia, as well as up and down Palestine. To anyone who would listen, Jews or Gentiles, they told about the life of Jesus, explaining the Good News that he had preached and that he was the Messiah and Savior of the world. They established the Church in various places. Among the members of the local churches, they settled disputes, answered questions and resolved difficulties. This was *the period of the apostolic oral tradition*, which was the second stage of the writing of the Gospels.

During the decades of this second stage, the Apostles and the other disciples retold the stories from Jesus' sermons, recalled his miracles, explained the effect that Jesus' personality, words and actions had on their own personal faith, and recounted the events surrounding Jesus' Passion (his suffering and Death) and Resurrection. It is likely that they made notes or memory aids, and collected lists of the sayings and actions of Jesus, to help them in their preaching, but these were only informal documents at this stage.

The year AD 70 was an important milestone. In that year, the Roman army captured Jerusalem, and the Temple, in which Jesus himself had worshiped and preached, was completely destroyed. Many Jews were dispersed and scattered, and the hope of an independent Jewish nation was dashed once again. The Apostles and other disciples who had known Jesus and walked the roads of Palestine with him were dying off, or being killed in the various persecutions of Christians that were taking place. It was in Antioch that the followers of Christ were first called Christians. (Read Acts of the Apostles 11:26.) In the hope of preserving the truth of the message and mission of Jesus, scribes (editors) began to compile the various written materials and the extensive oral traditions about Jesus into formal accounts. Different accounts were assembled in different communities. Four of these many accounts have been recognized by the Church as inspired by the Holy Spirit and are included in the canon of the New Testament. They are the accounts of the Gospel written by the Evangelists Matthew, Mark, Luke and John. This was *the third and final stage of the formation of the Gospels*.

Alongside the four Gospels of Matthew, Mark, Luke and John, the New Testament contains other writings recognized by the Church as inspired by the Holy Spirit. These writings are the Acts of the Apostles, thirteen Pauline epistles (written by or attributed to St. Paul), the Epistle to the Hebrews, seven other epistles attributed to Peter, James, John and Jude, and the Book of Revelation.

WHAT ABOUT YOU PERSONALLY?

- ⊙ The coming of Jesus offered new hope to all of God's people. What hope does Jesus offer you in your life right now?
- ⊙ Jesus called his disciples to trust that he was the fulfillment of God's promise; he was the Messiah. What can you learn from their faith-filled trust in him for how you can respond to Jesus today?

MOSAIC IN THE BASILICA OF ST. MARK, VENICE, ITALY

FAITH WORD

Covenant

A covenant is a solemn agreement made between human beings or between God and a human being involving mutual commitments or guarantees. The Bible speaks of covenants that God made with Noah and, through him, 'with every living creature' (Genesis 9:10). Then God made the special Covenant with Abraham and renewed it with Moses. The prophets constantly pointed to the New Covenant that God would establish with all humankind through the promised Messiah—Jesus Christ.

The Old Testament Covenant was fulfilled in Jesus

SUPPER AT EMMAUS | 15TH-CENTURY FRESCO, MOMO, ITALY

OPENING ACTIVITY

◉ Recall some of the many images of Jesus that you have encountered in your life up to now; for example, in this book, in other books, in your local church and so on. Share your thoughts about some of them. What is your own image of Jesus?

WHO WAS JESUS?

It is clear from the four accounts of the Gospel that the identity of Jesus and his mission remained, in part, an unanswered question, even to Jesus' disciples while Jesus was living among them. Luke's account of the conversation between the risen Jesus and two of his disciples while they were traveling to their homes in Emmaus speaks to this point. The two disciples, disappointed by the Death and burial of Jesus, expressed this uncertainty, saying to their risen Lord, whom they did not recognize, 'But we had hoped that he was the one to redeem Israel' (Luke 24:21).

It was only after their anointing with the Holy Spirit during the celebration of Pentecost that the Apostles boldly proclaimed that Jesus was the Messiah, the Christ, the long promised Savior of the world. Filled with the Holy Spirit, they entered the marketplace and started the work Jesus had given them and spread the Good News. They began to profess publicly their faith in Christ, which Peter had personally confessed to Jesus in Caesarea Philippi, 'You are the Messiah, the Son of the living God' (Matthew 16:16). Now their memories and experiences of Jesus and their faith in him began to make sense in the light of the Scriptures.

Jesus Christ is the New and Everlasting Covenant promised in the Scriptures of ancient Israel. Through his life, Death and Resurrection, all sins are forgiven, and a new 'heart', God's saving grace, is offered to all humankind (see Ezekiel 11:14–21, 37:1–6), the grace to live in deeper communion with God (see John 17:2–24).

Jesus, God-among-us (see Matthew 1:23), is truly 'the way, and the truth, and the life' (John 14:6) for all people. The risen Christ affirmed that, through his life, Death and Resurrection, he is the fulfillment of all that had been written in the Scriptures. He said to the two disciples who were travelling to Emmaus, ' "Oh, how foolish you are and how slow of heart to believe all that the prophets have declared! Was it not necessary that the Messiah should suffer these things and then enter into his glory?" Then beginning with Moses and all the prophets, he interpreted to them the things about himself in all the scriptures' (Luke 24:25–27).

Jesus is the center of the divine plan of Creation and Salvation. He is the fulfillment of God's promise to Adam and Eve and of the Covenants with Abraham, Moses and their descendants. Jesus is the New Covenant who reveals the depth of God's love for humankind and the love that is the 'heart' of striving to live the way of Jesus.

THE NEW BORN OUT OF THE OLD

For the Jewish people, all the Old Testament books are unfinished as they stand. They still await the coming of the Messiah, the Anointed One, who will establish the **Kingdom of God**. They continue to look forward to the fulfillment of the Promise or Covenant between their ancestors and God. For the Jewish people, the Covenant revealed in their Scriptures is still in force. Our Catholic faith agrees; Pope John Paul II often repeated, 'The First Covenant has never been revoked.'

Christians, on the other hand, refer to the Jewish, or Hebrew, Scriptures as the 'Old' Testament because they believe that God made the New Covenant with humankind in Jesus. At the Last Supper Jesus proclaimed, 'This cup that is poured out for you is the new covenant in my blood' (Luke 22:20). The new was born out of the old; the New Covenant completes that which was begun in the First Covenant. Jesus is the fullness of God's Revelation. The New Testament completes what was begun in the Old Testament. As the Letter to the Hebrews states: 'Long ago God spoke to our ancestors in many and various ways by the prophets, but in these last days he has spoken to us by a Son, whom he appointed heir of all things, through whom he also created the worlds' (Hebrews 1:1–2). Or the Gospel of John summarizes: in Jesus, God's 'Word became flesh and lived among us, and we have seen his glory, the glory as of a father's only son, full of grace and truth' (John 1:14).

OVER TO YOU

- ◉ How do you now understand the connection between the Old Testament and the life of Jesus?
- ◉ What have you learned about who Jesus really is? And how will this make a difference to the way you think of and relate to Jesus from here on?

A JEWISH TEENAGER PREPARING FOR BAR MITZVAH

How the Old Testament promises came to be fulfilled

OPENING CONVERSATION

When Jesus walked the earth, people had many different expectations and hopes about who he was and what he might do. At one stage Jesus asked, 'Who do people say I am?' The people who had read the Old Testament and had listened to the prophets were looking forward to the coming of the Messiah. They were waiting for the promises of the Old Testament to be fulfilled.

⊙ Think of a time when you were waiting for a promise to be fulfilled; for example, to get a present you were promised for your birthday. Describe how you felt.

THE NEW TESTAMENT—AS FRUIT FROM THE SEEDS OF THE OLD

Let's take a look now at some of the promises in the Old Testament; then imagine and talk over how they bore fruit—were fulfilled—in Jesus Christ.

After the Great Flood, God promised Noah, 'I am establishing my covenant with you and your descendants after you, and with every living creature . . . that never again shall all flesh be cut off by the waters of a flood, and never again shall there be a flood to destroy the earth' (Genesis 9:9–11). Later in the Book of Genesis we read that God promised Abraham, 'I will make of you a great nation, and I will bless you, and make your name great, so that you will be a blessing . . . and in you all the families of the earth shall be blessed' (Genesis 12:2–3).

God promised that the people he had chosen to be his own would become a great nation, and that he would be their God for ever and they would be a source of blessing for all humankind.

As the story of the Covenant God made with his chosen people continues, the Old Testament tells us that God entered into the Covenant with the Israelites through Moses. God told Moses to lead the Israelites out of slavery in Egypt, and promised, 'I will be with you' (Exodus 3:12). Through Moses, God made this promise to the Israelites: 'I am the Lord, and I will free you from the burdens of the Egyptians and deliver you from slavery to them. I will redeem you with an outstretched arm and with mighty acts of judgment. I will take you as my people, and I will be your God' (Exodus 6:6–7). In return, the

THE BUILDING OF THE ARK | 15TH-CENTURY BOOK OF HOURS

Israelites were challenged to keep their side of the Covenant that God had made with them. They were to live as God's own people by keeping the law of the Covenant, summarized in the Ten Commandments.

The Book of Psalms in the Old Testament gives us an insight into how the people saw themselves as being blessed by God, how they repented for their wrongdoing, and how they gave praise and thanks to God. Even in the worst of times, when they were in captivity or exile, they trusted that God was with them and that his promise to them would be fulfilled. The Psalms often express their confidence that God is trustworthy:

Even though I walk through the darkest valley,
    I fear no evil;
for you are with me;
    your rod and your staff—
        they comfort me.

—Psalm 23:4

Guard me as the apple of the eye;
    hide me in the shadow of your wings.

—Psalm 17:8

The greatest promise and sign of God's fidelity to his people and to the Covenant, made in the Old Testament, was the promise to send the Messiah, whom the prophets said would be a descendant of King David. During the period of the monarchy, God sent the prophet Nathan to say to David, 'When your days are fulfilled and you lie down with your ancestors, I will raise up your offspring after you . . . and I will establish his kingdom. . . . I will be a father to him, and he shall be a son to me' (2 Samuel 7:12–14). At the time of the Exile, the prophet Isaiah often reminded the Israelites of God's promise of the Messiah (Jesse was the father of King David):

A shoot shall come out from the stump of Jesse,
    and a branch shall grow out of his roots.
The spirit of the Lord shall rest on him,
    the spirit of wisdom and understanding,
    the spirit of counsel and might,
    the spirit of knowledge and the fear of the Lord.

—Isaiah 11:1–2

He shall judge between the nations,
    and shall arbitrate for many peoples;
they shall beat their swords into ploughshares,
    and their spears into pruning-hooks.

—Isaiah 2:4

So, when Jesus began his public ministry, the Jews, who were familiar with the Scriptures, were already looking forward to the coming of the Messiah. They were waiting for God's promise to be fulfilled. In Luke 7:18–22 we read that John the Baptist sent two of his disciples to Jesus to ask, 'Are you the one who is to come, or are we to wait for another?' As was often the case, Jesus did not answer the question directly. Instead he said, 'Go and tell John what you have seen and heard: the blind receive their sight, the lame walk, the lepers are cleansed, the deaf hear, the dead are raised, the poor have good news brought to them.' This same story is told in Matthew 11:2–19.

What would John the Baptist make of that? For a person who knew the Scriptures—and John the Baptist, son of Zechariah the priest, surely did—the words recalled passages from the Old Testament in which the prophet Isaiah spoke of the signs by which the Messiah would be known. (Check this out by reading the following passages: Isaiah 29:18–19; 35:5–6; 61:1–3.)

During his public ministry Jesus told his disciples, 'Wherever two or three gather in my name, there am I in the midst of you' (Matthew 18:20). He also said, 'I will not leave you orphaned' (John 14:18). Then, before Jesus, now the risen Christ, ascended to Heaven, he promised his followers that he would always be with them. He said, 'I am with you always, to the end of the age' (Matthew 28:20).

(Reread Exodus 3:15. What is the common message in Matthew 28:20 and Exodus 3:15?)

We can totally trust that Jesus, the Son of God, keeps his promises. The risen Christ is with us today, in our good times and in our bad times.

TALK IT OVER
- What do you think has been the main message in all of God's promises from Old Testament times down to the present day?
- What does this mean for your own life?

JUDGE AND ACT

LEARN BY EXAMPLE

The story of St. Stephen

THE STONING OF STEPHEN | GABRIEL-JULES THOMAS

Jesus' whole life witnessed to his love for his Father and to his commitment to fulfill faithfully his Father's will; namely, the mission he was sent to accomplish. Jesus suffered and died; he preached and lived his whole life for the Kingdom of God, when love and compassion, peace and justice for all people would reign 'on earth as in heaven'. He was ever faithful to his mission, even when the authorities warned him to stop. He told his followers that their fidelity to him and the mission he entrusted to them would be challenged; they too would suffer for being his disciples. 'Brother will betray brother to death, and a father his child, and children will rise against parents and have them put to death; and you will be hated by all because of my name. But the one who endures to the end will be saved' (Matthew 10:21–22).

From the days of the early Church to the present, disciples of Christ have suffered, sometimes even to death, for witnessing to and refusing to deny their faith in Christ. This will happen to the end of time. People who have lost their lives for the faith are called martyrs (from a Greek word meaning 'witnesses'). The very first martyr of the Church was St. Stephen, whose story is told in chapters 6 and 7 of the Acts of the Apostles.

As the number of followers of the risen Christ increased, the Apostles asked 'the whole community of disciples' to choose people to help preach the Good News. One person they chose was Stephen. Stephen preached fearlessly, but the rulers were 'enraged' by the wisdom with which he spoke. 'They stirred up the people as well as the elders and the scribes; then they suddenly confronted him, seized him, and brought him before the council.

ST. STEPHEN | 15TH-CENTURY STATUE, AHOLMING, GERMANY

They set up false witnesses who said, "This man never stops saying things against this holy place and the law; for we have heard him say that this Jesus of Nazareth will destroy this place and will change the customs that Moses handed on to us." And all who sat in the council looked intently at him, and they saw that his face was like the face of an angel' (Acts of the Apostles 6:13–15).

Stephen was brought before the Sanhedrin, the Jewish legal authorities. He was not afraid to speak—to give witness to—the truth. He recounted the whole history of the Jewish people, beginning with Abraham, explaining how God's promises were fulfilled in Jesus. He accused them of killing the prophets and also of killing Jesus. They rushed at him, dragged him out of the city and began stoning him to death. While they did so, Stephen prayed, 'Lord, do not hold this sin against them.' When he had said this he died (Acts of the Apostles 7:60). The feast of St. Stephen, deacon and martyr, is celebrated on December 26, the day after Christmas Day.

TALK IT OVER
⊙ What was it about Jesus that inspired people like Stephen to sacrifice themselves for love of him and of God?
⊙ What can you learn from the story of St. Stephen about witnessing to your faith?

DECISION TIME!
⊙ Pause and decide—honestly: How much of an inspiration is Jesus in your life? In your decisions about what is right and wrong? In your relationships with others? In what you believe to be the true purpose of your life?
⊙ Most likely, you will never be called upon to die for your faith in Jesus Christ; but every day you are called to give witness to it by living it. How will you do so today?

WHAT WILL YOU DO NOW?
⊙ What inspiration have you drawn from what you have heard in this chapter about how people down the centuries placed their trust in God's promises?

HAITIAN AMERICANS HOLD A VIGIL TO REMEMBER HAITI EARTHQUAKE

⊙ What changes will you make to your life now so as to trust fully in God's promises revealed in Jesus?

RESPOND WITH YOUR FAMILY

⊙ Check in with your family about the whole issue of placing trust in God and of living as trustworthy persons ourselves. Find out how they understand God's faithfulness and their own faithfulness. Share your convictions and a little of what you learned from this chapter with them.

STUDYING THE BIBLE

As you can see from what we have learned so far, it is not easy to understand correctly the writings in the Bible. There are often layers of meaning that only become clear when we spend time pondering and studying how and why the texts were written. There are many people who have spent their entire lives studying the Bible. One of the most famous Catholic biblical scholars was the Jesuit priest John McKenzie. He was born in 1910 in Indiana and died in July 1991 after a lifetime of Scripture study. The knowledge and wisdom that he has passed on in his many written works will enrich people's study of the Bible for years to come. He lectured in universities throughout the United States and wrote a number of books and articles. One of the works for which he is best known is his *Dictionary of the Bible*. With 900,000 words, this was a most unusual work for one person to have undertaken and completed successfully. Though first published over fifty years ago, it is still widely consulted today by other Scripture scholars (and authors of high school theology texts).

QUESTIONS TO PONDER BEFORE THE PRAYER REFLECTION

⊙ Some of the most important promises in your life as a Catholic are those made at your Baptism. Take a look at them now (in our closing prayer ritual).

⊙ What do these promises mean for your life today?

⊙ Why might it be difficult to keep them at times?

⊙ What can help you to keep these promises?

LEARN BY HEART

These are my words that I spoke to you while I was still with you—that everything written about me in the law of Moses, the prophets, and the psalms must be fulfilled.

LUKE 24:44

PRAYER REFLECTION

Pray the Sign of the Cross together.

LEADER

Some of the most important promises in the life of a Catholic are those that were professed on their behalf by their parents and godparents if they were baptized as an infant. Many people are also baptized as adults or as older children or teenagers and make the baptismal promises on their own behalf. Throughout our lives as Catholics, there are times when the Church asks us to renew our baptismal promises; for example, when we receive the Sacrament of Confirmation and at the celebration of the Easter Liturgy during the Easter Vigil or on Easter Sunday. Today we will renew our baptismal promises in class.

As we look at this holy water we are reminded of how great a role water plays in our lives. Where there is no water, there is no life. Water is one of

God's great gifts. It is a symbol of life and health and growth. It reminds us of how God led the people of Israel safely through the waters of the Red Sea. That Exodus event became a sign of what would be fulfilled in the waters of Baptism.

First, let us recall the story of the baptism of Jesus by John the Baptist in the River Jordan.

READER

A reading from the holy Gospel according to Matthew.

ALL

Glory to you, O Lord.

READER

Then Jesus came from Galilee to John at the Jordan, to be baptized by him. John would have prevented him, saying, 'I need to be baptized

Then Jesus came from Galilee to John at the Jordan, to be baptized by him

THE BAPTISM OF JESUS | ST. FINNIAN'S CHURCH, CLONARD, IRELAND

by you, and do you come to me?' But Jesus answered him, 'Let it be so now, for it is proper for us in this way to fulfill all righteousness.' Then he consented. And when Jesus had been baptized, just as he came up from the water, suddenly the heavens were opened to him and he saw the Spirit of God descending like a dove and alighting on him. And a voice from heaven said, 'This is my Son, the Beloved, with whom I am well pleased.'

—Matthew 3:13–17

LEADER
As we prepare to renew our baptismal promises, we remind ourselves of what it means to be a disciple of Jesus in the world today. Close your eyes now and think of times when you felt called to act in a particular way because you are a disciple of Jesus. (*Pause*)

Remember times when you may have failed to live up to your calling as a disciple. (*Pause*)

In your heart, ask God to grant you the courage and the wisdom to be able to live as a disciple of Jesus . . . in your family, in your school and in your neighborhood. (*Pause*)

Now let us stand and renew our baptismal promises.

We begin by promising to turn away from all evil and sin.

Do you reject sin, so as to live in the freedom of God's children?

ALL
I do.

LEADER
Do you reject the glamour of evil, and refuse to be mastered by sin?

ALL
I do.

LEADER
Do you reject Satan, father of sin and prince of darkness?

ALL
I do.

LEADER
Now let us profess our faith.

Do you believe in God, the Father almighty, creator of heaven and earth?

ALL
I do.

LEADER
Do you believe in Jesus Christ, his only Son, our Lord, who was born of the Virgin Mary, was crucified, died, and was buried, rose from the dead, and is now seated at the right hand of the Father?

ALL
I do.

LEADER
Do you believe in the Holy Spirit, the holy catholic Church, the communion of saints, the forgiveness of sins, the resurrection of the body, and life everlasting?

ALL
I do.

LEADER
This is our faith. This is the faith of the Church. We are proud to profess it, in Christ Jesus our Lord.

ALL
Amen.

> God, our Loving Creator, as we remember and renew the promises of our Baptism, we ask you to pour out abundant blessings on all here present

LEADER
Now, with holy water, make a sign of the cross on the forehead of the person on your left. As you do, say, 'Remember and keep the promises of your Baptism, in the name of the Father, and of the Son, and of the Holy Spirit.' The person answers, 'Amen'.

After the blessing:

LEADER
God, our Loving Creator, as we remember and renew the promises of our Baptism, we ask you to pour out abundant blessings on all here present. Make us always faithful members of your holy people, ever trusting in your promises.

ALL
Amen.

Pray the Sign of the Cross together.

CHAPTER 10

The Gospel Is Good News

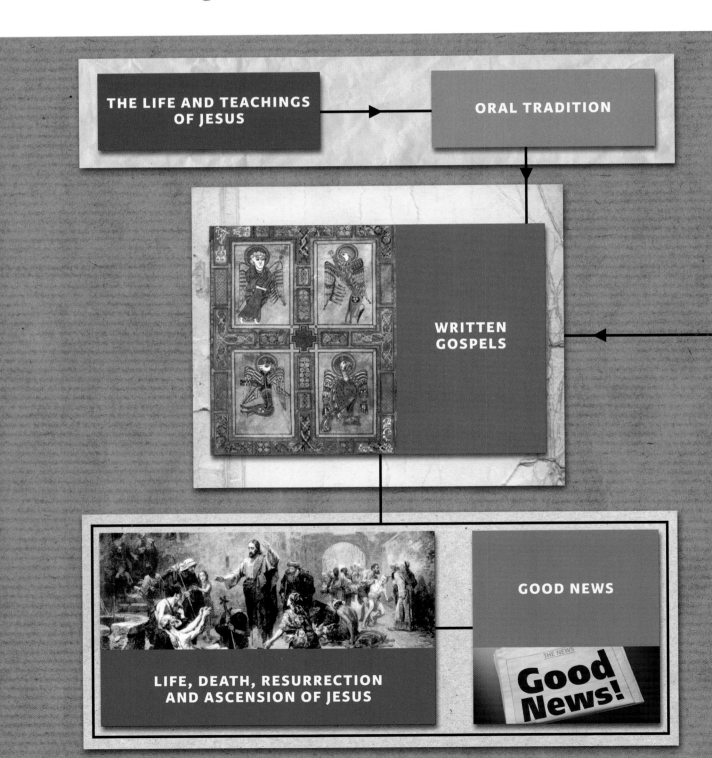

THE LIFE AND TEACHINGS OF JESUS

ORAL TRADITION

WRITTEN GOSPELS

GOOD NEWS

LIFE, DEATH, RESURRECTION AND ASCENSION OF JESUS

IN THIS CHAPTER WE EXPLORE THE GOSPEL AS Good News. We examine in more detail how the four books of the Gospels in the New Testament came to be written and we begin to look at the Synoptic Gospels; that is, the accounts of the Gospel according to Matthew, Mark and Luke.

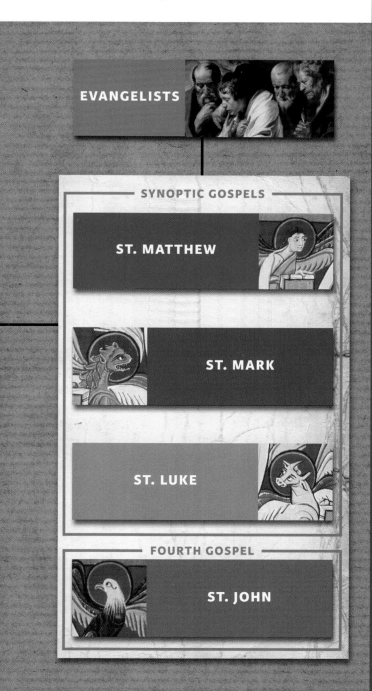

EVANGELISTS

SYNOPTIC GOSPELS

ST. MATTHEW

ST. MARK

ST. LUKE

FOURTH GOSPEL

ST. JOHN

Faith Focus: These teachings of the Catholic Church are the primary focus of the doctrinal content presented in this chapter:
⊙ The Gospels occupy a central place in Scripture.
⊙ The Gospels proclaim the Good News of Jesus Christ, the Incarnate Word of God and the definitive Revelation of God.
⊙ Central to the understanding of all four written accounts of the Gospel is Jesus Christ, the Incarnate Son of God, and his teachings and redeeming work.
⊙ There were at least three stages in the formation of the Gospels: the life and teaching of Jesus, the oral tradition, and the written Gospels.
⊙ The four Evangelists selected certain of the many elements that had been handed on by the Apostles and others, either orally or in written form, and, under the guidance of the Holy Spirit, explained them in such a fashion that they tell us the honest truth about Jesus.
⊙ The Gospels lead us to accept Jesus Christ in faith and to apply his teachings to our lives.

Discipleship Formation: As a result of studying this chapter and discovering the meaning of the faith of the Catholic Church for your life, you should be better able to:
⊙ understand and articulate how the Gospel is Good News for *you*;
⊙ consider the significance of Jesus for your life and how that impacts your choices, now and for the future;
⊙ come to see more clearly why the 'life, Death, Resurrection and Ascension' of Jesus is often called 'the greatest story ever told';
⊙ respond to the presence of the risen Jesus in your life;
⊙ choose a Gospel quotation as a motto for your life, and make a commitment to live according to this motto.

Scripture References: These Scripture references are quoted or referred to in this chapter:
NEW TESTAMENT: Matthew 1:1–17, 3:2 and 17, 4:23—7:29, 5:17, 6:9–13, 7:7, 13:52, 14:13–21, 15:32–39, 16:24–26, 28:16–20; **Mark** 1:1, 14–20 and 22, 5:25–26, 6:30–44 and 50, 8:1–10 and 34, 9:31, 12:28–34, 16:6 and 15; **Luke** 1:1–4, 6:27, 7:1–10, 19–23, 8:43, 9:10–17, 10:25–37, 11:1–4, 13:10–17, 15:11–32,16:19–31, 18:16, 23:34, 43 and 49; **John** 6:1–15, 13:31–35; **Acts of the Apostles** 4:13 and 29; **1 Corinthians** 15:3–5, 8, 28; **Ephesians** 3:12; **Philippians** 1:20, 2:1–11; **1 Timothy** 3:13

Faith Glossary: Familiarize yourself with the meaning of these key faith terms. Definitions are found in the Glossary: **Evangelist(s), Gentile(s), Gospel/Gospels, Kingdom of God, Messiah, miracle(s), oral tradition, paganism, parable, Passion Narrative, polytheism, public ministry of Jesus, Sermon on the Mount, Synoptic Gospels, typology, Yhwh**

Faith Words: Gospel/Gospels
Learn by Heart: Mark 16:15
Learn by Example: Chiara Lubich

What is good news?

There is something about the human heart that glories in good news. Good news lifts our spirits, brings us joy, gives us hope. It is a great delight to hear good news and, perhaps even more so, to share it. It lifts us up to lift up others. To hear good news even contributes to our good health; a lot of negative and discouraging (bad) news can make us sick, emotionally as well as physically.

As Christians, we have the 'best news' ever heard and given to us to share with others. But first, let's listen to a 'good news' story.

Miracle Babies

John and Debbie did not sleep very much on the twins' first night home from the hospital. They kept checking the two cribs at the end of the bed to see if their babies were still breathing. For the past eight weeks the twins had been in the intensive neonatal care unit of the local hospital after being delivered three months premature by an emergency caesarean section. John still shudders when he remembers how small and frail the twins looked in their incubators, hooked up to all sorts of machines and medicines. But the doctors had never given up hope, and gradually the twins put on weight and grew stronger. Debbie and John visited every moment they could, and their families really rallied round. Debbie's mother was a wonderful support and remained steadfast throughout in her prayers. There had been a couple of scares when the babies needed blood transfusions, but the medical team had dealt with every crisis calmly. Now their little miracles were at home and nearly at their normal weight, and John and Debbie were beside themselves with joy. What might have been an awful tragedy had truly turned into a good news story.

REFLECT AND SHARE
⊙ Do you have a good news story of your own? If so, share it with the class.

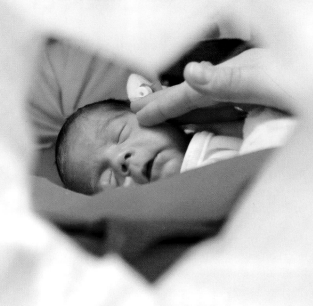

FAITH WORD

Gospel/Gospels

The term 'gospel' comes from the Old English word *godspel*, meaning 'good news'. *Godspel* was originally used to translate the Greek word *euangelion* (Latin *evangelium*), a term the early Church used for the Good News of Jesus. The Church uses the word 'Gospel' to refer to the four New Testament books that proclaim the life, teaching, Death and Resurrection of Jesus. More generally, however, the word 'Gospel' refers to the proclamation of the entire message of faith revealed in and through Jesus Christ, the Incarnate Son of God, the Second Person of the Blessed Trinity.

JESUS REVEALED AND WAS GOOD NEWS

Just over two thousand years ago, Jesus, the Incarnate Son of God, revealed most fully the best news the world has ever heard. ('Incarnate' means 'invested with a human nature and form'.) He revealed God's unconditional love for all people. He himself was the Good News. He was the **Messiah** and Savior of the world.

The **Gospel** according to Mark opens with the pronouncement that Jesus is good news: 'The beginning of the good news of Jesus Christ, the Son of God' (Mark 1:1). In the same first chapter of Mark's Gospel we read:

Jesus came to Galilee, proclaiming the good news of God, and saying, 'The time is fulfilled, and the **kingdom of God** has come near; repent and believe in the good news.'

As Jesus passed along the Sea of Galilee, he saw Simon and his brother Andrew casting a net into the sea—for they were fishermen. And Jesus said to them, 'Follow me and I will make you fish for people.' And immediately they left their nets and followed him. As he went a little farther, he saw James son of Zebedee and his brother John, who were in their boat mending the nets. Immediately he called them; and they left their father Zebedee in the boat with the hired men, and followed him.

—Mark 1:14–20

Devout Jews prayed three times every day for the coming of both God's Kingdom and the Messiah who would usher it in. This announcement by Jesus must have excited the first disciples. No prophet or Jewish leader before Jesus had ever declared the Good News that God's Kingdom had come. In the next chapter we will look in greater depth at what Jesus meant by the 'Kingdom of God'.

OVER TO YOU

- When Jesus called Simon and Andrew, they immediately left their nets and followed him. What does this tell us about Jesus and how he delivered his message?
- What does it tell us about Simon and Andrew?

WHAT ABOUT YOU PERSONALLY?

- What sacrifices or lifestyle changes do you think you would be prepared to make in order to follow Jesus?

In this chapter we explore how the Apostles and the other early disciples of Jesus came to faith in him and his message as the Good News of salvation. First, they wrote this Good News on their hearts, lived it in their lives and communities, and preached it to all who would listen. Eventually, and as the first disciples died, this Good News was written down to become the Gospels in the New Testament that we know today.

The formation of the Gospels

Catholics always approach the Bible as the Revelation of God's Word to our lives. We cherish the Gospels, in particular, because Jesus Christ is their center; they are the core stories, passing on to us the apostolic faith of the Church in Jesus Christ. Our Church also teaches that this 'Word of God' always comes to us 'in human language'.

For this reason, it is important to understand how the Gospels came to be written and to appreciate how they arose from **oral traditions** and within a storytelling culture.

OPENING CONVERSATION

⊙ With a partner, recall the different steps that led to the writing of the four accounts of the Gospel, which were presented briefly in chapter 9. How do you imagine an oral culture would have given rise to the written Gospels?

⊙ Think back over the past twenty-four hours and recall some personal story or news report that you heard. Where did it come from? Text messages, blogs, twittering? Is text-messaging the twenty-first-century equivalent of oral communication? Explain.

⊙ What kind of news is still transmitted orally today? In what ways is oral news more reliable or less reliable than written news?

THE FORMATION OF THE GOSPELS

Scripture scholars have discovered that there were at least three stages in the formation of the Gospels. The *Catechism of the Catholic Church*, quoting the Second Vatican Council's *Constitution on Divine Revelation*, summarizes these stages as follows:

1. THE LIFE AND TEACHING OF JESUS. The Church holds firmly that the four Gospels, 'whose historicity she unhesitatingly affirms, faithfully hand on what Jesus, the Son of God, while he lived among men, really did and taught for their eternal salvation, until the day when he was taken up.'

2. THE ORAL TRADITION. 'For, after the Ascension of the Lord, the Apostles handed

What kind of news is still transmitted orally today?

on to their hearers what he had said and done, but with that fuller understanding which they, instructed by the glorious events of Christ and enlightened by the Spirit of truth, now enjoyed.'

3. THE WRITTEN GOSPELS. 'The sacred authors, in writing the four Gospels, selected certain of the many elements which had been handed on, either orally or already in written form; others they synthesized or explained with an eye to the situation of the churches, while sustaining the form of preaching, but always in such a fashion that they have told us the honest truth about Jesus.'

—CCC, no. 126

In other words, first, there was the **public ministry of Jesus**, through which he revealed God's unconditional love for all people; announced the coming of the Kingdom of God; revealed himself to be the Messiah and Savior, the Son of God; and revealed how best to live as the People of God and his disciples.

Second, there was the preaching and living of his Good News by the first and early disciples, people who had witnessed the risen Jesus and come to believe that Jesus had, indeed, risen from the dead. At this second stage, different oral traditions could have varied slightly within the early Church, depending on the religious background and culture of those to whom the story of Jesus was being passed on; for example, Jew or **Gentile** (non-Jewish/pagan) converts to Christianity.

Third and finally, as the first witnesses died, people knew that subsequent generations would need a written account of Jesus' life, Death and Resurrection and of his teachings. And so the writing of the Gospels began. The four **Evangelists**, or sacred authors of the Gospels, tell 'the honest truth about Jesus', and all were inspired and guided by the Holy Spirit in their writing. Yet, each author had his own particular style, intended audience, emphasis and so on. The Evangelists were even influenced by their personal perspectives. The following exercises will help to illustrate this point.

SYMBOL OF ST. LUKE | 11TH-CENTURY MANUSCRIPT

SYMBOL OF ST. MATTHEW | 11TH-CENTURY MANUSCRIPT

READ AND DISCUSS

⊙ Read and compare Luke's version of the 'Our Father' (Luke 11:2–4) with Matthew's (Matthew 6:9–13). Matthew's version is the one with which we are more familiar. Discuss how the two versions vary slightly.

⊙ Then compare the following two versions of the same story very carefully.

Now there was a woman who had been suffering from hemorrhages for twelve years. She had endured much under many physicians, and had spent all that she had; and she was no better, but rather grew worse.

—Mark 5:25–26

Now, there was a woman who had been suffering from hemorrhages for twelve years; and though she had spent all she had on physicians, no one could cure her.

—Luke 8:43

⊙ Which account seems more critical of physicians and which is more excusing of them?

⊙ Why might Mark and Luke have had different perspectives while telling the same story? (Hint: Luke was himself a physician.)

The four
Evangelists, or
sacred authors
of the Gospels,
tell 'the honest
truth about
Jesus', and all
were inspired
and guided by
the Holy Spirit
in their writing

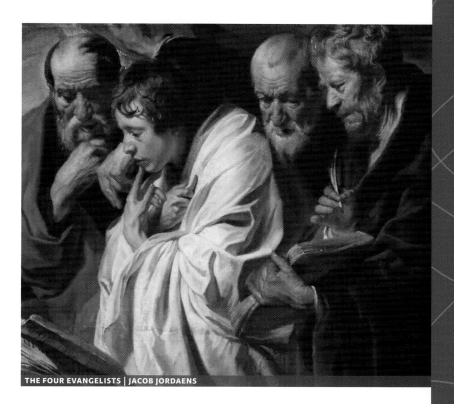

THE FOUR EVANGELISTS | JACOB JORDAENS

The Acts of the Apostles, you will recall, describes how the Apostles and other disciples, after receiving the gift of the Holy Spirit at Pentecost, came to a rock-solid faith in their risen Lord and Savior. Driven by a boldness of faith, the Apostles and the other disciples began traveling from one village to another, from one country to another, telling and retelling the stories that shaped the now emerging Tradition within the Church. (See Acts of the Apostles 4:13, 29; Ephesians 3:12; Philippians 1:20; 1 Timothy 3:13). Thus, they established the Church, the seed of the Kingdom of God made present in Jesus in his Death and Resurrection, but yet to come in its fullness at his Second Coming.

Gradually, collections of stories and sayings were brought together, comprising different snippets, or what the scholars call 'pericopes'. This 'pericope' material was first communicated orally and was gradually organized for practical use; for example, in worship. As needed, individual preachers made use of a saying or an event from the Church's growing Tradition. As a result, events were not always recounted in the actual time-frame in which they happened because those who were recalling them were more interested in what happened and what was said and the faith truth to be taught than they were in *when* exactly the incidents took place.

Sometimes teachings or sayings of Jesus, which he may have taught in a variety of places and at different times, were gathered together for emphasis. For example, Jesus' **Sermon on the Mount** (Matthew 5—7) is most likely a collection of Jesus' teachings from different times and places in his public ministry. Jesus himself may not have preached and taught all the elements in the Sermon on the Mount at one time and in one place. The people for whom Matthew wrote his Gospel—Jewish converts—would not have missed the significance of Jesus preaching a 'blueprint for living as his disciples' on a mount, or side of a mountain. Why is that? Teaching from a mountain played a significant part in their history as God's people. For example, God revealed his name, **YHWH**, to Moses near a mountain; during the Exodus, God entered the Covenant with his people near a mountain and revealed the Ten Commandments to Moses on a mountain; God appeared to Elijah the Prophet on a mountain. What is central is the *message* of the Sermon on the Mount. What matters to our faith is that it is the 'blueprint teaching' for the life of disciples of Jesus.

This helps to explain that when the teachings and stories of Jesus were put in written form in the Gospels, they often read like a series of loosely connected paragraphs without a chronological sequence. The time element and precise details were not as important for the early Church as that they accurately and authentically passed on the faith and teachings of the Apostles. For example, all four accounts of the Gospel recount Jesus' miraculous feeding of some five thousand people from 'five loaves and two fish'. However, John's Gospel is the only account of the Gospel that notes that they were 'barley loaves' and that a young boy—probably a teenager like yourself—had brought them (obviously his lunch that he now was willing to share).

A key point to remember is that the Gospels are not biographies as we understand that literary genre today. They are writings inspired by the Holy Spirit which are faith witnesses to the deep faith of those first Apostles and the early Church. The main intent of the Evangelists was to pass on the apostolic faith of the Church in Jesus Christ, the Incarnate Son of God, the Messiah and Savior of the world. For example, let's take another look at the account of the multiplication of the loaves and fish. In addition to the four accounts of the **miracle** of the five loaves and two fish to feed the five thousand, Mark and Matthew report another incident when Jesus fed 'four thousand men, besides women and children'. This time Matthew writes about 'seven loaves and a few small fish', while Mark mentions only the seven loaves. The details, again, are not the issue. What matters is the message: in feeding the hungry, Jesus was clearly revealing and making known God's 'caring' love for all people.

St. Paul the Apostle gives us a helpful summary of his own mission as an Apostle to pass on the core faith of the early Church. He writes:

For I handed on to you as of first importance what I in turn had received: that Christ died for our sins in accordance with the scriptures, and that he was buried, and that he was raised on the third day in accordance with the scriptures, and that he appeared to Cephas [Peter], then to the

All four accounts of the Gospel recount Jesus' miraculous feeding of some five thousand people from 'five loaves and two fish'

twelve. . . . Last of all, as to one untimely born, he appeared also to me.

—1 Corinthians 15:3–5, 8

This is the message that matters most.

GROUP WORK/DISCUSSION

◉ Look up and read the Feeding of the Five Thousand in Matthew 14:13–21, Mark 6:30–44, Luke 9:10–17 and John 6:1–15, and the Feeding of the Four Thousand in Matthew 15:32–39 and Mark 8:1–10. Compare the similarities and differences.

◉ Then, in groups, talk about how well you can recall an important occasion or event in which you were involved. Discuss how easy (or difficult) it is to remember the specific details. If the event or occasion was filled with emotion (like winning a big game or celebrating Confirmation), does that make recalling the details easier or more difficult? Would everyone involved remember all the details? What matters most—the details or the overall message? In conclusion, what do you think is more important—being able to record the details, or remembering and appreciating the spirit and meaning of an event or happening?

◉ How does what you have learned from this discussion help you to understand the intention and motivation of the inspired writers of the Gospels?

WHAT ABOUT YOU PERSONALLY?

◉ Looking at the overall message rather than the details of an event: how might this help you to read the Gospels more effectively for your life?

◉ Yet, the details can and do matter and have a message as well. For example, what might you learn from the young boy in the story of the multiplication of the loaves and fish about sharing with those in need—even when the odds seem impossible?

◉ From your reflections so far, how is the Gospel 'Good News' for you?

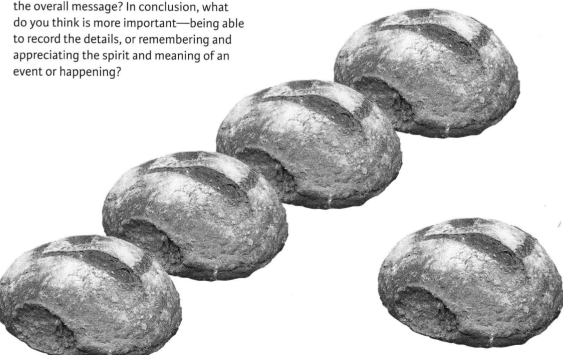

Introduction to the Synoptic Gospels—Mark, Matthew and Luke

The Gospels according to Matthew, Mark and Luke are known as the **Synoptic Gospels**. The word 'synoptic' comes from two Greek words that mean 'to see together'. These three accounts of the Gospel are called 'synoptic' because there are many similarities between them in terms of their content and the order in which the content is presented. Matthew, Mark and Luke have many stories and passages in common, and overall the main lines of the Gospel story are similar in all three.

OPENING CONVERSATION

⊙ What are some of your all-time favorite Gospel stories? Chances are that they are in one of the Synoptic Gospels; they have the great stories.

⊙ Look up and try to find your favorite. Share why you like it so much.

Reflecting on their own and other eyewitnesses' remembrances of the life, Death, Resurrection and Ascension of Jesus and his teachings, each of the Evangelists who wrote the Synoptic Gospels passes on the faith of the Apostolic Church in Jesus from a different perspective—as does the Fourth Gospel, John's Gospel. Each of the Evangelists, inspired by the Holy Spirit, wrote their account of the Gospel to appeal to a specific audience. Central to the understanding of all the accounts of the Gospel, however, is 'Jesus Christ, God's incarnate Son: his acts, teachings, Passion and glorification' (CCC, no. 124). The Good News that they all proclaim is that God's plan of Salvation for the world was brought to completion in the Person of Jesus of Nazareth, the Christ and Son of God, who suffered, died and was buried, and rose again. This Good News demands a response of faith from the reader, a change of heart that turns one's whole life toward God and to living as a disciple of Jesus. This 'change of heart' or 'direction of one's life' is what the New Testament calls 'conversion'.

The Gospel according to Mark

Most scholars now agree that Mark's Gospel was the first to be written, some time between AD 65 and 75. By this time, many of the great apostolic leaders—Peter, Paul, James the son of Zebedee, and James of Jerusalem—had already been martyred, or suffered and died because of their faith in Jesus Christ. Mark's primary source is thought to have been the oral preaching of Peter the Apostle, though it is clear that the Evangelist had a number of different sources at his disposal when he composed his work. These include an oral tradition concerning John the Baptist, some particular controversy stories, **parables**, miracle stories, community instruction and the earliest **Passion Narrative**.

Mark's account of the Gospel is full of emotion and drama, with a vividness and intensity that we do not find in the other Gospels. Many biblical scholars hold that Mark's Gospel was written for Christians in Rome who were suffering persecution or under threat of persecution. Suffering, lack of understanding and failure, which were part of their daily lives as Christians, are part of the presentation of the theme of discipleship that is such a prominent feature of Mark's Gospel.

Mark presents a clear picture of the apostolic faith in Jesus to be both true God and true man, fully divine and fully human in all ways but sin. The Catholic Church today continues to teach and pass on this faith. She teaches:

> The unique and altogether singular event of the Incarnation of the Son of God does not mean that Jesus Christ is part God and part man, nor does it imply that he is the result of a confused mixture of the divine and the human. He became truly man while remaining truly God. Jesus Christ is true God and true man.
>
> —CCC, no. 464

Jesus is truly the Son of God, the Second Person of the Blessed Trinity. In him and through his saving work, the Kingdom, or reign, of God was inaugurated and made present in human history. Mark teaches that through his miracles

ST. MARK | CHURCH OF ST MARY & ST LAMBERT, SUFFOLK, ENGLAND

Jesus revealed that he is truly God and gave witness to the reality and existence of the Kingdom he inaugurated but which is not yet present on earth. A miracle is a 'sign or wonder, such as a healing or the control of nature, which can only be attributed to divine power. The miracles of Jesus were messianic signs of the presence of God's kingdom' (CCC, Glossary).

Mark also teaches that Jesus is truly human. Jesus became angry and tired, was often misunderstood and not recognized, took children in his arms, and showed compassion for those who were suffering. While he freely expressed his feelings about his forthcoming suffering and death, Jesus freely accepted the Father's will and carried out the mission of Salvation. His suffering and dying revealed his love for his Father and for all humanity. Jesus obeyed his Father and served others. He emptied himself and suffered unto death—but his suffering and death was not the end. (Read Philippians 2:1–11.)

Mark presents Jesus launching his public ministry, announcing: 'The time is fulfilled, and the kingdom of God has come near; repent, and believe in the good news' (Mark 1:14–15). In so doing, he teaches a key demand of being a disciple of Jesus; namely, to become a disciple requires conversion, or 'a turning around', of one's whole life toward God, a total transformation of one's life. The depth of this conversion, or the cost of being a disciple, is revealed in the very life of Jesus, who said, 'If any want to become my followers, let them deny themselves and take up their cross and follow me' (Mark 8:34).

An essential characteristic of the life of a disciple of Jesus is to love and serve as he did, as he commanded his disciples at the Last Supper. (Read John 13:31–35.) This life of love includes denying oneself and embracing the suffering that will be part of that service. This is the demand and cost of 'following Jesus'. The reward of faithful discipleship is a life filled with a peace and joy that truly makes one 'blessed'. (Read Matthew 16:24–26).

Mark is sure to tell us that Mary Magdalene and two other women disciples of Jesus, on Easter Sunday morning, found Jesus' tomb empty, and were greeted with the words, the Good News, 'He has been raised; he is not here' (Mark 16:6). The risen Christ is God's great assurance that faithful disciples of Jesus will share in Jesus' final victory. God will raise us up from suffering and death—God is not the one who causes suffering and death. God is the Giver and Source of life. God helps us to carry our cross with hope, in service to him and others, to live the Great Commandment. When we do, we are not far from the Kingdom of God. (Read Mark 12:28–34.)

REFLECT AND DISCUSS

⊙ Given Mark's context and intended audience, why do you think he portrayed Jesus the way he did?

ST. MATTHEW | GUIDO RENI

⊙ Search through Mark's Gospel for some examples of the focus on Jesus' 'suffering'; you might look for the term 'suffering servant'.

WHAT ABOUT YOU PERSONALLY?

⊙ Mark focuses on Jesus' humanity and on his willingness to accept loneliness and suffering as the cost of obedience to his Father's will. How might this response of Jesus challenge you in your own response to suffering and pain in the world and in your own life? How might Jesus' trust in his Father help you in your own faith?

The Gospel according to Matthew

The Gospel according to Matthew was written between AD 70 and 85. Matthew, one of the Twelve—the first twelve Apostles—wrote mainly for Jews who had become believers in Jesus. Matthew, under the inspiration of the Holy Spirit, taught that Jesus was the Messiah promised from of old and that everything that happened to and through him was the fulfillment of the Scriptures of ancient Israel.

Matthew's genealogy of Jesus (Matthew 1:1–17) identifies Jesus as 'the son of David, the son of Abraham' (Matthew 1:1), which were revered titles in the Hebrew tradition. Matthew also clearly proclaims that Jesus is the Son of God. At Jesus' baptism by John, Jesus was anointed by the Holy Spirit 'and a voice from heaven said, "This is my Son, the Beloved, with whom I am well pleased" ' (Matthew 3:17).

Matthew's Gospel teaches that Jesus is the fulfillment of the Covenant that God and the people of Israel entered. For example, Matthew uses the literary genre of typology to teach that Moses prefigured Jesus. 'Typology indicates the dynamic movement toward the fulfillment of the divine plan when "God [will] be everything to everyone" [1 Corinthians 15:28]' (CCC, no. 130).

As Moses went to the top of Mount Sinai to receive God's Law, Matthew presents Jesus proclaiming 'the Sermon on the Mount'. (See Matthew 4:23—7:29.) Throughout the Sermon on the Mountain, Matthew presents

THE SERMON ON THE MOUNT | GUSTAV DORÉ

Jesus repeating, building upon and sometimes reinterpreting the Law of Moses—'You have heard it said, but I say. . . .' Later Jesus says what was likely key to Matthew's understanding of Jesus' mission: 'Every scribe who has been trained for the kingdom of heaven is like the master of a household who brings out of his treasure what is new and what is old' (Matthew 13:52). As Moses proclaimed the Old Law, Jesus proclaims its fulfillment. 'Do not think that I have come to abolish the law or the prophets; I have come not to abolish but to fulfill' (Matthew 5:17). 'Christians therefore read the Old Testament in the light of Christ crucified and risen. . . . As an old saying put it, the New Testament lies hidden in the Old and the Old Testament is unveiled in the New [St. Augustine of Hippo, *Seven Questions Concerning the Heptateuch* (First Seven Books of the Bible), 2, 73]' (CCC, no. 129).

The Passion (suffering and Death) and Resurrection of Jesus are at the center of Matthew's Gospel, as they are the center of all four accounts of the Gospel. Jesus, the Messiah, suffers, dies, is buried, raised from the dead, and appears to his disciples. At his last appearance, again on a mountain, the disciples finally recognize that the very same Jesus who walked the roads of Galilee with them, and journeyed up to Jerusalem, there to be crucified, had now risen from the dead 'three days after being killed' (Mark 9:31), as he predicted. There, on the mountain, the risen Christ, before he ascends to the Father, commissions the Apostles to go make disciples among all peoples. His parting promise to them is his assurance that he will always be with them 'to the end of the age'—or, as the Church has come to understand, until his Second Coming, when the Kingdom of God he inaugurated and established will come about in its fullness. (Read Matthew 28:16–20.)

OVER TO YOU

⊙ Try to summarize your own faith in who Jesus is and how that gives meaning to your life now.

were a sect of Judaism whom other Jews considered to have defiled the Law of Moses and they were despised even more than pagans.

Many people would consider Luke's Gospel to be the most polished and sophisticated of the Synoptics. At the beginning of his work, the Evangelist indicates that he made use of a number of sources and he outlines his aim and the procedure he followed in writing his Gospel:

> Since many have undertaken to set down an orderly account of the events that have been fulfilled among us, just as they were handed on to us by those who from the beginning were eye-witnesses and servants of the word, I too decided, after investigating everything carefully from the very first, to write an orderly account for you, most excellent Theophilus,* so that you may know the truth concerning the things about which you have been instructed.
>
> —Luke 1:1–4

The Gospel according to Luke

Luke put the Gospel message into a form that was understandable and meaningful to educated Greek converts from paganism. 'Paganism' was a term used in the early Church to designate a religion other than Christianity or Judaism whose values were contrary to the teachings of Sacred Scripture. Pagan religions practiced polytheism, or the belief in many gods. Luke, probably a native of Asia Minor and, by tradition, a doctor of medicine, was a Gentile (non-Jewish/pagan) convert to Christianity. So, one of his main concerns was to show that both Gentiles and Jews were invited to be followers of Jesus. In Luke 7:1–10, for example, Jesus praises the faith of a Roman (pagan) centurion, who would have been a Gentile and a hated symbol of the Roman occupation. Again, in Luke 10:25–37 Jesus makes a Samaritan the hero of a parable. Samaritans

The genealogy of Jesus in Luke's Gospel goes back to Adam. Jesus is the one who ushers in God's fulfillment of his promise of salvation, God's grand hope not only for the Israelites, the descendants of Abraham and King David, but for all humanity, the descendants of Adam. When messengers come from John the Baptist to Jesus, inquiring, 'Are you the one who is to come, or are we to wait for another?', Jesus points to his miracles as the inauguration, or in-breaking, of God's Kingdom: 'Go and tell John what you have seen and heard; the blind receive their sight, the lame walk, the lepers are cleansed, the deaf hear, the dead are raised, the poor have the good news brought to them.' (Read the whole story in Luke 7:19–23.)

God's saving love extends to all people. Jesus' mission as the Prophet of God's Kingdom,

---

* The name 'Theophilus' represents the Gentile (Greek) Christians to whom Luke's Gospel is addressed.

included the Revelation that God is at work establishing peace and justice, reaching out to the lost and outcast, and with special favor for the afflicted and oppressed. Jesus, the Incarnate Son of God, reached out to hated tax collectors and to Roman soldiers, to the despised Samaritans and the dreaded lepers, to public sinners, uneducated shepherds and all the underprivileged. Luke's account of the Gospel also teaches that God loves the poor and admonishes the rich for their lack of concern for the poor. An example of this is Jesus' teaching in the parable of the rich man and Lazarus in Luke 16:19–31.

Women also had an inferior place and little status in society at the time. They were not granted the same rights as men and were not valued highly by many Jews of Jesus' time. Luke's Gospel presents women quite differently. Jesus openly includes women among his disciples—a fact that many Jews of Jesus' time would have considered scandalous. The pre-eminent story about women and their role in the divine plan is of course the story of the Blessed Virgin Mary, whom God chose to become the Mother of the Incarnate Son of God through the power of the Holy Spirit. Luke also includes many other women. Among these were the women at the foot of the Cross, 'including the women who had followed him from Galilee' (Luke 23:49). In other words, they had been his disciples from the beginning. Read the story of Jesus curing the woman on the Sabbath (Luke 13:10–17).

In Luke's Gospel, Jesus is the Revelation of the infinite mercy of God, offering hope to those who seem to have lost hope and given up. Only Luke has the parables of the Lost Sheep, the Lost Coin and the Lost Son—the Prodigal (read Luke 15). Even on the Cross, we see the depth of the saving love of God revealed. Jesus forgave those who crucified him, praying to his Father, 'Father, forgive them; for they do not know what they are doing' (Luke 23:34). One of Jesus' last acts was to extend mercy and hope to the 'good thief' crucified alongside him, assuring him, 'Today you will be with me in Paradise' (Luke 23:43). Throughout his Gospel, Luke proclaims that Jesus is the saving God of all people, Jews and Gentiles. In this message we discover what is required of us as disciples of Jesus. The teachings and life of Jesus reveal what God requires of us and, thus, how we as the People of God should live.

READ AND DISCUSS

- Read the story of the rich man and Lazarus in Luke 16:19–31.
- Discuss what you think this story means.
- What does it mean for your life?

THE RICH MAN AND LAZARUS | FRESCO FROM FANEFJORD CHURCH, DENMARK

The greatest story ever told

OPENING ACTIVITY

⊙ Imagine you are creating a newspaper on behalf of the Evangelists Mark, Matthew and Luke. Based on what you have learned in this chapter so far, work in pairs or small groups to come up with three 'News Headlines'. Each headline should try to capture the unique message about Jesus that Matthew, Mark and Luke wanted to convey in their account of the Gospel.

THE GREATEST STORY EVER TOLD

The coming of Jesus and his story, told for us in the Gospels, was to change the history of the world. That is why it is often called the 'greatest story ever told'. Even nonbelievers acknowledge the power and force of Jesus' life (story) and how it has shaped all of human history since then.

Here is how one man, Dr. James Allen Francis, described the life of Jesus. He wrote 'One Solitary Life' in 1926.

One Solitary Life

He was born in an obscure village,
the child of a peasant woman.
He grew up in another obscure village
where he worked in a carpenter shop
until he was thirty.

He never wrote a book.
He never held an office.
He never went to college.
He never visited a big city.
He never travelled more than two hundred miles
from the place where he was born.
He did none of the things
usually associated with greatness.
He had no credentials but himself.

He was only thirty-three.
His friends ran away.
One of them denied him.
He was turned over to his enemies
and went through the mockery of a trial.
He was nailed to a cross between two thieves.
While dying, his executioners gambled for his clothing,
the only property he had on earth.

JESUS IN HIS FATHER'S WORKSHOP | MAYNOOTH, IRELAND

When he was dead
he was laid in a borrowed grave
through the pity of a friend.

Nineteen centuries have come and gone
and today Jesus is the central figure of the human race
and the leader of mankind's progress.
All the armies that have ever marched,
all the navies that have ever sailed,
all the parliaments that have ever sat,
all the kings that ever reigned put together
have not affected the life of mankind on earth
as powerfully as that one solitary life.

WOODEN CRUCIFIX, MEXICO

TALK IT OVER

⊙ What do you think the writer wanted to convey most of all about Jesus?

⊙ Why do you think Jesus had such an impact, given that he did not have any of the trappings of wealth and status that we might expect an influential person to have?

LET'S PROBE DEEPER

⊙ What is the most important thing that this piece of text says about Jesus? What does this mean for you personally?

⊙ One of the earliest comments made by Mark the Evangelist about Jesus was that 'he taught them as one having authority' (Mark 1:22). But Jesus had no official position in his community; he was not a member of the Sanhedrin (the ruling Council) nor even officially appointed a rabbi. So, what do you think was his 'authority'?

JUDGE AND ACT

In this chapter we have focused on the Gospel as the Good News of Jesus Christ. Now we must ask ourselves: Is the Gospel Good News in my life? How and why? How will I put this Good News to work?

WHAT DIFFERENCE DOES THE GOSPEL MAKE IN YOUR LIFE?

Find some quotations from Matthew, Mark or Luke that you consider to be life-giving or 'good news' for you. Notice, however, that the Gospel as Good News does not mean it is all 'nice' and 'sweet'; it is always both consoling and confronting, pleasing as well as challenging. Here are some possible examples:

'Repent, for the kingdom of heaven has come near.'
—Matthew 3:2

'Take heart, it is I; do not be afraid.'
—Mark 6:50

'Ask, and it will be given you; search, and you will find; knock, and the door will be opened for you.'
—Matthew 7:7

'But I say to you that listen, Love your enemies.'
—Luke 6:27

'Let the little children come to me, and do not stop them; for it is to such as these that the kingdom of God belongs.'
—Luke 18:16

JUDGE AND DECIDE
⊙ If you had to take one of your chosen Gospel quotations as a motto for your life at present, which one would you choose?
⊙ Why did you choose that particular quotation and what does it say to your life?
⊙ Better still, how will you try to live it?

DISCUSS
⊙ Does the world still needs Jesus' Good News? Why or why not?

CLASS ACTIVITY
⊙ Imagine you were to wake up tomorrow and read only good news headlines in the newspapers; what might they say? Have a go at writing some and stick them around the room.

PROTESTERS LOBBY FOR THE REBUILDING OF NEW ORLEANS AFTER HURRICANE KATRINA

Gospel as Good News does not mean it is all 'nice' and 'sweet'; it is always both consoling and confronting

The story of Chiara Lubich

Born in 1920 in the northern Italian city of Trento, Chiara Lubich was baptized Silvia but changed her name to Chiara (Clare) on joining a branch of the Franciscan Third Order in her teens. Members of the Franciscan Third Order, or tertiaries, try to live the values and spirituality of St. Francis of Assisi in their daily life. Chiara was brought up with the traditional Catholic spirituality of her mother but was equally influenced by her father's socialist and anti-fascist views. Chiara saw the Gospel as Good News in her own life, and she wanted to share it. To do so, she set up what has become a worldwide movement, known as Focolare. Its members are wonderful laypeople who support one another in living the Gospel as Good News in their day-to-day lives.

Chiara was a twenty-four-year-old primary school teacher when she launched her movement with a group of young women, some of them former pupils, in her native Trento in 1944. Despite its ordinary name—*focolare* means 'hearth' or 'family fireside'— the organization had a revolutionary impact on the stagnating Catholicism of its time. Many of Focolare's innovations are a reaffirmation of the importance of the laity in the mission and ministries of the Church: a return to Scripture as the center of Catholic faith; a joyful Liturgy using popular tunes of the day; an emphasis on the key Gospel message of love and unity that anticipated the direction the Second Vatican Council would take twenty years later.

Under Chiara's leadership, Focolare spread to more than 180 countries, with 140,000 members as well as 2.1 million people affiliated to the movement. Besides Catholics, Focolare now includes Protestant and Orthodox members as well as people of other faiths.

Chiara Lubich died at the age of eighty-eight in 2008.

TALK IT OVER

- How did Chiara Lubich live out the values of the Gospel in her life?
- What can you learn from Chiara's example about how you might face the challenges of the Gospel in your own life today?

WHAT WILL YOU DO NOW?

- What commitment are you willing to make to try to live the message of the Gospel in your day-to-day life, in your interactions with family, friends, neighbors and others, thereby making the Gospel 'Good News' for both yourself and the people with whom you come into contact?

RESPOND WITH YOUR FAMILY AND FRIENDS

- The world needs people of hope, people who bring 'good news' rather than despair and negativity. Think about ways that you can be this kind of person with your friends and family.

And he said to them, 'Go into all the world and proclaim the good news to the whole creation.'

MARK 16:15

PRAYER REFLECTION

Pray the Sign of the Cross together.

LEADER
The risen Christ Jesus promised his disciples, 'I am with you always, to the end of the age' (Matthew 28:20). May this candle help us to remember that the risen Lord is with us today as he promised.

Jesus came to reveal good news. 'Gospel' means 'good news'. The Gospel is Good News for our lives because it assures us of God's love, reveals Jesus as our Savior, teaches us how to live as his disciples, and guarantees us the grace we need to live as the People of God, after the way of Jesus.

As you prepare to spend a little time reflecting on some of the Good News that Jesus revealed for each one of us, relax and close your eyes. . . . Settle into your seat, with your feet on the floor and your hands on your lap. . . . Become aware of your breathing. *(Pause)*

Breathe in . . . and out . . . , in . . . and out. . . . Each breath is God's gift of life flowing through your body.

As we sit here, the risen Christ is with us. *(Pause)*

Now listen to what he has to say to you:

'Ask, and it will be given you; search, and you will find; knock, and the door will be opened for you.' *(Repeat)*

Allow these words of Jesus to take root in your mind and in your heart, just as they took root in the hearts of the Apostles and the other disciples who lived in Jesus' time.

Jesus is speaking these words to you right now:

'Ask and it will be given you; search, and you will find; knock, and the door will be opened for you.'

What do you ask for? *(Pause)*

Where do you search? *(Pause)*

Which doors are you knocking on now? *(Pause)*

Now we will leave all our requests, all our searching and all the closed doors in our life in the hands of Jesus. Know that Jesus is listening to all that you say. . . . Remember what he has said to you:

'Ask, and it will be given you; search, and you will find; knock, and the door will be opened for you.'

As you prepare to open your eyes, get ready to leave this prayer time with renewed confidence that the risen Christ is with you in all you do. He is aware of all your needs. Ask him for the grace you need to live as a true disciple—an apprentice to him.

Open your eyes and let us pray together.

ALL
Christ be with me.
Christ be beside me.
Christ be before me.
Christ be behind me.
Christ at my right hand.
Christ at my left hand.
Christ be with me everywhere I go.
Christ be my friend for ever and ever. Amen.
(From the 'Breastplate of St. Patrick')

Pray the Sign of the Cross together.

CHAPTER 11

Jesus and His Message in the Gospels

according to Matthew, Mark and Luke

INFANCY NARRATIVES

THE BAPTISM OF JESUS

THE TEMPTATION OF JESUS

JESUS—THE NEW MOSES

JESUS—THE NEW DAVID

JESUS' PUBLIC MINISTRY

JESUS INAUGURATES THE KINGDOM OF GOD

JESUS' PARABLES

JESUS' MIRACLES

JESUS IN THE SYNOPTIC GOSPELS

IN THIS CHAPTER WE DELVE MORE DEEPLY INTO the Synoptic Gospels. The inspired authors of these accounts of the Gospel communicated the message that Jesus, the Incarnate Son of God, the Second Person of the Blessed Trinity and the Savior of the world, came to reveal the extent of God's love for all people. They invited their readers to take up the challenge of the Gospel and allow their lives to be transformed by the words and example of Jesus.

LIVING THE VALUES OF THE KINGDOM

JUSTICE

PEACE

MERCY

LOVE

Faith Focus: These teachings of the Catholic Church are the primary focus of the doctrinal content presented in this chapter:

⊙ The Blessed Virgin Mary is truly the Mother of God, the Mother of Jesus, the Incarnate Son of God. Joseph accepted and fulfilled the role of adoptive father of Christ.

⊙ The baptism of Jesus was his manifestation as the Messiah of Israel and the Son of God and of the redemptive work that he would accomplish by his Passion, Death and Resurrection.

⊙ The temptation of Jesus in the desert shows Jesus triumphing over Satan by his total adherence to the plan of Salvation willed by the Father.

⊙ The Beatitudes, which are at the heart of Jesus' preaching, shed light on the actions and attitudes characteristic of the Christian life.

⊙ The Kingdom of God was inaugurated on earth by Christ and will come in its fullness at his Second Coming at the end of time, when he returns in glory.

Discipleship Formation: As a result of studying this chapter and discovering the meaning of the faith of the Catholic Church for your life, you should be better able to:

⊙ consider how you can resist temptations in your own life, in light of what you have learned from the Gospel accounts of the temptation of Jesus;

⊙ compare the values of the Beatitudes with your own attitudes and actions, and realize how the Beatitudes challenge you to live and work to build the Kingdom of God;

⊙ reflect on what you have learned for your own life from the parables and miracle stories you have read;

⊙ appreciate more fully the meaning of the Our Father;

⊙ decide how you will bring God's mercy, love and compassion into people's lives today.

Scripture References: These Scripture references are quoted or referred to in this chapter:
OLD TESTAMENT: Exodus 2:1–10; **Isaiah** 9:6–7, 11:1–9
NEW TESTAMENT: Matthew 1:18—2:15, 3:13–17, 4:1–11, 5:3–12, 8:1–3, 9:27–30, 13:3–9, 44–45 and 55, 14:13–23, 15:32–39, 21:28–32, 22:1–14, 25:1–36; **Mark** 1:2, 9–13, 15, 21–28, 3:1–6, 5:1–11, 23–29, 6:3; **Luke** 1:5—2:52, 3:21–38, 4:1–13, 16 and 18, 5:1–11, 40–44, 6:20–49, 7:22, 8:4–15, 22–25 and 40–56, 13:6–9, 11–13 and 18–19, 14:7–24, 16:19–31, 18:1–8, 16, 35–43, 19:1–10; **John** 1:1–44, 8:8 and 40–56, 10:10; **Acts of the Apostles** 1:22; **Romans** 6:4; **Galatians** 1:1; **Titus** 3:3–7; **Hebrews** 4:15; **James** 2:14–16; **1 John** 4:9, 16

Faith Glossary: Familiarize yourself with the meaning of these key faith terms. Definitions are found in the Glossary: **Baptism, baptism of Jesus, Beatitudes, Infancy Narratives, Kingdom of God, miracle(s), parable, Satan, Second Coming (of Christ), Sermon on the Mount, temptation, Works of Mercy, worship**

Faith Words: Kingdom of God
Learn by Heart: Corporal Works of Mercy
Learn by Example: *Nothing But Nets*

What influences our lives?

Many people believe that the time and place and circumstances of a person's birth can have a major influence on how their life takes shape—the kind of person they become, the things they value in life and even their choice of career. When someone makes a particularly important contribution to the world, for example, in sport, music, art or politics, or, indeed, through significant acts of charity or altruism, people are immediately interested in finding out about the person's background and what it was that gave rise to such courage or giftedness and so on.

When you were an infant, your family saw you as being full of promise, a bundle of potential, a range of possibilities. What do you know about your birth and very early life? Do you know, for example, when and where you were born? Not just the date, but the time of day—or night—as well?

RECALL ACTIVITY

Most of you will have heard stories about your birth and early childhood. See how many of the following questions you can answer. You might like to share your memories and stories with a partner.

- ⊙ Who visited you during the first joyous days of your life?
- ⊙ Did anything out of the ordinary, any particular event, occur during your first weeks of life?
- ⊙ Why were you given your particular name and who chose it?
- ⊙ How did your parents feel when they saw you for the first time?
- ⊙ Did they imagine what kind of person you would turn out to be?
- ⊙ Was there anything about you that struck them from the start?
- ⊙ Were you born in a different place from where you live today? If so, do you know the story of why you moved from there?

As a young child:
- ⊙ Were there any signs in your early years that might indicate your path or direction in life; for example, musical ability, athletic ability, fluency in language, artistic ability, interest in cars or machinery, in cooking and so on?
- ⊙ What personality traits came to the fore early on; for example, caring/kind; fiery/hot tempered, or calm/easygoing; natural leader/organizer, team person or solo player; outgoing or shy and so on?
- ⊙ What is your own earliest memory? Does it have any significance for your life today?

REFLECT ON YOUR OWN
- ⊙ What aspects of your early life do you think might have influenced the person you are today?

APPLICATION FORM

Name: _____

Father and mother: _____

_____

Place of birth: _____

Place of residence: _____

Date of birth: _____

Close relatives: _____

_____

_____

Education: _____

_____

_____

⊙ There is a proverb that says, 'The child is father to the man (or mother to the woman!).' What do you think this means? Is it true for you?

NOW LET'S TURN TO JESUS

What do you know about Jesus' birth and early life? Everyone today has to fill in application forms. Suppose Jesus had to fill in such a form when he was your age. Could you do it for him? Have a hand at it by copying the form on this page into your journal and filling in the details. There may be a few facts that you got wrong or did not know. Here are the correct responses:

Name: Jesus, son of Joseph, or Jesus of Nazareth. (In first-century Palestine, people were usually known by their father's name or by the place they came from. So Jesus would have been called 'Jesus, son of Joseph', or *Bar Joseph* in Hebrew, in his native village; and as 'Jesus of Nazareth' when he traveled elsewhere.)

Father and mother: Joseph and Mary. (Jesus is the Second Divine Person of the Blessed Trinity, the only begotten Son of God the Father, who 'was incarnate of the Virgin Mary, and became man' [Nicene Creed]. Jesus' contemporaries knew him as the son of Joseph the carpenter [see Matthew 13:55, Mark 6:3]. Joseph accepted the role of adoptive father of Christ, as it was revealed to him that Mary, to whom he was betrothed, had conceived by the Holy Spirit [see Matthew 1:18–25].)

Place of birth and place of residence: Bethlehem and Nazareth. (You probably got those right!)

Date of birth: Before 4 BC. (We do not know the exact date but it was not December 25, AD 1. That day is the celebration of the event, not an historical commemoration. The year 0 BC is mistaken as well. There was no year zero. The counting went from 1 BC to AD 1. Jesus, of course, was meant to be born on AD 1, hence it was called 'In the Year of the Lord' or AD, standing for *Anno Domini;* but a scholar got the counting of the years wrong in the early days of the Church and we have been out by four or five years ever since. Jesus was probably born before 4 BC, because that was the year Herod died. The Gospel of Matthew tells us that Herod was king when Jesus was born.)

Close relatives: John, Elizabeth and Zachary. (The Gospel of Luke tells us that Elizabeth was a 'relative' of Mary. This means that John the

Baptist, son of Elizabeth and Zachary, was a distant relative of Jesus as well.)

Education: Very good. (In all likelihood, Jesus had an excellent education. First of all, he could read [see Luke 4:16] and write [see John 8:8]. Jewish men were very well educated because they had to be able to read the Scriptures in the synagogue. When Jesus was only twelve years old he impressed the teachers in the Temple with his knowledge of the Scriptures [see Luke 2]. Also, Jesus was the son of a carpenter, so it is quite likely that he was trained in this skill and trade.)

THE ACCOUNTS OF JESUS' BIRTH AND EARLY LIFE AS RECORDED IN THE SYNOPTIC GOSPELS

There are two **Infancy Narratives**, or Gospel accounts of the birth of Jesus, in the Gospels of Matthew and Luke. Each approaches the event from a different point of view. In pairs, read Matthew, chapters 1 and 2, and Luke, chapters 1 and 2. Mark's Gospel begins with Jesus' public ministry and does not contain an account of Jesus' birth.

The story according to Matthew

Matthew teaches that the birth of Jesus was foretold in the Old Testament. He writes:

All this took place to fulfill what had been spoken by the prophet: 'Look, the virgin shall conceive and bear a son, and they shall name him Emmanuel,' which means, 'God with us'.
—Matthew 1:22–23

In his account Matthew places the birth of Jesus during the rule of Herod the Great, who was king from 73 BC to 4 BC. Herod was a tyrannical ruler, known for the ruthless protection of his position as king. When Herod heard that 'wise men' (magi or astronomers) from the East had come looking for the child who would be 'king of the Jews' in order that they could **worship** him, Herod summoned the wise men and told them to let him know when they found the child so that he too could pay homage to him. After paying homage to the Infant Jesus, the wise men 'warned in a dream not to return to Herod . . . left for their own country by another road' (Matthew 2:12).

Jewish priests, though they knew the prophecies, did not even bother to travel the eight miles from Jerusalem to Bethlehem to see the child for themselves. When Herod realized that he had been tricked by the wise men, he ordered that all children of two years old and under be killed. Joseph, warned in a dream, fled with Mary and the infant Jesus to Egypt. (Who else in the history of Israel is connected with Egypt?)

For Matthew, Jesus was the new Moses. Both Jesus and Moses were rescued from a tyrant. (Read Exodus 2:1–10.) Both Jesus and Moses had escaped a massacre of infant boys. Both eventually came out of Egypt and overcame the hostility to save their people. And because of the hostility, Jesus had to move to Nazareth, where he prepared for his ministry.

HEROD'S TOMB IN HERODION

The story according to Luke

Luke, by contrast, places his account of Jesus' birth within the rule of the Roman emperor Augustus Caesar, who reigned from 63 BC to AD 14. Luke's account begins with the emperor calling for a census of the population. Because Joseph was a descendant of the family of David, he had to go to Bethlehem, the city of David, to be registered. This was how it came to pass that Jesus was born in Bethlehem, in a place where animals were kept and fed, as there was no room in any of the inns on account of the crowds gathered for the census. Shepherds on the hillside heard of the birth from the angels— 'To you is born this day in the city of David a Savior, who is the Messiah, the Lord' (Luke 2:11)—and came to worship the infant. For Luke, Jesus was the new David, the one who would bring justice and peace to the whole world. This latter point is also highlighted in Luke's genealogy, which he traces back to Adam. (Read Luke 3:23–38.)

AUGUSTUS CAESAR

Each of these Infancy Narratives moves beyond the plain facts of how, when and where Jesus came to be born. As you will have discovered in researching the circumstances of your own birth, the significance of a baby's arrival into the world is about what the baby brings to that world, what its arrival means to the family, relatives and friends, and the expectations, hopes and dreams that surround it. Matthew and Luke sought to convey the significance of Jesus' birth both to the Jewish people (the descendants of David) and to all humanity (the descendants of Adam) in light of what had been foretold in the Scriptures and fulfilled in Jesus.

TALK IT OVER

- What significant pieces of information about Jesus can you glean from the stories of his birth?
- What would these lead one to believe about the kind of person Jesus would become?

In this chapter we will learn how the story of Jesus is the most important influence in our lives, as Catholics, as we try to answer his call to become more like him.

The significance of a baby's arrival into the world encompasses the hopes and dreams that surround it

Jesus begins his public ministry

OPENING CONVERSATION

- ⊙ What event or person from your early childhood is having the most influence on your life right now?
- ⊙ From what you have read of Jesus' infancy, what influence do you think the events of that time would have had on him as he grew into adulthood?

THE BAPTISM OF JESUS (MATTHEW 3:13–17; LUKE 3:21–22; MARK 1:9–11)

All three of the Synoptic Gospels give an account of the **baptism of Jesus** by John the Baptist in the Jordan River. This is the account from Mark:

In those days Jesus came from Nazareth of Galilee and was baptized by John in the Jordan. And just as he was coming up out of the water, he saw the heavens torn apart and the Spirit descending like a dove on him. And a voice came from heaven, 'You are my Son, the Beloved; with you I am well pleased.'

—Mark 1:9–11

People from Jerusalem and all over Judea had been coming to John the Baptist to confess their sins and be baptized. John saw himself as preparing the way for the coming of Jesus, and Mark identifies John as the one spoken about by Isaiah the Prophet to fulfill that mission, 'See, I am sending my messenger ahead of you, who will prepare your way; the voice of one crying out in the wilderness: "Prepare the way of the Lord, make his paths straight" ' (Mark 1:2). John called people to be baptized as a sign that they

would turn away from their sins. It was surprising even to him that Jesus presented himself for baptism. In Matthew's account, John says to Jesus, 'I need to be baptized by you. . . .'

In presenting himself for baptism, Jesus was affirming John's call to the people to repentance. Obviously Jesus did not need to be baptized in order to have his sins forgiven, but, as the

THE BAPTISM OF JESUS | PIERO DELLA FRANCESCA

Catechism of the Catholic Church states, 'he allows himself to be numbered among sinners' (CCC, no. 536).

According to Apostolic Tradition, Jesus, when he was about thirty years old, began his public life and ministry 'with his baptism by John in the Jordan' (CCC, no. 535). (See Luke 3:23, Acts of the Apostles 1:22.) All three Synoptic Gospels (Mark, Matthew and Luke) speak of the Spirit of God, the Holy Spirit, descending like a 'dove', the 'Spirit whom Jesus possessed in fullness from his conception' (CCC, no. 536), and a voice from Heaven proclaiming, 'This is my Son, the Beloved' (Matthew 3:17).

Mark's readers would have made the connection between the Spirit coming down on Jesus at his baptism and the descent of the Spirit of God on the Israelites, the Chosen People, during their Exodus from slavery in Egypt. The dove is one of the many 'symbols' used in the Old Testament for the Spirit of God (see CCC, no. 701). The baptism of Jesus 'is the manifestation ("Epiphany") of Jesus as Messiah of Israel and Son of God' (CCC, no. 535). The coming of Jesus, the promised Messiah, marked the beginning of the new and final Exodus. This new and final Exodus is the Spirit-led journey from slavery to sin to living in the freedom of the **Kingdom of God** (Mark 1:15). Jesus' invitation to live for the Kingdom is God's call to all people to move out of their enslavement to sin and live a life of justice and holiness. 'The Christian must . . . go down into the water with Jesus in order to rise with him, be reborn of water and the Spirit so as to become the Father's beloved son in the Son and "walk in newness of life" [Romans 6:4]' (CCC, no. 537).

REFLECT AND DISCUSS

⊙ What different responses might the people of Jesus' time have had to his action of presenting himself for baptism?

WHAT ABOUT YOU PERSONALLY?

⊙ Look up and read Titus 3:3–7. What does the fact that you have been reborn of water and the Spirit in **Baptism** say to you about your faith journey as a disciple of Jesus Christ?

TALK IT OVER

⊙ There have been many television documentaries made about people who take up the challenge of going into the wilderness to see if they can survive alone. Can you recall seeing such a program? Share your examples.

⊙ Why do you think people sometimes choose to get away from it all and spend time alone like this?

THE TEMPTATION OF JESUS | DUCCIO DI BUONINSEGNA

⊙ What might they be hoping to get away from? To find?

⊙ What do you think a person could gain from such an experience?

THE TEMPTATION OF JESUS (MARK 1:12–13; MATTHEW 4:1–11; LUKE 4:1–13)

Matthew, Mark and Luke all give an account of the **temptation** of Jesus in the desert. It is significant that Jesus spent forty days in solitude in the desert at the beginning of his public ministry. Matthew's readers, who were primarily converts from Judaism, would have paid careful attention to the number forty. They would have made the connection with the well-known Scripture accounts of God's saving acts among his people. In particular, Matthew's account would have called to mind how Moses and David both spent time in the desert at the beginning of their ministry. Matthew's readers would also have connected the number forty with the forty years the Israelites spent in the desert on their way to the Promised Land.

Here is Matthew's account of the temptation of Jesus:

Then Jesus was led up by the Spirit into the wilderness to be tempted by the devil. He fasted forty days and forty nights, and afterwards he was famished. The tempter came and said to him, 'If you are the Son of God, command these stones to become loaves of bread.' But he answered, 'It is written, "One does not live by bread alone, but by every word that comes from the mouth of God." '

Then the devil took him to the holy city and placed him on the pinnacle of the temple, saying to him, 'If you are the Son of God, throw yourself down, for it is written, "He will command his angels concerning you," and "On their hands they will bear you up, so that you will not dash your foot against a stone." ' Jesus said to him, 'Again it is written, "Do not put the Lord your God to the test." '

Again, the devil took him to a very high mountain and showed him all the kingdoms of the world and their splendor; and he said to him, 'All these I will give you, if you will fall down and worship me.' Jesus said to him, 'Away with you, **Satan**, for it is written, "Worship the Lord your God, and serve only him." '

Then the devil left him, and suddenly angels came and waited on him.

—Matthew 4:1–11

The message in the Gospel account of Jesus' temptations was not just for the first disciples of Jesus. It is for us and our lives as disciples of Jesus today. The New Testament Letter to the Hebrews, which presents Jesus in light of the Scriptures of ancient Israel, passes on this meaning for us as disciples of Jesus Christ. 'For we do not have a high priest [Jesus] who is unable to sympathize with our weaknesses, but we have one who in every respect has been tested, as we are, yet without sin' (Hebrews 4:15).

REFLECT AND DISCUSS

⊙ What importance do you think Lent holds for Christians today?

WHAT ABOUT YOU PERSONALLY?

⊙ How might Jesus' example of resisting temptation help you in your own life?

Jesus inaugurates the Kingdom of God

OPENING ACTIVITY/CONVERSATION

As a group, compile a list of the attitudes and actions that you would regard as essential in building an 'ideal' world. You may initially come up with a very long list, but try to agree eventually on about five or six. We will be looking back at this list later in this lesson.

WHAT DID JESUS MEAN BY THE 'KINGDOM OF GOD'?

A central theme in the Synoptic Gospels is the Kingdom of God. (The word 'kingdom' appears over 115 times in the Synoptics.) It is difficult for us today, living in a democratic country, to appreciate exactly what the notion of a 'kingdom' meant to people long ago, especially the Jewish people in Jesus' time, who had been living under the rule of hostile foreign kingdoms and were looking forward to the restoration of their 'kingdom' under the rule of their only true King, God. People in the time of Jesus looked forward to the coming of a good king as someone who would bring hope, security, safety, prosperity and peace.

Jesus frequently taught about 'the coming of the Kingdom'. The Kingdom Jesus announced and inaugurated was not a 'political or geographical' kingdom. It was the Kingdom of God without boundaries, without borders. As we explored in chapter 9, the Kingdom of God that Jesus inaugurated was made present in him and was established in his Death and Resurrection, but has yet to come in its fullness at his **Second Coming** at the end of time when he comes again in glory. This was the Good News—a message of hope and the promise of a new abundant life (see John 10:10) that would begin now and last forever.

The Gospel describes the Kingdom of God as involving love, forgiveness, equality and openness to all, especially the poor. To be part

of this Kingdom requires a conversion of heart, a change of attitude and a new way of acting. Most people do not think that such a world is possible in this life. But Jesus taught that the Kingdom is here, now, among us, in our hearts. All we have to do is recognize it and believe. But the Kingdom does not end there. As we shall see, the Kingdom will grow even stronger, in this life and in the next, to its climax in the sharing of the life and love of God in eternity.

OVER TO YOU

⊙ Do you think that the type of world Jesus described is possible in this life? Why or why not?

READ AND DISCUSS

⊙ Read the following extracts from Isaiah, chapters 9 and 11.

In the first passage, Isaiah 9:6–7, Isaiah describes the coming of Jesus as King.

For a child has been born for us,
    a son given to us;
authority rests upon his shoulders;
    and he is named
Wonderful Counselor, Mighty God,
    Everlasting Father, Prince of Peace.
His authority shall grow continually,
    and there shall be endless peace
for the throne of David and his kingdom.
    He will establish it and uphold it
with justice and with righteousness
    from this time onward and forevermore.
The zeal of the LORD of hosts will do this.

—Isaiah 9:6–7

In the second passage, Isaiah 11:1–9, Isaiah was providing a vision of the kind of world the Messiah, whom we know is Jesus, would inaugurate and establish:

THE JESSE TREE | CATHEDRAL OF LIMBURG, GERMANY

A shoot shall come out from the stump of Jesse,
    and a branch shall grow out of his roots.
The spirit of the LORD shall rest on him,
    the spirit of wisdom and understanding,
    the spirit of counsel and might,
    the spirit of knowledge and the fear of the
        LORD.
His delight shall be in the fear of the LORD.

He shall not judge by what his eyes see,
    or decide by what his ears hear;
but with righteousness he shall judge the poor,
    and decide with equity for the meek of the
        earth;
he shall strike the earth with the rod of his mouth,
    and with the breath of his lips he shall kill
        the wicked.
Righteousness shall be the belt around his waist,
    and faithfulness the belt around his loins.

The wolf shall live with the lamb,
    the leopard shall lie down with the kid,
the calf and the lion and the fatling together,
    and a little child shall lead them.
The cow and the bear shall graze,
    their young shall lie down together;
    and the lion shall eat straw like the ox.
The nursing child shall play over the hole of the
        asp,
    and the weaned child shall put its hand on
        the adder's den.
They will not hurt or destroy
    on all my holy mountain;
for the earth will be full of the knowledge of the
        LORD
    as the waters cover the sea.

—Isaiah 11:1–9

⊙ What are some of the 'signs of our times' you see through the eyes of faith in our culture today that point to the fulfillment of Isaiah's vision?

LIVING FOR THE KINGDOM

Jesus' 'Sermon on the Plain' in Luke's Gospel is similar to the 'Sermon on the Mount' in Matthew's Gospel, though it is shorter. Luke presents Jesus teaching his disciples and the crowds on the plain below the mountain where

Jesus had spent the night in prayer before choosing the Twelve Apostles. The Beatitudes are included in both the Sermon on the Mount (Matthew 5:3–12) and the Sermon on the Plain (Luke 6:20–23).

The **Beatitudes** take up and fulfill the promises made to Abraham and God's chosen people since then. They 'are at the heart of Jesus' preaching' (CCC, no. 1716). 'They shed light on the actions and attitudes characteristic of the Christian life' (CCC, no. 1717) and are a summary of the blessings and rewards the faithful disciple of Jesus will experience, and a source of hope in times of suffering and other tribulations we encounter in living out our faith in Christ.

THE SERMON ON THE MOUNT | JAN LUYKEN

Here are the Beatitudes as presented by Luke:

Blessed are you who are poor,
    for yours is the kingdom of God.
Blessed are you who are hungry now,
    for you will be filled.
Blessed are you who weep now,
    for you will laugh.
    Blessed are you when people hate you, and when they exclude you, revile you and defame you on account of the Son of Man. Rejoice in that day and leap for joy, for surely your reward is great in heaven; for that is what their ancestors did to the prophets.

—Luke 6:20–23

Luke, unlike Matthew, then adds these consequences of not making the actions and attitudes proclaimed in the Beatitudes part of one's everyday life; that is, of not living in the hope of and promise for the Kingdom of God.

But woe to you who are rich,
    for you have received your consolation.
Woe to you who are full now,
    for you will be hungry.
Woe to you who are laughing now,
    for you will mourn and weep.
Woe to you when all speak well of you, for that is what their ancestors did to the false prophets.

—Luke 6:24–26

This first Beatitude in Luke, 'Blessed are you who are poor, / for yours is the kingdom of God', teaches that the kingdom made present in Jesus belongs, above all, to the poor. Luke proclaims, as the Scriptures of ancient Israel so often do, a message that was contrary to the predominant and pervasive actions and attitudes of the world of Jesus and the early Church, just as it is today. As is the case for many people in the world today, those who lived at the time of Jesus would probably have preferred to be able to live comfortably or to be wealthy, respected, popular, well-known, honored rather than 'poor'. Contrary to popular attitudes and actions of people who place their trust and hope in prosperity (wealth, good health, status) as both a source and a sign of God's blessing, the truly 'blessed' are the poor—those who place their hope and trust in God before and above all else. The poor are the 'humble and meek' who 'rely solely on their God's mysterious plans, who await the justice, not of men but of the Messiah' (CCC, no. 716).

Jesus points to the 'poor' as those who will share in the blessings of the Kingdom

Luke also proclaims not only the poor's love for God but also God's special love for the poor and vulnerable. Jesus, who shared in 'the life of the poor, from the cradle to the cross' and experienced 'hunger, thirst and privation' (CCC, no. 544), is sent to 'bring good news to the poor' (Luke 4:18; see also 7:22). Jesus reaches out to and ministers with the poor and other vulnerable people. He holds them up as models of those who are faithful to God and his Law, and makes active love for the poor and vulnerable 'the condition for entering his kingdom' (CCC, no. 544; see also Matthew 25:31–46).

TALK IT OVER

⊙ How do the actions and attitudes identified in the Beatitudes correspond with or differ from the list you drew up for the bringing about of 'your' ideal world?

⊙ In what ways are the Beatitudes contrary to the actions and attitudes you might often see driving young people in the world today?

⊙ 'Blessed are you who are poor, for yours is the kingdom of heaven.' How does living this Beatitude challenge families today? Challenge young people today?

WHAT ABOUT YOU PERSONALLY?

⊙ 'Blessed are you who are poor, for yours is the kingdom of heaven.' How does this Beatitude challenge your attitude toward 'wealth' in its many forms? Challenge you to act?

JOURNAL EXERCISE

⊙ Each time you pray the Our Father you pray 'Thy kingdom come'. How might your growing in the attitudes named in the Beatitudes move you to work with the Spirit of Christ toward bringing about the Kingdom that Christ inaugurated and established?

⊙ Write your reflections in your journal and revisit them often.

Exploring the notion of the Kingdom of God

OPENING REFLECTION

⊙ Look up and read the following references from the Gospel of Luke: Luke 6:27–35, Luke 6:36–42, Luke 6:43–49, Luke 16:19–31 and Luke 19:1–10. Then write in your own words what Jesus taught about the Kingdom of God.

JESUS USED THE POWER OF STORY IN HIS PREACHING

Story can teach and invite people to understand 'truth' in ways simple statements cannot do. A story draws us in, helps us to see ourselves, makes us active participants, as we have to figure out what the story 'means'. Jesus was a master storyteller, and he used a form of 'story', the **parable**, in his preaching.

A parable is a literary form, or genre, that speaks to the imagination of the listeners in order to make a point. A parable is based on experiences widely known by the audience to whom the parable is addressed. Jesus' parables aimed to draw his listeners' attention, to prick at their conscience, to cause them to pause, reflect and make good choices; in other words, convert his listeners to live for the Kingdom. Here is a summary of the teaching of the Catholic Church on Jesus' use of parables.

Through his parables [Jesus] invites people to the feast of the kingdom, but he also asks for a radical choice: to gain the kingdom, one must give everything [see Matthew 13:44–45, 22:1–14].

JESUS THE STORYTELLER | 19TH-CENTURY ENGRAVING

Words are not enough, deeds are required [see Matthew 21:28–32]. The parables are like mirrors for man: will he be hard soil or good earth for the word [see Matthew 13:3–9]? What use has he made of the talents he has received [see Matthew 25:14–30]?

—CCC, no. 546

WHAT ABOUT YOU PERSONALLY?

- ⊙ Many of Jesus' parables have become very well known. Which is your favorite parable and why?
- ⊙ Which of Jesus' parables prick your conscience and cause you to pause and reflect? Explain.

THE KINGDOM OF GOD IN THE PARABLES OF JESUS

Jesus used parables to teach his listeners about the Kingdom of God. 'Jesus and the presence of the kingdom in this world are secretly at the heart of the parables' (CCC, no. 546). By using everyday images and ordinary everyday experiences, Jesus helped people to understand the true meaning of the Kingdom of God.

Jesus taught his listeners (as he continues to teach us) about their need to accept God's invitation to change their lives and live for the Kingdom. He explored with them who truly belonged to and would be welcomed into the Kingdom. For example, in the parable of the Great Feast Jesus used the image of a banquet or feast (Luke 14:7–24). In this parable, which he addressed to the Pharisees, Jesus contrasts the Pharisees (those who thought they were invited to the feast and worthy of the Kingdom promised by God) with those whom the Pharisees judged to be unworthy and 'not invited'. Imagine the Pharisees' reaction when Jesus concludes by having the master say, 'For I tell you, none of those who were invited will taste my dinner' (Luke 14:24). In short, all are invited to share in the Kingdom of God but not all will take up that invitation.

OVER TO YOU

- ⊙ Look up the following passages and identify the stories (parables) in the Gospel of Matthew that involve feasts or banquets: Matthew 14:13–21, 15:32–39, 22:1–14 and 25:1–13.
- ⊙ What have you learned for your own life from each of these stories?

THE GROWTH OF THE KINGDOM OF GOD

Another image that Jesus used frequently in his parables was that of growth, especially of seeds and plants. Jesus' listeners would have comprised many farming folk, who knew all about seeds and harvests, bad weather and crop failure. They

MUSTARD SEEDS (SEE MARK 4:30–32)

FAITH WORD

Kingdom of God

The actualization of God's will for human beings proclaimed by Jesus Christ as a community of justice, peace, mercy and love, the seed of which is the Church on earth, and the fulfillment of which is in eternity.

—United States Catholic Catechism for Adults, 517

knew that progress comes slowly and that the growth of the harvest also depended on carefully tending to the crop. You do not pull up a cabbage to see how it is doing! You have to wait until it is fully grown and ripe for harvesting. Similarly with the Kingdom, it may seem to be progressing slowly, almost imperceptibly, but it is growing.

You must have faith and be patient. The harvest time will come. The Church has come to see this teaching as pointing, in part, to the activity of the Church on earth, preparing for the coming of the Kingdom of God in this world. 'The kingdom of heaven was inaugurated on earth by Christ. . . . The Church is the seed and beginning of this kingdom' (CCC, no. 567). Through our Baptism we are made sharers in this work.

OVER TO YOU
- Look up and read the following passages and identify the stories (parables) in the Gospel of Luke that involve growth and harvest: Luke 6:43–45, Luke 8:4–15, Luke 13:6–9, 18–19 and Luke 18:1–8.
- What have you learned for your own life from each of these stories?

REFLECT AND DISCUSS
- What comes to mind when you hear the term 'miracle'?
- Can you tell the story of a 'miracle' that happened in your own life?

THE KINGDOM OF GOD AND THE MIRACLES OF JESUS
Everything Jesus did and said revealed the truth that 'God is love' (1 John 4:16). Jesus was the Incarnate Son of God living among us; he is the Revelation of God's love for all people and of God's loving presence and work in the world: 'God's love was revealed among us in this way: God sent his only Son into the world so that we might live through him' (1 John 4:9).

Jesus' proclamation of the Kingdom of God revealed the same truth. Wherever he traveled, people were drawn to him, moved by his message and the power of his words and attracted by his preaching of the Kingdom of God. One of the most powerful ways Jesus revealed the Kingdom was through his **miracles**. The miracles of Jesus were '"mighty works and wonders and signs"', which manifest that the kingdom [of

JESUS HEALING THE BLIND MAN | 19TH-CENTURY COLORED PRINT

God] is present in him and attest that he was the promised Messiah' (CCC, no. 547). The miracles of Jesus manifested 'that the kingdom of God is present in him'—the Kingdom announced by the prophets and inaugurated and established in him: the blind will be able to see, the sick will be cured, the poor are truly blessed, and those isolated to the edge of society will be included.

In biblical times, illness was taken as a sign of God's displeasure and was sometimes understood as a punishment for one's sins or perhaps the sins of the ill person's parents. Thus, when Jesus enabled a blind man to see (Matthew 9:27–30), helped a woman bent low to stand erect (Luke 13:11–13), or cured a leper of his illness (Matthew 8:1–3), he was revealing God's loving care for those who suffer; illness and other forms of suffering are not a sign of God's displeasure or a punishment for sin.

In the Kingdom of God there is plenty for all (read the account of the multiplication of the loaves and fish in Matthew 14:13–21); there is no need to be afraid (read the account of Jesus calming the storm in Luke 8:22–25); death has no power over God (read about the raising of Lazarus in John 1:1–44 and of Jairus' daughter in Luke 8:40–56). God's love embraces all; all

people, men and women, the sick, the needy, those on the margins of society, are welcomed into the embrace of a loving and just God.

The Gospel writers who recorded and passed on these 'wonders and signs' of Jesus were reassuring their audience, the members of the early Church, that the risen Jesus was indeed with them, and that he would always be with them, just as he had promised. The miracles of Jesus reveal that Jesus was the promised Messiah and the Son of God. The Gospel accounts of the miracles of Jesus reveal that the promised Kingdom had been established in Jesus Christ, the Incarnate Son of God.

READ, REFLECT AND DISCUSS

⊙ Read one of the following miracle stories: Matthew 14:22–23; Mark 1:21–28, 3:1–6 and 5:23–29; Luke 5:1–11, 40–44 and 18:35–43.

⊙ What do you think the story you have chosen reveals about Jesus? About the Kingdom of God?

JOURNAL EXERCISE

⊙ Write about what the story you chose says to you in your own life.

JUDGE AND ACT

REFLECT ON WHAT YOU HAVE LEARNED

⊙ Think about what you have learned in this chapter concerning the values of the Kingdom as lived and preached by Jesus. Reflect especially on how the values of the Beatitudes speak to you at this present stage of your life.

READ AND DECIDE

⊙ Read the following extract from the Letter of St. James, which aimed to advise people on how to live as disciples of Jesus Christ:

> If a brother or sister is naked and lacks daily food, and one of you says to them, 'Go in peace; keep warm and eat your fill,' and yet you do not supply their bodily needs, what is the good of that?
> —James 2:14–16

⊙ What parts of the teaching of Jesus do you think James had in mind when he wrote this piece?
⊙ What does this challenge you to do in your own life?

LEARN BY EXAMPLE

Nothing But Nets

There are many people in our world today who want to live by the values of the Gospel and bring the good news and the joy of the Kingdom of God into people's lives. Some do this by joining organizations that work for the well-being of people either at home or abroad. *Nothing But Nets* is a global campaign that brings together youth and adult members of churches to join their efforts with partners such as the National Basketball Association (NBA) and Women's National Basketball Association (WNBA) and others in working to end malaria in Africa. *Nothing But Nets* reports:

⊙ Malaria kills more than a million people per year; 90 percent of those who die are African children.
⊙ Every thirty seconds in Africa a child dies of malaria.
⊙ Malaria incapacitates people, keeping countries poor. In addition to the health burden, illness and death from malaria cost Africa about $12 billion per year.

Nothing But Nets mobilizes people and resources to raise funds to purchase and distribute simple insecticide-treated bed nets and to educate people on how to use them to protect themselves from the deadly bite of malaria-carrying mosquitoes. The simple bed-nets are saving millions of lives. Church groups who take part in *Nothing But Nets* follow the two-thousand-year-old model of Jesus: they bring healing and hope to the suffering sick and their families.

TALK IT OVER

- How are those who work for *Nothing But Nets* bringing the values that Jesus spoke of into the lives of people in our world today?
- What other individuals or groups do you know about who bring God's love into people's lives? How does this happen?

WHAT ABOUT YOU PERSONALLY?

- In what ways do you bring God's love into people's lives?
- Are there more ways in which you could bring God's love to people in your life right now?
- Do you have dreams of helping people in other ways when you get older? If so, you might like to share them.

RESPOND WITH YOUR FAMILY, FRIENDS, NEIGHBORS

- Try to find a local project or initiative in which you and your family or friends could become involved . . . and put some of the Kingdom values you have learned about into action.

LEARN BY HEART

The seven Corporal Works of Mercy are works found in the Gospel by which we help our neighbors meet their bodily needs. They are:

Feed the hungry
Give drink to the thirsty
Shelter the homeless
Clothe the naked
Visit the sick and those in prison
Bury the dead
Give alms to the poor

PRAYER REFLECTION

Pray the Sign of the Cross together.

LEADER
Today we will reflect on Jesus' teaching in the Beatitudes. As we recall how Jesus described what life is like when people live according to the values of God's Kingdom, let us resolve to work for the coming of the Kingdom in our world from this moment onward.

READER 1
God, help me to believe that the poor are blessed;
that the Kingdom of Heaven is theirs.
Help me to allow this belief to shape my attitude to those I know who are poor,
poor for lack of material things or poor for lack of love. (*Pause*)

READER 2
Sustain those who are hungry today.
Prompt me to contribute to their sustenance by sharing what I have with them. (*Pause*)

READER 3
When I am sad or in mourning,
may I know your comfort.
Help me to be a source of your comfort for others who are in mourning. (*Pause*)

READER 4
When I suffer for doing what I know to be right,
when I am excluded, bullied or ridiculed,
help me to know that I am blessed by you.
Give me the courage always to do what I know Jesus had in mind when he spoke the Beatitudes. (*Pause*)

READER 5
When I live as Jesus has called me to live,
may I rejoice in the sure knowledge that I will be rewarded in Heaven. (*Pause*)

READER 6
Teach me to be wise about worldly possessions,
to avoid seeking those that are unnecessary,
and to recognize instead what I truly desire.
(*Pause*)

READER 7
When I long for more,
help me to remember all those who have so little.
(*Pause*)

READER 8
Even at times of my greatest happiness,
help me to remember those who are sad.
Teach me how to be a source of comfort for others. (*Pause*)

READER 9
Teach me never to depend on human praise,
in the knowledge that it is you alone, God,
who knows the depths of my heart. (*Pause*)

LEADER
As we go forth to transform our world according to the values of the Beatitudes, make us loving, forgiving and generous, so that we will be true disciples of Jesus and builders of the Kingdom of God in our world.

Pray the Sign of the Cross together.

Blessed are you who are hungry now,
for you will be filled.

– Luke 6:21

CHAPTER 12

The Gospel According to John

—Jesus Is God's Word to the World

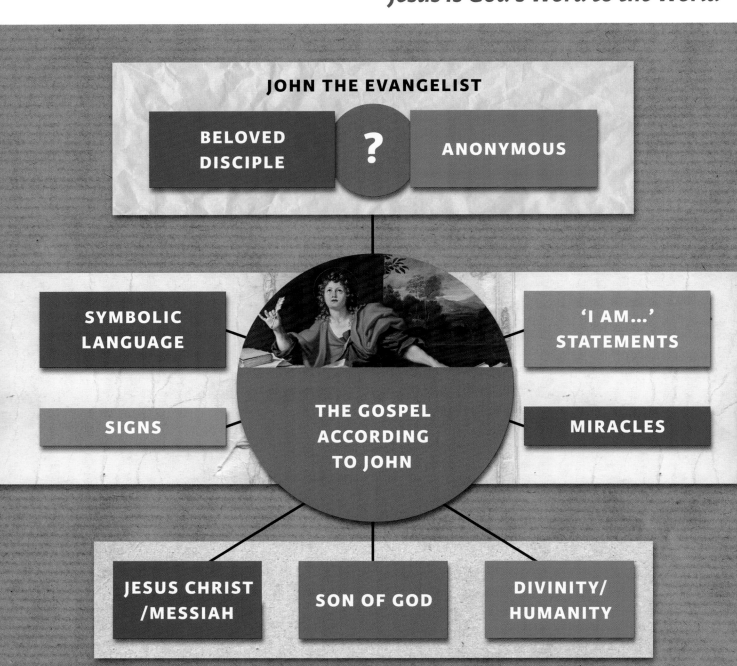

JOHN THE EVANGELIST

BELOVED DISCIPLE

?

ANONYMOUS

SYMBOLIC LANGUAGE

'I AM...' STATEMENTS

SIGNS

THE GOSPEL ACCORDING TO JOHN

MIRACLES

JESUS CHRIST /MESSIAH

SON OF GOD

DIVINITY/ HUMANITY

IN THIS CHAPTER WE EXPLORE THE GOSPEL according to St. John and discuss the identity of its author. John's Gospel is so distinct from the three Synoptics that it is sometimes referred to simply as the Fourth Gospel. It is a mature theological presentation of Jesus Christ, the Light of the World, the Incarnate Son of God, the Second Divine Person of the Blessed Trinity, who was with God at the beginning of creation and who took on flesh to live among us and show us 'the way'.

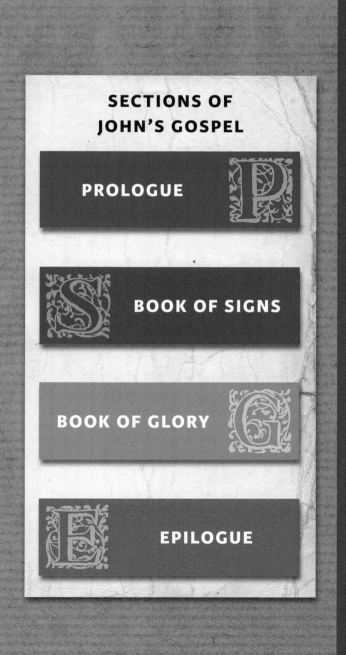

SECTIONS OF JOHN'S GOSPEL

PROLOGUE

BOOK OF SIGNS

BOOK OF GLORY

EPILOGUE

Faith Focus: These teachings of the Catholic Church are the primary focus of the doctrinal content presented in this chapter:

- In human life, signs and symbols occupy an important place. As a being at once body and spirit, man expresses and perceives spiritual realities through physical signs and symbols.
- Jesus Christ is the Incarnate Son of God; he is truly God and truly man.
- Jesus is the living Revelation of God and the means by which God's love can bring all people to eternal life.
- The treatment of Christ's dialogues and personal testimony in John's Gospel is more 'mystical' than in the Synoptics.
- The seven 'I AM' statements of Jesus reveal the identity of Jesus and his mission.
- John treats Jesus' miracles as signs of his divinity and glory.
- The miracle stories in John's Gospel reveal the saving presence of God active in the world and anticipate Jesus' great victory over Satan.
- Eternal life is God's gift to all who believe in Jesus. The Paschal Mystery of Jesus is the source of that life.

Discipleship Formation: As a result of studying this chapter and discovering the meaning of the faith of the Catholic Church for your life, you should be better able to:

- identify and appreciate the power of symbols to uncover the deeper meaning of reality;
- reflect on your own belief in Jesus, the Incarnate Son of God and Messiah, and how that faith impacts your life;
- discern the meaning of Jesus' prayer at the Last Supper for your life;
- appreciate how the humanity of Jesus, who is true God and true man, fully divine and fully human, can help you in your efforts to live as a disciple of Jesus;
- recognize people in your family and neighborhood who make significant sacrifices for others.

Scripture References: These Scripture references are quoted or referred to in this chapter:
OLD TESTAMENT: **Exodus** 3:13–14, 12:1–32; **Leviticus** 19:18; **Deuteronomy** 6:5; **Psalms** 27:1; **Proverbs** 6:23; **Isaiah** 2:5
NEW TESTAMENT: **Matthew** 22:15–22; **Mark** 1:19, 12:1–12; **Luke** 2:32, 20:9–19; **John** 1:1–14, 18, 29 and 35–40, 2:1–11, 3:16, 4:5–29 and 46–54, 5:1–47, 6:1–14, 16–24, 35, 41 and 48, 8:12, 9:1–12, 10:9, 11, 14, 25 and 31–44, 11:25 and 38–44, 12:31, 13:14–15, 23–25 and 34–35, 14:3, 6, 16–17, 21, 23 and 27, 15:1, 4–5 and 11–15, 16:13 and 24, 17:20–24, 18:15–16, 19:25b–27, 20:1–2, 6–7, 17, 22–23, 30 and 31, 21:7, 20 and 24

Faith Glossary: Familiarize yourself with the meaning of these key faith terms. Definitions are found in the Glossary: **Advocate, eternal life, hypostatic union, 'I AM' statements, Incarnation, Last Supper discourse, Messiah, miracles, Paschal Mystery, Passion, Passover, Resurrection, salvation, symbols/symbolic language, Word of God**

Faith Word: hypostatic union
Learn by Heart: John 13:34–35
Learn by Example: St. Maximilian Kolbe

How important are symbols in the search for meaning in life?

The human person is a unity of body and soul, the physical and the spiritual. Since the beginning of time, human beings have known that there is more to life than what we can see, touch, taste, hear and feel—the life of our body. This has driven us to strive to figure out the meaning of life. We are aware that there are two levels to reality: the obvious, and then what is not so obvious, the visible and the invisible, and these invite us to 'go figure it out'.

A primary path by which we delve deeper into the meaning of reality is through the use of signs and **symbols**. Signs and symbols help us discern and make meaning out of life and express and share the meaning that we find. In John's Gospel we encounter a symbol-laden world of meaning; deciphering the symbols in the Fourth Gospel will shed light on the meaning of God's Revelation for our lives.

OPENING CONVERSATION

- ◉ What is a symbol?
- ◉ What symbols can you think of from everyday life? Make a list.
- ◉ How and when can symbols have more than one meaning?
- ◉ Why do people use symbols?

Signs and symbols touch us on many different levels. Signs and symbols can communicate the meaning of realities, both seen and unseen, when the literal meaning of words and the simple visible reality of signs are not enough. Symbols point to deeper realities and convey meaning when an experience is so profound that it is difficult to find the words to communicate its meaning. For example, the inspired sacred authors of Scripture used several symbols for the Holy Spirit to reveal God's presence and work among his people. These included 'water', 'anointing', 'fire', 'cloud and light' and 'the dove' (*Catechism of the Catholic Church* [CCC], nos. 694–697, 701). On the role of signs and symbols in human life, the Catholic Church has this to say:

> In human life, signs and symbols occupy an important place. As a being at once body and spirit, man expresses and perceives spiritual realities through physical signs and symbols. As a social being, man needs signs and symbols to communicate with others, through language, gestures, and actions.
>
> —CCC, no. 1146

We need to strive to understand the deeper meaning of the signs and symbols used by the inspired human authors of the Bible.

This is necessary if we are to come to a true understanding of what God, the primary author of the Bible, is revealing.

TALK IT OVER

The inspired human authors of the Old Testament often used 'light' as a symbol. For example, look up and read Psalm 27:1, Proverbs 6:23 and Isaiah 2:5.
⊙ Why is light a very powerful symbol?
⊙ What might light be used to symbolize?

OVER TO YOU

⊙ What might someone be saying about you if she or he were to describe you this way: 'You are the light of my life'?

THE USE OF THE LITERARY GENRE OF SYMBOL IN JOHN'S GOSPEL

As we turn to St. John's symbol-laden Gospel, you will need to be all the more attuned to the language of sign and symbol that the Evangelist uses to communicate the Gospel of **Salvation**. John the Evangelist uses the vivid imagery of many signs and symbols known by his audience. In this way, under the inspiration of the Holy Spirit, John communicates the meaning of God's Revelation in Jesus Christ, the eternal **Word of God** who 'became flesh and lived among us' (John 1:14).

There are four distinct parts in John's account of the Gospel. All are symbol-laden with meaning:
The Prologue (1:1–18)
The Book of Signs (1:19—12:50)
The Book of Glory (13:1—20:31)
The Epilogue: Appearances in Galilee (21)

The Prologue (John 1:1–18)

John's Gospel begins with the Prologue, which is like an introduction that captures the essence of the message to come. The very opening statement in the Prologue uses *light* and *darkness* as symbols to identify the true nature of Jesus and his saving work among us. We read:

What has come into being in him was life, and the life was the light of all people. The light shines in the darkness, and the darkness did not overcome it.

—John 1:4–5

When John's Gospel was written, the world was very different from our world today, where we can dispel darkness with the flick of a switch. People back then were all the more aware of the necessity of light for daily living. To say that 'light' could not be overcome by 'darkness' was a statement that would have caught his readers' attention and contributed to their understanding of his teaching.

READ, REFLECT AND SHARE

Read the Prologue of the Fourth Gospel. As you read, mark all the symbols the Evangelist uses; then discuss the possible meaning of each with a partner.

In the beginning was the Word, and the Word was with God, and the Word was God. He was in the beginning with God. All things came into being through him, and without him not one thing came into being. What has come into being in him was life, and the life was the light of all people. The light shines in the darkness, and the darkness did not overcome it.

There was a man sent from God, whose name was John. He came as a witness to testify to the light, so that all might believe through him. He himself was not the light, but he came to testify to the light.

The true light, which enlightens everyone, was coming into the world. He was in the world, and the world came into being through him; yet the world did not know him. He came to what was his own, and his own people did not accept him. But to all who received him, who believed in his name, he gave power to become children of God, who were born, not of blood or of the will of the flesh or of the will of man, but of God.

And the Word became flesh and lived among us, and we have seen his glory, the glory as of a father's only son, full of grace and truth.

—John 1:1–14

The Prologue of the Fourth Gospel includes a variety of signs and symbols that provide insight into the faith of the Apostolic Church in the identity of Jesus and his mission: Jesus is God; he is the Word who 'was with God', pre-existing with God from all eternity, and 'was God'. The Word participated in the divine work of Creation: 'All things came into being through him, and without him not one thing came into being' (John 1:3). The Word is indeed the Giver of life: 'What has come into being in him was life, and the life was the light of all people' (John 1:3a–4).

John concludes his Prologue with the amazing statement that 'the Word'—God—'became flesh and lived among us, and we have seen his glory, the glory as of a father's only son, full of grace and

ST. JOHN THE EVANGELIST | VANI GOSPELS

truth' (John 1:14). To those who 'received him, who believed in his name, he gave power to become children of God, who were born, not of blood or of the will of the flesh or of the will of man, but of God' (John 1:12–13). (See also John 17:20–24.)

LET'S PROBE DEEPER

Let us look more closely at five examples of the Prologue's use of symbol, or symbolic language, to help us come to a deeper understanding of the mystery of the **Incarnation**:

In the beginning was the Word and the Word was with God and the Word was God. He was in the beginning with God.

—John 1:1–2

The Word was there from the beginning and was with God and was God. Jesus is God. He is the Word who became incarnate; he assumed human nature and became man.

All things came into being through him, and without him not one thing came into being.

—John 1:3

Through the Word, all things were created. The Word is God, who is the Creator. While we attribute the divine work of Creation to the Father, Creation is the work of God, who is Father, Son and Holy Spirit. Creation is the work of the Blessed Trinity. While the three divine Persons are distinct from one another, they are inseparable in what they do—there is one God.

What has come into being in him was life, and the life was the light of all people. The light shines in the darkness, and the darkness did not overcome it.

—John 1:4–5

In the Nicene Creed we profess the Holy Spirit to be 'the Lord [God], the giver of life'. Throughout John's Gospel, the reason for the Word coming into the world is to bring life: 'I came that they may have life, and have it abundantly' (John 10:10). Life is not possible without Christ, the only begotten Son of the Father. God, Father, Son and Holy Spirit, is the 'giver of life'.

Through Jesus Christ our lives have profound meaning, and we can live the meaning that they have to the full

The true light, which enlightens everyone, was coming into the world.

He was in the world, and the world came into being through him; yet the world did not know him.

—John 1:9–10

The Church from apostolic times has professed Jesus to be the 'Light of the world' (see Luke 2:32; John 1:8–9, 8:12). Jesus is the only true light to guide us on our path to life. He is the fulfillment of the psalmist's profession of faith in God: 'The Lord is my light and my salvation' (Psalm 27:1). In John's Gospel Jesus declares, 'I am the way, and the truth, and the life' (John 14:6). His Death and **Resurrection** scattered the shadows of doubt, death and despair.

And the Word became flesh and lived among us.

—John 1:14

The Incarnation is the high point of God's Revelation of himself (whose name is Emmanuel, or 'God-with-us') and of the divine plan. We profess this faith of the Apostolic Church in the Nicene Creed: 'I believe in one Lord Jesus Christ, / the Only Begotten Son of God, / born of the Father before all ages. / God from God, Light from Light, / true God from true God, / begotten, not made, consubstantial with the Father; / through him all things were made. / For us men and for our salvation / he came down from heaven, / and by the Holy Spirit was incarnate of the Virgin Mary, / and became man'.

Jesus is indeed the source of 'grace and truth'. Through him our lives have profound meaning, and we can live that meaning to the full in communion with the Blessed Trinity, now and forever.

TAKE ANOTHER LOOK
⊙ What other symbolic language can you find in the Prologue? The footnotes in your *Catholic Study Bible* may help.

WHAT ABOUT YOU PERSONALLY?
⊙ The Son of God assumed a human nature and became man in all things but sin. How do you think this will help you in your search to know, love and serve God?

The authorship and content of John's Gospel

OPENING CONVERSATION

⊙ If someone were writing about an event they had experienced, how might their account or analysis be different if they were writing:
  a. immediately after it happened?
  b. some years later?

⊙ What might be the strengths and weaknesses of each account?

THE IDENTITY OF JOHN THE EVANGELIST
Scholars all agree that John's account of the Gospel was written well after the three Synoptics had come together; as we shall see, John's Gospel presumes that the reader is familiar with the Synoptic Gospels. This advantage probably contributed to the writer's ability to create a more mature presentation—after years of preaching and praying, living and reflecting—on Jesus and the work his Father sent him to do. But first, who was John? Get ready for some detective work!

From the days of the early Church, the Tradition of the Church has named John the Apostle, the brother of James, and who is thought to be the 'beloved disciple' (John 13:23, 19:26, 20:2 and 21:7, 20), to be the author of the Fourth Gospel. (Read Mark 1:19 for Jesus' call of James and John.) The basis for identifying John the Apostle as the 'beloved disciple' or 'the disciple whom Jesus loved' is that John and James are the only members of the Twelve not named in the Fourth Gospel. This has led some people to assert that the author of John's Gospel modestly refers to himself by that phrase. Summarizing the early Tradition of the Church, St. Irenaeus, writing about the year 190, attested: 'John, the disciple of the Lord, who also had leaned upon his breast, did himself publish a Gospel during his residence at Ephesus in Asia.'

Let's take a look at the references to 'the disciple whom Jesus loved' in the Gospel

ST. JOHN THE EVANGELIST | KARL-BORROMÄUS-KIRCHE, VIENNA

according to John. It is at the Last Supper that the 'disciple whom Jesus loved' first appears. There we see that he is the one leaning on the Lord's breast, asking the question about who is the traitor among them. (Read John 13:23–25.) Later on, this beloved disciple appears at the foot of the Cross with Mary, the Mother of Jesus, and with 'his mother's sister, Mary the wife of Clopas, and Mary Magdalene', and it is to this disciple that Jesus entrusts the care of his mother; and to Mary Jesus entrusts the care of this disciple, who is a symbol of the Church. (Read John 19:25b–27.)

There are also three references to the beloved disciple in the Resurrection Narratives. In chapter 20, Mary Magdalene goes to Jesus' tomb 'early on the first day of the week' after Jesus' Death and burial. When she sees that 'the stone had been removed from the tomb', she runs and tells Peter and 'the other disciple, the one whom Jesus loved'; both immediately run there. (Read John 20:1–2.) Second, the disciple whom Jesus loved is a faster runner than Peter (Is he younger?), and gets there first. But he waits for Peter to go into the tomb before he enters. They both see the 'linen wrappings' lying there and 'the cloth that had been on Jesus' head'. (Read John 20:6–7.) Ironically, both of them leave, whereas Mary Magdalene stays on, and she is the one rewarded with the first appearance of the risen Christ. Third, in chapter 21, this disciple is the only one who recognizes Jesus by the lake: 'That disciple whom Jesus loved said to Peter, "It is the Lord!"' (John 21:7). At the conclusion of this passage, in which Peter professes his love for Jesus and Jesus entrusts the care of the Church to Peter, we read: 'Peter turned and saw the disciple whom Jesus loved following them; he was the one who had reclined next to Jesus at the supper. . . . This is the disciple who is testifying to these things and has written them, and we know that his testimony is true' (John 21:20, 24).

Elsewhere in John's Gospel, there are other references to an anonymous disciple; could this also be John? The first reference is to the companion of Andrew, who had been a disciple of John the Baptist when they both stayed with Jesus for a day. (Read John 1:35–40.) The other reference concerns the disciple known to the high priest, who managed to get himself and Peter into the high priest's house during the trial of Jesus. (Read John 18:15–16. Is this a clue to the author?)

But does this settle the question: did John the Apostle really write the Fourth Gospel? Is the 'disciple whom Jesus loved' the same as John the Apostle, and the same as the anonymous disciple who was with John the Baptist and at the high priest's house? And if so, did this John write the Fourth Gospel?

Some scholars say 'Yes', as does the ancient tradition of Irenaeus.

However. . . .

In modern times many scholars have suggested that John's Gospel was written by an author who was not himself one of the Twelve but a close companion of the early disciples. Their reasoning is based on the fact that this Gospel is so different from the three Synoptic Gospels. Another reason for this opinion is that, in the ancient world, authorship was attributed as much to the one who inspired a particular work and whose views and teachings were authentically and accurately presented in the work, as to the one who actually wrote it. So, regardless of who wrote the Fourth Gospel, we have in John's Gospel an account of the Gospel that the Church recognizes to be inspired by the Holy Spirit and that accurately passes on the apostolic faith in Jesus Christ, the Son of God, the Second Divine Person of the Blessed Trinity.

REFLECT AND DISCUSS

◉ In light of what you have read in this section, what evidence is there that John the Apostle was the author of the Fourth Gospel?

MARY MAGDALENE RECOGNIZES THE RISEN JESUS | FRA ANGELICO

⦿ How might the facts that the author of John's Gospel wrote his account of the Gospel after the other Evangelists and that he had known Jesus personally have helped him?

WHAT IS DISTINCTIVE ABOUT JOHN'S ACCOUNT OF THE GOSPEL?

The writer of the Gospel of John wrote from the perspective of one who had spent time with Jesus, listened to his words, accompanied him during his public ministry, witnessed his Death and Resurrection, and whose faith had been profoundly shaped by the experience of Jesus' Resurrection. The following key differences distinguish John's Gospel from the Synoptics:

First, the Gospel of John presumes that the reader is already familiar with the Synoptic Gospels. Why is that? Very little is repeated in John from the three Synoptics. There are no parables, for instance, no Sermon on the Mount, no (or very little) mention of the Kingdom of God, nor of Christ's body and blood given at the Last Supper.

Second and more significant, the Fourth Gospel focuses more on the divinity of Christ, while the Synoptics each present a very human Jesus who is gradually recognized to be divine, the Son of God. In John's Gospel, Jesus from the beginning is clearly divine. The Evangelist writes: 'In the beginning was the Word, and the Word was with God, and the Word was God. . . . And the Word became flesh and lived among us. . . .' (John 1:1, 14). John's Gospel was written around the year 90, during a time of conflict between Jews who accepted Jesus and those who did not, to support the faithful and to encourage them to remain faithful to Christ in their time of suffering. Jesus

The seven 'I AM' statements of Jesus

THE LIGHT OF THE WORLD | HOLMAN-HUNT

A key and unique writing technique in John's Gospel is his use of seven 'I am' sayings or statements to teach that Jesus is divine, truly God. These two words, 'I am', have their roots in the Book of Exodus when God reveals his identity, his name, to Moses. When Moses asks the voice in the burning bush, 'If I come to the Israelites and say to them, "The God of your ancestors has sent me to you", and they ask me, "What is his name?", what shall I say to them?', God says to Moses, 'I AM WHO I AM. . . . Thus you shall say to the Israelites, "I AM has sent me to you"' (Exodus 3:13–14). These words had very clear meaning for the audience for whom John's Gospel was written; namely, Jews who came to believe in Jesus. How significant it is, then, that Jesus so often echoes this divine name and applies it to himself.

The seven '**I AM' statements** of Jesus are included in and are part of longer sermons, or discourses, of Jesus. They are: 'I am the bread of life' (6:35); 'I am the light of the world' (8:12); 'I am the gate' (10:9); 'I am the good shepherd' (10:11); 'I am the resurrection and the life' (11:25); 'I am the way, and the truth, and the life' (14:6); and 'I am the vine' (15:5).

'I am the resurrection and the life. Those who believe in me, even though they die, will live' (11:25). What an extraordinary promise—those who believe in Jesus will live forever. No wonder John can say, 'For God so loved the world that he gave his only Son, so that everyone who believes in him may not perish but may have **eternal life**' (3:16).

> # I am the vine, you are the branches. Those who abide in me and I in them bear much fruit, because apart from me you can do nothing.
>
> **JOHN 15:5**

clearly favors those who do believe in him, and sounds harsh against those who do not. We need to read his condemnations in this context—a struggle to hold on to Christian converts—and apply the meaning of their message to situations that we face in our time.

John's central theme is Jesus, the **Messiah** and Son of God. John summed up his aim in writing his Gospel for Jews who had come to believe in Jesus (and thus for disciples in every age and every place) when he said: 'These things are written so that you may come to believe that Jesus is the Messiah, the Son of God, and that through believing you may have life in his name' (John 20:31). The **Paschal Mystery** of Jesus, the Incarnate Son of God, is the source of that life. It is the triumph of light over darkness, truth over untruth, freedom over slavery, life over death, goodness over sin. Jesus' **miracles**—seven great 'signs' in John's Gospel—'attest that the Father has sent him' (CCC, no. 548). 'They invite belief in him [see John 5:36, 10:25, 38] . . . they bear witness that he is the Son of God [see John 10:31–38]' (CCC, no. 548), who is the 'bread of life' (John 6:41, 48) and 'the way, and the truth, and the life' (John 14:6). The miracles of Jesus anticipate Jesus' great victory over Satan, 'the ruler of this world' (see John 12:31).

Another theme in John's Gospel is Jesus' affection and care for his disciples, whom he calls 'friends' (John 15:14–15). There is a deep intimacy between Jesus and his disciples; when he said, 'I am the vine', he immediately added, 'and you are the branches' (15:5). His whole last discourse on the night before he died, chapters 14 to 17, speaks of his great love and concern for his disciples, praying 'that they may all be one' (17:21) and that 'my joy might be in you, and that your joy may be complete' (15:11). And he promised to send the Holy Spirit upon them to enable them to continue his own saving work throughout the world and down through human history: 'I will ask the Father, and he will give you another **Advocate**, to be with you forever. This is the Spirit of truth. . . .' (14:16–17). God's saving work in the divine Son, Jesus, continues now through the Church—his community of disciples—through the power of the Holy Spirit.

TALK IT OVER

- What is your initial impression of Jesus as John represents him?
- Discuss why you think John might have chosen to explore the meaning for us of Jesus' words and actions rather than simply narrate them.

WHAT ABOUT YOU PERSONALLY?

- John sums up his aim in writing his Gospel when he says: 'These things are written so that you may come to believe that Jesus is the Messiah, the Son of God, and that through believing you may have life in his name' (John 20:31). Reflect on your own belief that Jesus is the Messiah. What difference does this belief make to your hopes and fears for your life?

A *different perspective on miracles*

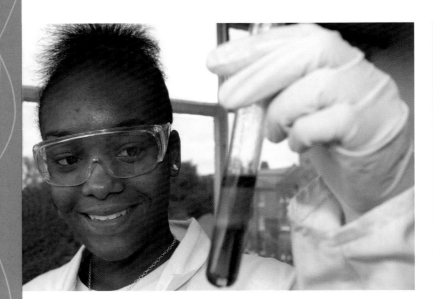

> Unless you see signs and wonders you will not believe.
>
> **JOHN 4:48**

OPENING CONVERSATION

⊙ Jesus once said to the people, 'Unless you see signs and wonders you will not believe' (John 4:48). What do you think he meant?

⊙ In our everyday lives, where do we see 'signs' or evidence of God's presence?

⊙ Do you think miracles still happen? Why or why not?

The Book of Signs (John 1:19–12:50)

The second section of John's Gospel is the Book of Signs. In this section of the Fourth Gospel there are seven 'sign' (or miracle) stories. In John, 'works' or 'signs' are used to mean 'evidence' of God's presence in Jesus. This echoes the Old Testament, which refers to the freeing of the Israelites from Egypt as the 'works of God', and describes the 'signs of God' which Moses performed. The signs or miracles of Jesus in the Gospel of John are evidence of a new reality— that God is in Jesus saving the world. Jesus is the Word of God made flesh in the world for our salvation. He is the true and complete Revelation of the Father. 'No one has ever seen God. It is God the only Son, who is close to the Father's heart, who has made him known' (John 1:18). In summary, the writer of John's Gospel includes these signs not only to reveal that Jesus is the saving, Incarnate Son of God who lived among us, but also to invite his readers to faith in Jesus and to understand the new life that is God's gift to all who believe in Jesus.

GROUP WORK/DISCUSSION

⊙ Look up and read some of the seven signs in the Book of Signs (John 1:19—12:50): The wedding at Cana (John 2:1–11); Jesus heals an official's son (John 4:46–54); the cure of the paralytic man at the pool (John 5:1–47); the feeding of the five thousand (John 6:1–14); the walking on water (John 6:16–24); the restoring of sight to a man born blind (John 9:1–12); the raising of Lazarus to life (John 11:38–44).

- Notice in these stories how people seem to discuss the sign or evidence *after* it has happened. Whether they are Jesus' close disciples and companions, Jews who have come to believe in Jesus, the crowd who are attracted to him, or his Jewish opponents, or even the people for whom the 'work' was done, they are often confused about what the 'miracle' might mean. They needed to 'go deeper'—as we do!
- Pick out some phrases in the passages you read that indicate what the listeners thought these 'works of Jesus' meant; see for example John 6:14. What do you think these works 'said' to the people who witnessed them?
- Pick out the words of Jesus in each passage. What is the deeper meaning of these words in the context of the stories?
- Search for passages in the stories that show that faith had a role in these 'works' of Jesus. What do they mean for our own faith today?

The Book of Glory *(John 13:1–20:31)*

In this third section of John's Gospel, the writer passes on the apostolic faith in the meaning of Jesus' identity, life and work. Many of the chapters in this section are part of the **Last Supper discourse**, one of several long discourses in John's Gospel. In the Last Supper discourse, Jesus makes no secret of who he is or what he is doing. As in the opening Prologue, he is the Son, sent by God to bring light to the world.

THE LAST SUPPER DISCOURSE (JOHN 13–17)
In chapter 13, John's account of the Gospel has the Last Supper of Jesus with his disciples take place on the day when the lambs were killed for the **Passover** meal, clearly referring to and recalling the release of the Israelites from slavery in Egypt. The Old Testament tells us that the Israelites sprinkled lambs' blood on the doorposts of their houses. The angel of the Lord who slew the first born of the Egyptians passed over these houses and their first born were spared. (Read Exodus 12:1–32.) John's Gospel describes Jesus as the Lamb of God, whose blood, shed on the Cross, freed all people from the slavery of sin.

Unlike the Synoptics, John's Gospel does not give an account of the institution of the Eucharist at Jesus' final Passover meal with the disciples. Instead, it tells the story of Jesus washing the disciples' feet before the meal and his final discourse with his disciples. The washing of the feet sets the context for Jesus' teaching on the true meaning of being his disciple. It was an amazing and most symbolic act by Jesus. He, their leader, was performing a task for them that not even a slave was required to perform. When he had finished, Jesus said to them, 'If I, your Lord and Teacher, have washed your feet, you also ought to wash one another's feet. For I have set you an example, that you also should do as I have done to you' (John 13:14–15).

Jesus was teaching that his disciples must become as servants, as he was the Servant. We, his disciples, are 'apprenticed'—the meaning of 'disciple'—to a Master who shows us the way, a way whose heart is service to others.

ADORATION OF THE MYSTIC LAMB | JAN VAN EYCK

'Parakletos', which means comforter or advocate.

> I will ask the Father, and he will give you another Advocate, to be with you forever. This is the Spirit of truth, whom the world cannot receive, because it neither sees him nor knows him. You know him, because he abides with you, and he will be in you.
> —John 14:16–17

He also asks his disciples to love him by living as he modeled and taught. Then he and the Father will be present in them. He says, 'Those who love me will keep my word, and my Father will love them, and we will come to them and make our home with them' (John 14:23). Jesus concludes this section of the discourse by sharing with them the gift of his peace: 'Peace I leave with you; my peace I give to you' (John 14:27).

In the next section of the discourse, Jesus speaks of his relationship with his disciples (his first disciples and his future disciples). This is one of the best known and most important passages in the New Testament. It is the final 'I am' saying in John's Gospel. In it Jesus speaks of himself as the vine, his Father as the vinegrower, and the disciples as branches. He tells them (and us) that, like shoots on a vine, he ('I AM' or God) is the source of all life for them (and us): 'I am the true vine, and my Father is the vinegrower. . . . Just as the branch cannot bear fruit by itself unless it abides in the vine, neither can you unless you abide in me. I am the vine, you the branches' (John 15:1, 4–5). United with him, his disciples will have the true life and bear the richest fruit. They will have the gift of peace or 'shalom' from God.

Jesus continues to speak of the depth of his relationship with his disciples. He commands them to witness to their love of him by loving one another as he has loved them, saying, 'This is my commandment, that you love one another as I have loved you' (John 15:12). He then sums up the depth of his love for them, calling them 'friends': 'No one has greater love than this, to lay down one's life for one's friends. You are my friends if you do what I command you' (John

Jesus was teaching that his disciples must become as servants, as he was the Servant

TALK IT OVER

◉ We remember Jesus' washing of the feet of his disciples in our Liturgy on Holy Thursday. How is 'the rite of the washing of the feet' remembered in your church?

◉ What do you think Jesus was teaching all disciples—forever after—through this action?

In chapters 14 to 17 of his final discourse to his disciples, Jesus speaks to them about the fact that soon he will leave them. It is as if he is telling them all the things he would want them to remember once he is no longer with them. He explains that he is giving this final instruction 'so that my joy may be in you, and that your joy may be complete' (John 15:11). To live as a disciple of Jesus, embracing his Good News, is to find true joy and real peace in life.

Jesus urges his disciples to remain strong and united. He promises to send them the Holy Spirit as a helper, describing the Spirit as the

15:13–14). His coming Death on the Cross, his hour of glory, will be the greatest sign of his love for and commitment to them, his friends. Jesus seems to raise the level of demand in the Great Commandment of love, which is at the heart of living the New Covenant (see Matthew 22:15–22, Mark 12:1–12 and Luke 20:9–19), as it was of the Old (see Leviticus 19:18 and Deuteronomy 6:5), binding God and his people. Indeed, we are to love God by loving our neighbor as ourselves; however, the model here is that of Jesus' own love for his friends and for his Father.

In chapter 16 Jesus prepares his disciples for his own Death and the suffering and persecution they will suffer for their faith in him—being a disciple always has been and always will be very demanding. Jesus repeats his promise to send 'the Spirit of truth' who 'will guide you into all the truth' (John 16:13). We know that the Holy Spirit continues to guide the Church toward the truth today. Jesus alerts his disciples that he is about to leave them—his Crucifixion is the very next day—but, like a woman who forgets her labor pangs after the child is born, so, too, their joy will be made 'complete' (John 16:24). John knows well that Jesus' Death led to Resurrection and new life.

The discourse concludes with chapter 17, which is Jesus' prayer to his Father for his disciples. As the prayer ends, Jesus prays, 'Father, I desire that those also, whom you have given me, may be with me where I am, to see my glory, which you have given me because you loved me before the foundation of the world' (John 17:24).

REFLECTIVE EXERCISE

⊙ Stop for a moment and imagine yourself as a disciple sitting at the Last Supper table with Jesus. What are you hearing from him? What do his words mean to you?

JESUS' SUFFERING AND DEATH AND RESURRECTION

From chapter 18 on, John's Gospel recounts the story of Jesus' **Passion** (his suffering and Death) and Resurrection. However, the theme is quite different from that in the Synoptic Gospels. Now, the writer can tell us, from the vantage point of the end of the first century, what the Death of Jesus means. Here, Jesus' Death is not seen as tragic at all—it is a necessary step in his glorious return to the Father. This account of the Gospel assures us that trust in God will be rewarded.

And if I go and prepare a place for you, I will come again and will take you to myself, so that where I am, there you may be also.

—John 14:3

No one has greater love than this, to lay down one's life for one's friends.

JOHN 15:13

APPEARANCE ON LAKE TIBERIUS | DUCCIO DI BUONINSEGNA

READING ACTIVITY

⊙ Working in pairs, read chapters 18 and 19 of John's Gospel. Each person, in turn, could read a paragraph while the other listens; then the 'listener' summarizes what he or she has heard. Continue like this until you have read the two chapters.

⊙ Then see if you can remember the three places where Peter denied Jesus. Discuss why you think Peter did this. See if you can remember the words Jesus said on the Cross.

After the Resurrection, according to John's Gospel, Jesus appeared first to a woman, Mary Magdalene. He called Mary by name, and she recognized him as the Lord. Then the risen Jesus sent her to bring the Good News of the Resurrection to the other disciples (John 20:17). The risen Jesus also appeared to the disciples who had gathered together and were hiding behind a locked door. He commissioned them to continue the work he had begun.

Receive the Holy Spirit. If you forgive the sins of any, they are forgiven them; if you retain the sins of any, they are retained.

—John 20:22–23

The Epilogue (John 21)

In the final chapter of John's Gospel Jesus appears to the disciples on the shores of Lake Galilee, where he shares a breakfast of bread and fish with them.

GROUP WORK

⊙ Look up the different appearances of the risen Jesus after the Resurrection as told by John in chapters 20 and 21. In small groups, choose *one* of these post-Resurrection stories and act it out. Think about how the different people would feel in the situation—excited, shocked or maybe even afraid! Try to convey this in your short role-play or by using a freeze-frame (which is like a still photo).

Exploring the meaning for us in John's Gospel

OPENING ACTIVITY/CONVERSATION

⊙ Work in small groups to produce a diagram or mind-map titled 'What's Wrong with the World?' When you have done this, try to agree as a group on what is the single biggest problem in the world. Then have a class discussion based on your ideas.

⊙ Do you think the world still needs a Savior? Why or why not?

⊙ How does a Christian perspective on the world help us to address our many problems?

⊙ What hope and challenge does John's Gospel put before us in the context of today's world?

JESUS—TRUE GOD AND TRUE MAN

John wrote his account of the Gospel for the early Church in Ephesus. In their prayer and in their reflection, these believers were in danger of losing sight of the fact that Jesus was true God and true man. John wanted to affirm and strengthen their faith that the Son of God had truly become a man in Jesus. As John says in the Prologue: 'The Word became flesh and lived among us' (John 1:14). John wanted his readers to come to believe that Jesus is the Son of God. God was really and truly revealing himself in the life, words and actions of Jesus, the Word who became a man and lived and died and rose from the dead among us. We profess this same faith today in the Nicene Creed. *Pause and pray the second part of the Nicene Creed, which begins 'I believe in one Lord Jesus Christ, / the Only Begotten Son of God'.*

Jesus is the living Revelation of God and the means by which God's love can bring all people to eternal life. This is the hope revealed in him.

For God so loved the world that he gave his only Son, so that everyone who believes in him may not perish but may have eternal life.

—John 3:16

John also alerted his readers to the fact that Jesus called his disciples to reflect in their own lives the love with which he loved them, the very love of God.

I give you a new command, that you love one another. Just as I have loved you, you also should love one another. By this everyone will know that you are my disciples, if you have love for one another.

—John 13:34–35

This is the 'new commandment' that Jesus gave to the disciples—we are to aspire to the unconditional love that we see in him and that reveals to us the very love of God. When we keep

Hypostatic Union

The union of the divine and human natures in the one divine Person (Greek: *hypostasis*) of the Son of God, Jesus Christ. (CCC, Glossary)

12TH-CENTURY FRESCO, CHURCH OF THE HOLY TRINITY, SARDINIA, ITALY

Jesus' commandments, we show our love for him. Jesus said, 'They who have my commandments and keep them are those who love me; and those who love me will be loved by the Father, . . . and we will come to them and make our home with them' (John 14:21, 23).

JUDGE AND DECIDE
- Why do you think God chose to become man and live among us?
- How does knowing and understanding Jesus help you to know and understand God? To know and understand yourself?
- What is the hope that John's Gospel offers to all who believe?

RELATIONSHIPS IN JOHN'S GOSPEL
John's account of the Gospel describes many significant encounters between Jesus and various persons. One of the great stories in John's Gospel tells of the meeting between Jesus and the Samaritan woman. Read this story now in John 4:5–29.

TALK IT OVER
- What do you think of the response of the Samaritan woman when Jesus asked for a drink? (Remember that it was the custom for Jews not to associate or share things with Samaritans because Jews considered that Samaritans were guilty of false worship. The woman alludes to this in verse 20 when she says to Jesus, 'Sir, I see that you are a prophet. Our ancestors worshipped on this mountain but you say that the place where people must worship is Jerusalem.')
- Why do you think the disciples reacted as they did when they saw Jesus talking to the woman? (Clue: In first-century Israel, men did not talk to women in public.)
- The woman obviously did not know what Jesus meant when he spoke of 'living water'. What do you think is the 'living water' that Jesus promised to her—and to disciples ever after?
- In the end, how did the woman react toward Jesus?
- What do you think of the question that the woman asks in verse 29?
- How many times in this story does Jesus show that he is not bound by customs and stereotypes when the message of the Gospel is at stake?
- How can you have access to the 'living water' that Jesus spoke of?
- What is the 'life' that it can give you?

GROUP WORK/DISCUSSION
- Find more stories in John's Gospel that tell of significant encounters between Jesus and others. List the references.

- What do each of these stories reveal about Jesus and his attitude to other people?
- What do each of these stories say to you in your life right now?

IMAGES FOR JESUS IN JOHN'S GOSPEL

The following are some of the images of Jesus presented in John's Gospel:

The Word made flesh (John 1:14)
The Light of the World (John 8:12)
The Good Shepherd (John 10:11)
The Way, the Truth and the Life (John 14:6)

The Lamb of God (John 1:29)
The Vine (John 15)
The Bread of Life (John 6:35)
The Resurrection and the Life (John 11:25)

OVER TO YOU

- Choose the image of Jesus that means most to you. Read the passage in which it is contained.
- What does this image mean to you in your daily life?
- How does it help you?
- How does it challenge you?

We next read about the great promise that God made to Abram, whom he later named Abraham. God chose Abram and made a Covenant with him and, in turn, with the descendants of himself and his wife Sarai, whose name God later changed to Sarah. God offered to be their God, to give them numerous descendants and a special land to live in, and to bring blessings upon all peoples through them and their offspring. In return, God asked them to believe in his promises and to be obedient to the commands of the Covenant. It is important to remember that Abram, Sarai and their family were part of a people who believed in 'many gods'. The challenge for Abram and Sarai to trust in God was made greater by the fact that they were very advanced in years and well past child-bearing age. Yet, Abram and Sarai trusted in God and agreed to enter into the Covenant with him. Abram had faith that God was trustworthy and would be faithful to all his promises. We read:

God changed Abram's name to Abraham. (Read Genesis 17:5.) In Old Testament times, the changing of a person's name often signified that God had chosen the person for a special task. Because of his great faith and trust in God and in his promises, Abraham is known as the Father of all believers. Jews, Christians and Muslims all look to Abraham as their common ancestor in faith.

—Genesis 12:1–3, 4–5, 7

Now the Lord said to Abram, 'Go from your country and your kindred and your father's house to the land that I will show you. I will make of you a great nation, and I will bless you, and make your name great, so that you will be a blessing. I will bless those who bless you, and the one who curses you I will curse; and in you all the families of the earth shall be blessed.'

So Abram went, as the Lord had told him . . . and they set forth to go to the land of Canaan. . . .

Then the Lord appeared to Abram, and said, 'To your offspring I will give this land.' So he built there an altar to the Lord, who had appeared to him.

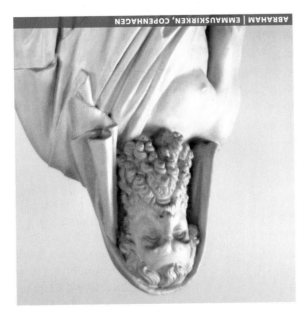

ABRAHAM | EMMAUSKIRKEN, COPENHAGEN

WHAT ABOUT YOU PERSONALLY?

- God's promise called for a response from Abraham. What can you learn from Abraham's story for your own life and how to place your trust in God?
- For what special purpose in life might God be calling you? How does this make you feel?
- How and why can you trust in God?

GOD'S SPECIALLY CHOSEN PEOPLE

The descendants of Abraham and Sarah became the Hebrew people, also known as the Israelites (a name indicating that they were descendants of Israel), grandson of Abraham and son of Isaac, and later known as the Jews. The Old Testament traces their story through good times and bad, through their captivity in Egypt and their eventual freedom, through their Exile and return to their homeland. It tells of times when they turned their backs on God, of how the prophets admonished them for the folly of what they were doing, and how God was always faithful to the Covenant and to them and had mercy on them, as God does on us.

In this chapter we will learn that God promised a Messiah, a Savior for all peoples, who would rise from the descendants of Abraham and Sarah. This promise was fulfilled in Jesus, whose story is told in the New Testament. In Jesus we have the definitive Revelation and proof that God is forever faithful and trustworthy, the greatest keeper of promises.

JUDGE AND ACT

REVIEW AND DISCUSS

- What stands out for you as the greatest 'good news' from John's Gospel?
- What do you like best about John's portrayal of Jesus?

- How will you take to heart the 'grace and truth' revealed in John's Gospel?

LEARN BY EXAMPLE

The story of St. Maximilian Kolbe

In John's Gospel, Jesus asked his disciples to be prepared to serve, even if they had to suffer in doing so. Here is the story of someone who did as Jesus asked.

Maximilian Kolbe was born in January 1894 in what was then a part of Russia. In 1907 he and his brother joined the Conventual branch of the Franciscan Order. He was ordained in 1918 and returned to the newly independent Poland, where he founded the monastery of Niepokalanów near Warsaw. Between 1930 and 1936 he led a number of missions to Japan, where he built another monastery. During the Second World War he provided food and safety for some two thousand Jewish refugees from Poland in his monastery at Niepokalanów. For this, he was arrested by the German Gestapo and transferred to Auschwitz concentration camp in May 1941, where he was simply known as Prisoner 16670.

Three months after he arrived in Auschwitz, a prisoner escaped from Kolbe's barracks. In order to dissuade other prisoners from attempting to escape, the commander announced that ten prisoners would die. He chose ten men at random as he walked along the line. One of the men, Franciszek Gajowniczek, cried out for mercy, saying that he had a wife and family. Immediately Maximilian Kolbe stepped forward and said that he would like to take this man's place.

'Who are you?' asked the commander. Kolbe replied, 'A priest.' The commander was dumbfounded. He kicked Gajowniczek out of the line and ordered Father Kolbe to join the other nine.

In the 'block of death' the men were ordered to strip naked, and the slow starvation of the ten men began. Maximilian Kolbe led the men in song and prayer. After three weeks of starvation and dehydration, only Kolbe and three others were still alive. Finally, on August 14, the eve of the Feast of the Assumption, Maximilian Kolbe was killed by an injection of carbolic acid. The Church beatified him in 1971 and canonized him in 1982.

FRANCISCAN CHURCH IN SZOMBATHELY, HUNGARY

KEEPING PROMISES

Being faithful and trustworthy involves every aspect of our lives; indeed, it concerns every minute of our day. Let's delve a little deeper and look at one aspect of being faithful and trustworthy, namely, keeping promises.

All of us make promises, some of which may be very significant, others less so. We probably make most of our promises out of a personal choice to please, help, support, surprise or offer hope to another person. But we may also feel coerced or pressurized into making certain promises. For example, someone might be asked to make a promise not to tell anyone that a friend is using drugs.

TALK IT OVER

- Name some promises—explicit or implicit—that you keep every day.
- Talk about a particular and important promise you made and kept. Why did you keep it?
- Have you ever broken a promise? Why did you not keep it? How did not keeping the promise make you feel? How did it make the other person feel?
- Talk about an important promise someone made to you. Did anyone ever break a promise that they had made to you? How did that make you feel?

GOD'S PROMISE AND FAITHFULNESS TO ABRAHAM

The **Old Testament** is the faith story of God's dealings with humankind and, in particular, with his chosen people, the Israelites. The story begins

always experienced and passed on, over and over again, in Sacred Scripture, that he is always faithful and always keeps promises. What do you know about some of the promises that God has made to humankind? How is God faithful to them?

REFLECT

- How do you experience God's faithfulness in your own life?

GOD'S COVENANT WITH ABRAHAM | WENCESLAUS HOLLAR

Just as I have loved you, you also should love one another. By this everyone will know that you are my disciples, if you have love for one another.

JOHN 13:34—35

JOURNAL EXERCISE

⊙ Jesus called upon his followers to lay down their lives for their friends. You are not likely to be asked to die for your faith, but as a disciple you are invited to live it. What is the biggest challenge this holds for young people today? For you personally? Write your thoughts on this.

GROUP DISCUSSION

Sometimes people make great sacrifices for others that go unnoticed. People in families do without things so that others can have what they need. In local communities people often work as volunteers so that others can have a better life.

⊙ Share some stories of such people in your families or in the communities where you live.

⊙ Then discuss how the people you chose as examples are living as Jesus taught in the Gospel according to John.

RESPOND WITH YOUR FAMILY AND FRIENDS

⊙ Jesus prayed for peace for his followers before he left them. You might decide to pray the following prayer of St. Francis with your family or friends.

Lord, make me an instrument of your peace;
Where there is hatred, let me sow love;
Where there is injury, pardon;
Where there is doubt, faith;
Where there is despair, hope;
Where there is darkness, light;
And where there is sadness, joy.
Grant that I may not so much seek
To be consoled as to console;
To be understood as to understand;
To be loved as to love;
For it is in giving that we receive,
It is in pardoning that we are pardoned,
And it is in dying that we are born to eternal life.

WHAT WILL YOU DO NOW?

⊙ Are there things that you do that break rather than build peace at home? In your neighborhood? With your friends? Decide how you will change your behavior.

⊙ What practical things might you do in your day-to-day life to serve and love others as Jesus commanded?

PRAYER REFLECTION

Pray the Sign of the Cross together.

LEADER
Let us remember and reflect upon some of the things Jesus said about himself in John's Gospel.

READER 1
Jesus said: 'I am the vine, you are the branches' (John 15:5).

(Pause)

Jesus is the source of your life and my life in faith.

Lord Jesus, help us to bear in our lives the abundant fruit of love for others.

READER 2
Jesus said: 'I am the good shepherd. I know my own and my own know me' (John 10:14).

(Pause)

Jesus knows us through and through. He loves us always and unconditionally.

Lord Jesus, help us to show our families and friends that we love them.

READER 3
Jesus said: 'I am the bread of life. Whoever comes to me will never be hungry and whoever believes in me will never be thirsty' (John 6:35).

(Pause)

When we take time to grow in our relationship with Jesus, he answers all our real needs.

Lord Jesus, help me to make space to talk to you every day. Help me to listen so that I will hear your promptings in my heart and respond as your disciple.

READER 4
Jesus said: 'I am the light of the world. Whoever follows me will never walk in darkness, but will have the light of life' (John 8:12).

(Pause)

Jesus is our constant companion. He shines a light on our path, showing us the way to live as disciples.

Lord Jesus, be a light for me always, but especially when I seem to be surrounded by darkness.

LEADER
Lord Jesus Christ,
who said to your Apostles:
Peace I leave you, my peace I give you;
look not on our sins,
but on the faith of your Church,
and graciously grant her peace and
    unity
in accordance with your will.
Who live and reign for ever and ever.

ALL
Amen.

Pray the Sign of the Cross together.

CHAPTER 13

Jesus' Death and Resurrection

Heralds a New Hope

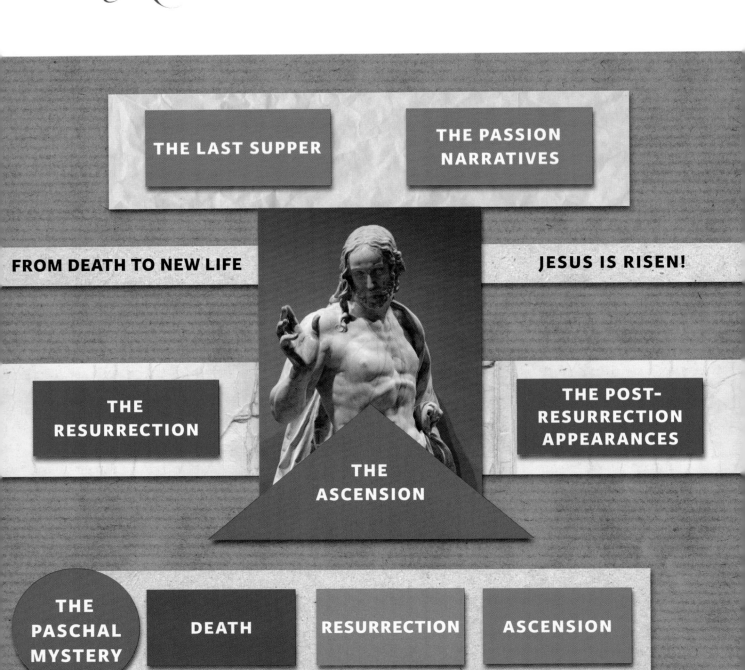

THE LAST SUPPER

THE PASSION NARRATIVES

FROM DEATH TO NEW LIFE

JESUS IS RISEN!

THE RESURRECTION

THE POST-RESURRECTION APPEARANCES

THE ASCENSION

THE PASCHAL MYSTERY

DEATH

RESURRECTION

ASCENSION

IN THIS FINAL CHAPTER WE RETELL THE STORY OF Jesus' last days on earth, beginning at the end (which is also a beginning)—with our faith in the Resurrection. Aware of how the life and work of Jesus will turn out (a perspective the first disciples did not have), we sit at the table with him at the Last Supper; we walk with him on his painful journey to Crucifixion; and then we experience the reality of his glorious Resurrection.

JESUS CHRIST

SAVIOR

REDEEMER

LORD

LIBERATOR

Faith Focus: These teachings of the Catholic Church are the primary focus of the doctrinal content presented in this chapter:

- ⊙ Jesus Christ has won the victory over sin and death for all humanity through the redeeming work of his Paschal Mystery.
- ⊙ We share in the Paschal Mystery in and through the sacramental life of the Church and through the gift of the Holy Spirit who is at work with the Father and the Son in the divine plan for our salvation.
- ⊙ Christ's Death on the Cross is the sacrifice of the New Covenant that reconciles humanity with God and enables us to live in communion with God.
- ⊙ Through Baptism one enters into communion with Christ's Death and rises with him.
- ⊙ The Eucharist is the memorial of Christ's Passover—that is, of the work of salvation accomplished by his life, Death and Resurrection.
- ⊙ The Resurrection is both a historical event that is verifiable and attested by signs and testimonies and a work of God that transcends and surpasses history.
- ⊙ The Ascension reveals that Jesus Christ is the Lord who now in his humanity reigns in the everlasting glory of the Son of God and constantly intercedes for us before the Father.

Discipleship Formation: As a result of studying this chapter and discovering the meaning of the faith of the Catholic Church for your life, you should be better able to:

- ⊙ articulate the causes of fear, concern and worry in the lives of young people and in your own life in particular;
- ⊙ become aware of how the Paschal Mystery of Christ can be a source of hope for you in the midst of such anxieties;
- ⊙ appreciate the Eucharist as a source of hope for your life;
- ⊙ discover inspiration for repentance in your life from Jesus' response to Peter's denial and repentance;
- ⊙ relate the Passion of Jesus to situations in today's world through taking part in praying the Stations of the Cross;
- ⊙ identify how your faith in the Paschal Mystery can make you an agent of hope in the world.

Scripture References: These Scripture references are quoted or referred to in this chapter:
OLD TESTAMENT: Genesis 3:15
NEW TESTAMENT: Matthew 25:34, 26:15, 33–34 and 36–58, 27:32, 46 and 55–56, 28:2–3; **Mark** 5:21–43, 6:12, 14:32–65, 67–68 and 72, 15:33–34, 39 and 43–47, 16:1–10 and 12, 27:55; **Luke** 7:11–17, 8:2, 22:20, 39–53 and 70–71, 23:5–16, 21, 32–43 and 46, 24:13–43 and 50–53; **John** 6:51, 54 and 56, 11:1–44, 12:13 and 31, 18:1–11, 19:26–28 and 30, 20:3–29, 21:12; **Acts of the Apostles** 1:14 and 22, 2:1–47, 3:15; **Romans** 1:16, 3:25, 4:25, 6:4; **1 Corinthians** 1:30, 11:23–26, 15:3–4, 6, 14, 22, 35–50 and 55; **2 Corinthians** 3:16–18, 4:14; **Galatians** 2:16–21, 4:4–6, 5:1, 6:15; **Philippians** 1:21; **1 Timothy** 2:4; **1 Peter** 1:3

Faith Glossary: Familiarize yourself with the meaning of these key faith terms. Definitions are found in the Glossary: **Ascension, blasphemy, Crucifixion, hope, Last Supper, life everlasting, Lord, New Commandment, Paschal Mystery, Passion Narratives, Passover, Redeemer, redemption, Resurrection, Resurrection Narratives, Sacrament(s), sacrifice, Sacrifice of the Cross, sanctification, Savior, Stations of the Cross**

Faith Words: sacrifice; Paschal Mystery
Learn by Heart: Matthew 25:34
Learn by Example: Mary Magdalene

Can you believe it?
—Always hope!

OPENING CONVERSATION

⊙ First, pause and reflect on the rock-solid and amazing faith of the members of the early Church—that 'God raised from the dead' (Acts of the Apostles 3:15) their beloved Jesus Christ. Further, reflect on how their **hope**, founded in Jesus' Resurrection, changed everything for them and for all people until the end of time, so that now there will always be hope for us all.

⊙ After Jesus' Death and Resurrection, no cross is too heavy to carry, no evil will ever finally triumph, no trouble can rob us of hope, no sin can enslave us, no dependency is beyond recovery, no oppression can hold us bound, no hurt is beyond healing. Why? As St. Paul assured us, even death has 'lost its sting' (1 Corinthians 15:55)—all because of the dying and rising of Jesus.

⊙ What is your own 'gut' reaction to such faith and to the hope that it lends? How deeply can you believe it?

THE RESURRECTION DIFFERENCE

'Christ's Resurrection is *the fulfillment of the promises* both of the Old Testament and of Jesus himself during his earthly life' (*Catechism of the Catholic Church* [CCC], no. 652). The members of the early Church anchor our faith in the Resurrection. Paul proclaimed what was handed on to him; namely, that Jesus had lived, died and then was raised up by God the Father on our behalf (Romans 4:25), and he knew well how high the stakes for Christians (and for all humankind) 'if Christ has not been raised': 'then . . . your faith has been in vain' (1 Corinthians 15:14).

While some of the first disciples were initially skeptical of and not expecting the Resurrection (recall Luke 24:13–35: the story of Jesus traveling the road to Emmaus with the two disciples; and John 20:24–28: Thomas the Apostle's expression of doubt in the Resurrection), the faith of the early Church was centered in Jesus' Death and Resurrection, God's saving acts in Christ accomplished 'for us and for our salvation'.

Bonded with Christ by Baptism, we are given the grace to 'walk in newness of life' (Romans 6:4). For God 'who raised the Lord Jesus will raise us also' (2 Corinthians 4:14). Of course, everyone still must die; yet after death 'all will be made alive in Christ' (1 Corinthians 15:22). The belief and hope of the early Church in the Resurrection of Christ and in the bodily resurrection of the dead at the Last Judgment became the hallmark of the faith of the Apostolic Church and

THE RESURRECTION OF CHRIST | 12TH-CENTURY ARMLET

of the Church today—even our bodies will rise to new life. (Check out the Apostles' Creed, second to last line.)

Through the saving mystery of his **Paschal Mystery** Christ has won the victory over sin and death. Because 'in his incarnate divine person he has in some way united himself to every man, "the possibility of being made partners, in a way known to God, in the paschal mystery", is offered to all men [Vatican II, *Constitution on the Church in the Modern World*, no. 22]' (CCC, no. 618).

Even when we reject the saving grace of God and freely choose to sin, we still live in hope. We believe that we now share in and anticipate that victory in and through the sacramental life of the Church and through the gift of the Holy Spirit, who is 'at work with the Father and the Son from the beginning to the completion of the plan for our salvation' (CCC, no. 686).

All people can sing the hymn of praise and have the living hope with which Peter opens his first Epistle: 'Blessed be the God and Father of our Lord Jesus Christ! By his great mercy he has given us a new birth into a living hope through the resurrection of Jesus Christ from the dead' (1 Peter 1:3).

GROUP WORK/DISCUSSION

- ⊙ Together, make a list of the greatest concerns, worries, fears that beset young people today. Try to agree on the 'top ten'.
- ⊙ Go deeper into the possible reasons for such concerns. Some reasons are from inside of us; some from outside. Which are which?
- ⊙ Try to distinguish the valid concerns from the false ones; the worthy ones from those we should dismiss.
- ⊙ Now discuss how a deep faith in Jesus' Death and Resurrection can prompt a 'living hope' in young people's lives—no matter how heavy their burdens.
- ⊙ If you feel comfortable doing so, share your thoughts on these questions: Have you ever plumbed the depths of despair? Has any event ever made you think that there was no hope left—perhaps the break-up of a friendship, or the death of someone close to you? Talk about what happened, how you felt then, and what helped you to regain hope for the future.

THE ASCENSION OF JESUS | ANDREI RUBLEV

- ⊙ How might the life, Death, Resurrection and Ascension of Jesus lend a clear sense of meaning and purpose to life for young people today?

REVIEWING JESUS' LAST DAYS—AFTER THE RESURRECTION

The Evangelists and other writers of the New Testament looked back on the closing events of Jesus' life on earth in light of their faith in his Death, **Resurrection** and **Ascension**, the Paschal Mystery and source of his glory. In other words, the climax of Jesus' work on earth shaped how they interpreted what went before. The same is true for us: we interpret Jesus' last days, indeed his whole life, in light of our faith that God raised him from the dead. That is why we began with our Resurrection faith here. Now, let us go back and take up the story step by step, beginning with Jesus' **Last Supper**.

THE LAST SUPPER | MATTHIAS GRÜNEWALD

JESUS' FAREWELL MEAL WITH HIS FRIENDS

On the Sunday before his Passion (his suffering and Death), Jesus entered Jerusalem as many other Jewish pilgrims were coming to the city for the annual celebration of **Passover**. This was the time when Jews recalled and celebrated God's great saving act for his people, in particular the Exodus, God's freeing the Israelites from slavery in Egypt. Jews still celebrate Passover today.

By now, Jesus' reputation had spread far and wide. Many people had come to acknowledge that he was the Messiah and were beginning to place their hopes in him to be the 'king' whom God had promised to send to them. A 'great crowd' greeted Jesus, expressing that hope. They 'took branches of palm trees and went out to meet him, shouting, "Hosanna! Blessed is the one who comes in the name of the Lord—the King of Israel" ' (John 12:13). There is great symbolism in this event. Jesus entered the city in a parade, as hero-conquerors and victorious kings routinely did! But Jesus was a different kind of king, symbolized by his riding on a young donkey as opposed to a horse, as a victorious king would. His popularity with the people, and their hailing

him as king, made the authorities all the more determined to kill him. Christians celebrate this event each year on Palm Sunday of the Lord's Passion—the Sunday before Easter and the beginning of Holy Week.

During the next few days after his triumphant entry into Jerusalem, Jesus preached in the Temple. On one occasion he vehemently protested against the money-changing and commercial activities that were taking place in the Temple. This action sealed his fate with the religious authorities and would lead to his arrest, trial and **Crucifixion** on that Friday.

The focus of the celebration of Passover is the celebration of the Passover meal. During this meal the events of the Exodus, of God freeing the Israelites from slavery in Egypt, are recalled in a very precise ritual. In his final days in Jerusalem Jesus celebrated this great memorial meal with his disciples for the last time. Christians have named this meal the Last Supper. It is only by reading all four accounts of the Gospel that we can gather and learn about the full details of this meal. For example, it is only in John's Gospel that we read of Jesus washing the disciples' feet and bestowing on them gifts of joy and peace, of his

It was at the Last Supper that Jesus transformed the Passover meal and instituted the Eucharist

prayer for their unity, his promise of the Holy Spirit, and his '**new commandment**' to love as he had loved and, so, as God loves; while the details of the meal itself are found only in the Synoptics and in 1 Corinthians 11:23–26. It is this meal that the Church commemorates each year on Holy Thursday at the celebration of the Evening Mass of the Lord's Supper.

It was at the Last Supper that Jesus transformed the Passover meal and instituted the Eucharist. At each celebration of the Eucharist, the Church fulfills Jesus' command to celebrate the Eucharist and 'proclaim the Lord's death until he comes' (1 Corinthians 11:26).

For when the hour had come . . .
he took bread, blessed and broke it,
and gave it to his disciples, saying,
TAKE THIS, ALL OF YOU, AND EAT OF IT,
FOR THIS IS MY BODY,
WHICH WILL BE GIVEN UP FOR YOU.

In a similar way,
taking the chalice filled with the fruit of the
    vine,
he gave thanks,
and gave the chalice to his disciples, saying:
TAKE THIS, ALL OF YOU, AND DRINK
    FROM IT,
FOR THIS IS THE CHALICE OF MY BLOOD,
THE BLOOD OF THE NEW AND ETERNAL
    COVENANT,
WHICH WILL BE POURED OUT FOR YOU
    AND FOR MANY
FOR THE FORGIVENESS OF SINS.
DO THIS IN MEMORY OF ME.

Jesus' actions expressed the meaning of his Death, which would follow shortly: it would be a **sacrifice**, the price to be paid for salvation, redemption, liberation, reconciliation and the forgiveness of sins. It would advance the coming of God's Kingdom of love and freedom, goodness and holiness, justice and peace for all.

The Eucharist is the heart and summit of the Church's work. It is the 'memorial of Christ's Passover, that is, of the work of salvation accomplished by the life, death, and resurrection of Christ', a work made present in the celebration of the Eucharist (CCC, no. 1409).

From her very beginning, the Church has fulfilled Jesus' command to celebrate this **Sacrament**, the Eucharist, in his memory. The members of the early Church firmly believed, as we do today, that the bread and wine become the Body and Blood of Jesus; that the risen Christ is truly and really present under the appearances of bread and wine and to be received in the Eucharist. When we receive the Eucharist we realize the meaning of the promise Christ made in the 'I am' statement:

I am the living bread that came down from heaven. Whoever eats of this bread will live forever; and the bread that I will give for the life of the world is my flesh. . . . Those who eat my flesh and drink my blood have eternal life. . . . Those who eat my flesh and drink my blood abide in me and I in them.
—John 6:51, 54, 56

Further, our receiving this Body and Blood of Christ not only bonds us more closely to Christ but also to the Body of Christ in the world, the Church, and gives us the grace to live faithfully as his disciples.

OVER TO YOU
- From what you have reviewed here already, how might you grow in your appreciation of the Eucharist?
- How might it be a constant source of hope for you?

We will now continue to recall the story of the final events in Jesus' life on earth, and then the meaning of his Death and Resurrection for our lives.

The arrest, trial and Crucifixion of Jesus

THE AGONY IN THE GARDEN | ANDREA MANTEGNA

JESUS—BETRAYED AND DENIED

All four accounts of the Gospel pass on a narrative of Jesus' arrest, trial and Crucifixion on Calvary. Though each of the Gospels vary in their perspectives and details, essentially they all tell the same 'story'. These narratives are often referred to as the **Passion Narratives**. You will hear the account of the Passion proclaimed many times at the Liturgy celebrated during Holy Week.

OPENING CONVERSATION

- From your own memory of the 'Passion' of Jesus, recall and name its main events.
- Then bring to mind your present concerns and joys, fears and hopes, and reflect together on what you think these events mean—for you personally; for all people.

THE EVENTS OF THE PASSION

At the end of the Last Supper, Jesus cautioned his disciples that, under the pressure of the events ahead, they would all desert him. Peter protested loudly, 'Though all become deserters because of you, I will never desert you' (Matthew 26:33). Jesus forewarned him, 'Truly I tell you, this very night, before the cock crows, you will deny me three times' (Matthew 26:34).

Jesus and his disciples then left the place where the Last Supper was celebrated and went to Gethsemane, a garden area just outside Jerusalem near the Mount of Olives. The word 'gethsemani' comes from two Hebrew words meaning 'olive press'. When they arrived there, Jesus said to his disciples, 'Sit here while I pray.' Then he invited Peter, James and John to come with him. He opened his heart to his closest companions and friends, saying, 'I am deeply grieved, even to death; remain here, and stay with me' (Matthew 26:38). Going off alone to pray, Jesus then opened his heart to his Father and prayed, 'My Father, if it is possible, let this cup pass from me; yet not what I want but what you want' (Matthew 26:39). Returning to Peter, James and John, Jesus found them sleeping and rebuked them. Jesus then went off a second time to pray and his disciples fell asleep a second time, so he left them and went off alone to pray to his Father a third time. This event of the Passion, when Jesus anticipated the terrible death he was about to die, is known as the Agony in the Garden. Meanwhile his disciples fell asleep. (Read about Jesus' agony in the garden of Gethsemane in Matthew 26:36–46 or Mark 14:32–42 or Luke 22:39–46.)

Soon after Jesus finished praying and had returned to the disciples, Judas the Apostle, who had betrayed him, led a mob to arrest Jesus. Judas identified and betrayed Jesus with a kiss, addressing him as 'Rabbi', or Teacher. They then arrested Jesus; meanwhile all of Jesus' disciples deserted him and fled. The reward for betraying his friend earned Judas 'thirty pieces of silver' (Matthew 26:15). (Read Matthew 26:47–58 or Mark 14:43–52 or Luke 22:47–53 or John 18:1–11.)

Jesus' accusers first took Jesus to the house of Caiaphas the high priest, where the scribes and members of the Sanhedrin, the council of elders, had gathered. Meanwhile 'Peter had followed him at a distance' and sat by the fire in the high priest's courtyard (Mark 14:54). When a young servant girl recognized Peter to be one of Jesus' disciples, she said, ' "You also were with Jesus, the man from Nazareth." But he denied it. . . . Then the cock crowed' (Mark 14:67–68). Three times in all, someone identified Peter as a disciple of Jesus, but he continued to deny it— thus becoming one of the 'deserters' he claimed he would never be. However, when the cock crowed a second time after his third denial, 'Peter remembered that Jesus had said to him, "Before the cock crows twice, you will deny me three times." ' At this Peter 'broke down and wept' (Mark 14:72).

REFLECT AND DISCUSS
Remember that Peter was the very one whom Jesus had appointed to lead his disciples, his Church. Now. . . .

- ◉ Reflect on Peter's denial of Jesus. What can you learn from it?
- ◉ What hope might this give you in your own life?
- ◉ How might Christians 'deny Jesus' today? How might you?
- ◉ All three Synoptic Gospels state that Peter 'wept bitterly'. What do you think of his repentance?
- ◉ Do you and the other members of the Church on earth today still need such moments of repentance? Explain.

WHY WAS JESUS PUT ON TRIAL?
Biblical scholars have argued long and hard over the legal details of the trial of Jesus, which is probably the most studied trial in history. When the chief priests and scribes questioned Jesus before an assembly of people, they focused on their greatest fears; namely, Jesus' claim to be not only the Messiah but also God, and the growing acceptance of these claims by many Jewish people and their coming to believe in him. When they brought Jesus before the Sanhedrin, they asked him, 'Are you, then, the Son of God?' He said to them, 'You say that I am.' Then they said, 'What further testimony do we need? We have heard it ourselves from his own lips!' (Luke 22:70–71). Mark refers to what they heard as 'blasphemy'—because Jesus had claimed to be

The simple 'conditions' for true repentance— or any sincere apology—are to say sincerely: 'I did wrong.' 'I am sorry.' 'Please forgive me.' 'I won't do it again.'

the Son of God. (Read Mark 14:53–65.) They had Jesus where they wanted him! His own words, in their view, sealed his fate! They could now bring him to Pilate and demand his execution.

The people, led by the chief priests and scribes, then brought Jesus before Pilate, the local Roman governor. They accused him of claiming to be king, which in Roman law was an act of treason. When Pilate said that he could find no legal standing to their claims against Jesus, the crowd modified their accusations, claiming he was a rabble rouser and a threat to Pilate's own rule. They said, 'He stirs up the people by teaching throughout all Judea, from Galilee where he began even to this place' (Luke 23:5).

When he learned that Jesus was a Galilean and technically a subject of Herod, Pilate found a way out of his dilemma without freeing Jesus and stirring up the crowds against him. So Pilate sent them off to Herod, the king of Judea with responsibility for religious matters. After Herod had questioned Jesus at length and Jesus did not respond, Herod sent him back to Pilate. (Read Luke 23:6–12.) The chief priests' civil and religious accusations against Jesus had failed!

Pilate called together the chief priests and leaders and the people and said to them, 'You brought me this man as one who was perverting the people; and here I have examined him in your presence and have not found this man guilty of any of your charges against him. Neither has Herod, for he sent him back to us. Indeed, he has done nothing to deserve death. I will therefore have him flogged and release him' (Luke 23:14–16).

This group of Jewish leaders and the people who assembled with them continued to demand that Jesus be put to death. In the eyes of this group of Jews, Jesus had blasphemed, or claimed to be God. By Jewish law, this claim deserved the death penalty, which in Roman law was implemented by the horrendous act of crucifixion. Incited by this small group of chief priests, the crowd shouted, 'Crucify, crucify him!' (Luke 23:21). Eventually, still arguing with them that Jesus was innocent, Pilate gave in to their demands and rendered his verdict that Jesus be crucified. Although none of their accusations against Jesus stood up to questioning, Jesus was sentenced to death. Why? Ultimately it may simply be that living for God's Kingdom, or reign, is always dangerous, and those who do good often incur the wrath of others.

When we read this account of the arrest, trial and Crucifixion of Jesus, we must remember that the Jewish people, then or since or today, were and are not responsible personally for the accusation, condemnation and death of Jesus. We must accurately assess the historical facts and truth: Jesus' Crucifixion was the result of the demands of a few of the Jews of Jesus' time. We must avoid falsely generalizing this historical act as the demand of all Jews of Jesus' time, of the Jewish People. It was not. Tragically, this false interpretation did occur throughout history and contributed greatly to the sin of anti-Semitism, and many Jewish people have suffered and been persecuted, even to death, by 'some' Christians. The Church has both condemned this false judgment and apologized to the Jewish People.

OVER TO YOU

⊙ Have you ever been deliberately falsely accused of doing something, or do you know someone who has? How did that feel?

JESUS BEFORE PILATE | WENZEL HOLLAR

⊙ How do you think Jesus felt at being wrongly condemned to death? Why were the chief priests, scribes and people who brought Jesus to Pilate and Herod so insistent that he be put to death?

TO CALVARY: THE WAY OF THE CROSS

Piecing together the four accounts of his Passion, we learn that Jesus was scourged—whipped—most cruelly, mocked by his captors, had a crown of thorns placed upon his head, was spat upon, and then was forced to carry his own Cross to Calvary. The Greek name of the place was Golgotha, which means 'the place of the skull'. It is significant to note that crucifixion—being nailed to a cross and hung

CHRIST CARRYING THE CROSS | HIERONYMUS BOSCH

there to die—was the Romans' cruel way of executing political prisoners to deter revolt of any kind. Along the way, the Roman soldiers, fearful that Jesus might not make it to the place of his execution, forced a man in the crowd, Simon of Cyrene, to help (Matthew 27:32). All four Gospels give the same three-word summary statement of what happened at Calvary; namely, 'they crucified him'.

All three of the Synoptics agree that some women disciples of Jesus stayed by him, accompanying him to Calvary. Matthew writes: 'Many women were also there, looking on from a distance; they had followed Jesus from Galilee and had provided for him. Among them were Mary Magdalene, and Mary the mother of James and Joseph, and the mother of the sons of Zebedee' (27:55–56). All the male disciples (with the exception of the disciple whom Jesus loved) had deserted him as Jesus forewarned them.

Based on all the Passion Narratives, the Church has identified 'seven last words' from Jesus upon the Cross.

The Seven Last Words of Jesus

'Father, forgive them; for they do not know what they are doing.' (Luke 23:34)

'My God, my God, why have you forsaken me?' (Matthew 27:46)

He said to his mother, 'Woman, here is your son.' Then he said to the disciple, 'Here is your mother.' (John 19:26–27)

'I am thirsty.' (John 19:28)

'Truly I tell you, today you will be with me in Paradise.' (Luke 23:43)

'It is finished.' (John 19:30)

'Father, into your hands I commend my spirit.' (Luke 23:46)

Perhaps Jesus' two most amazing statements were his prayer for forgiveness for those who executed him: 'Father, forgive them; for they do not know what they are doing' (Luke 23:34); and his promise to the 'good thief', one of the two criminals being crucified alongside him. The other criminal had berated Jesus as a false messiah but this one defended Jesus and asked, 'Jesus, remember me when you come into your kingdom.' In response, Jesus forgave him his sins and assured him, 'Today you will be with me in Paradise.' (Read Luke 23:32–43.)

Jesus was put to death in a particularly brutal manner, crucified between two common criminals.

When it was noon, darkness came over the whole land until three in the afternoon. At three o'clock Jesus cried out with a loud voice, 'Eloi Eloi, lema sabachthani?' which means, 'My God, my God, why have you forsaken me?'

—Mark 15:33–34

After Jesus died, the Roman centurion at the foot of his Cross was moved to faith and said, 'Truly this man was God's Son!' (Mark 15:39). Thereafter, 'Joseph of Arimathea, a respected member of the [Jewish] council . . . went boldly to Pilate and asked for the body of Jesus'. His request granted, Joseph wrapped Jesus' dead body in linen cloth, laid him in a tomb and 'rolled a stone against the door of the tomb' (Mark 15:43–46). It seemed as if it was all over!

Jesus' mission as Messiah and Savior now seemed an abject failure. The Kingdom he had proclaimed to be present among us looked now to be but a dream. Jesus' plans appeared to be in shambles, his movement gone to ground and his disciples scattered. For his followers and close friends, hope now seemed dead. (Read Mark 15 to get a feeling for the air of despair and loss that surrounded Jesus' Crucifixion.)

Christ's Death on the Cross accomplished the salvation of all people. He is the Lamb of God who takes away the sin of the world. Christ's Death is also the sacrifice of the New Covenant, which reconciles humanity with God and enables us to live in communion with him. Christ's sacrifice fulfills and surpasses all other sacrifices. It is the source of salvation for all. We are made sharers in this sacrifice through our participation in the Eucharist, the Holy Sacrifice and the memorial of the Lord's Passion and Resurrection. The Mass calls us to become 'a living sacrifice of praise' to God—by how we live our lives in the world now (Fourth Eucharistic Prayer).

OVER TO YOU

⊙ Try to imagine the thoughts and feelings of Peter, Mary Magdalene and the other disciples that evening after Jesus' body was placed in the tomb. What might have been their

KAMIEŃ POMORSKI CATHEDRAL, POLAND

FAITH WORD

Sacrifice

Sacrifice is a free offering, a gift, made by a person for the welfare of others. The word 'sacrifice' comes from two Latin words meaning 'to make sacred'. Such a gift is deemed to be sacred—a special and a sincere sign of love and life. The greatest sacrifice of all is to give one's life for another. In a religious context a sacrifice is 'a ritual offering made to God by a priest on behalf of the people as a sign of adoration, gratitude, supplication, penance, and/or communion' (*United States Catholic Catechism for Adults*, 527).

predominant emotion? How do you think you would have felt if you were there?

⊙ The story of the Passion, the suffering and Death of Jesus, is told in all four Gospels. Begin with Mark's account of the Passion, the first written account, and read it reflectively from start to finish (Mark 14—15). Place yourself in the story; occasionally, pause and reflect on what you are seeing and hearing, and what you are feeling. What is the story saying to you!

JOURNAL EXERCISE

⊙ What part of the Passion Narrative moves you most? How would you represent it visually or musically? Describe this in your journal.

THE STATIONS OF THE CROSS RE-ENACTED IN SYDNEY FOR WORLD YOUTH DAY 2008

THE WAY OF THE CROSS IN TODAY'S WORLD

Right down through the history of the Church, people have remembered and meditated upon Jesus' last days on earth. Through the practice of the **Stations of the Cross**, also known as the Way of the Cross (or *Via Crucis*), people recall in a prayerful way Jesus' journey to Calvary and his Crucifixion.

This rich spiritual practice originated when pilgrims who journeyed to Jerusalem wanted to visit and pray at significant places along the way of Jesus' last journey. Now, just about every Catholic church throughout the world has a set of Stations of the Cross, a practice that began around the fourteenth century to meet the spiritual needs of Christians unable to travel to the Holy Land.

There are many ways to pray the Stations, either individually or in community. The typical pattern is for people to: (a) move to a Station and announce what it is (for example, 'The first station, Jesus is condemned to death'; (b) say the traditional prayer, while genuflecting, *'We adore you, O Christ, and we praise you, because*

by your holy Cross you have redeemed the world'; (c) pause and meditate for a brief moment on the event represented by the Station; (d) pray an Our Father, a Hail Mary and a Glory be to the Father, and (e) then move to the next Station.

We can be creative in how we remember the sufferings of Jesus and those of our own time as well. Some communities publicly re-enact the Stations with the help of young volunteers. This practice is common among Catholics in Latin America, Europe and Asia. By entering, literally, into the drama of the Passion, people relive those difficult moments in the life of Jesus by walking with him. At the same time, we are reassured that Jesus walks with us in our own sufferings. In some cities it is not unusual for Catholics to join together on Good Friday to process through their neighborhood, stopping to read, pray and reflect over each Station. The community reflects on Jesus' falls; for example, by standing in the parking lot of a housing project in their neighborhood where they pray for many of their troubled youth who are exposed to violence and drugs, and who may have become involved in some type of violent or harmful activity. This connects the suffering of Jesus to people's daily experience.

Reversing death into new life

OPENING CONVERSATION

- ⊙ Place yourself in the 'sandals' of one of Jesus' disciples—imagining that you do not yet know about the Resurrection. How are you feeling? What are your thoughts? What do you want to do next?
- ⊙ Many of Jesus' friends fled in fear and disappointment. But a group of faithful women stayed until the end. Why do you think the women disciples stayed on? Why do you think the others ran away? (Don't be too judgmental; we do it often ourselves!)

JESUS IS RISEN!

All four Gospels include the story of the Resurrection of Jesus and several accounts of his post-Resurrection appearances. Different Gospels emphasize different aspects of the Resurrection. All three Synoptic Gospels, especially Mark (Mark 16:1–8), tell the story of the women disciples first finding the empty tomb; Luke places the emphasis on Jesus being alive in the breaking of the bread (a traditional phrase for the Eucharist) and in the Word of God (Luke 24:13–32); Matthew highlights God's power, with such dramatic symbols as earthquakes and lightning (Matthew 28:2–3); John's Gospel emphasizes Jesus commissioning the Apostles to be his witnesses and to carry on the work he had begun.

Mark's Gospel tells us that, after Jesus' burial, 'Mary Magdalene and Mary the mother of Joses saw where the body was laid' (Mark 15:47), and that on the third day Mary Magdalene and some other women went back to the tomb to anoint Jesus' body:

> When the sabbath was over, Mary Magdalene, and Mary the mother of James, and Salome bought spices, so that they might go and anoint him. And very early on the first day of the week, when the sun had risen, they went to the tomb.
>
> —Mark 16:1–2

When they arrived, they saw that the tomb was empty, even though a large stone had been put in front of it in case anyone should try to steal the body. As they entered the tomb, they 'saw a young man, dressed in a white robe, sitting on the right side. . . .', who greeted the women with the astounding announcement: 'He has been raised; he is not here', and then instructed them to 'go, tell his disciples and Peter that he is going ahead of you to Galilee'. (Read Mark 16:1–8.)

In John's Gospel, it is only Mary Magdalene who comes to the tomb and finds it empty. She runs to tell Peter and 'the other disciple, the one whom Jesus loved'.

> Then Peter and the other disciple set out and went toward the tomb. The two were running together, but the other disciple outran Peter and

THE THREE MARYS AT THE TOMB | FRA ANGELICO

reached the tomb first. He bent down to look in and saw the linen wrappings lying there, but he did not go in. Then Simon Peter came, following him, and went into the tomb. He saw the linen wrappings lying there, and the cloth that had been on Jesus' head, not lying with the linen wrappings but rolled up in a place by itself. Then the other disciple, who reached the tomb first, also went in, and he saw and believed; for as yet they did not understand the scripture, that he must rise from the dead. Then the disciples returned to their homes.

—John 20:3–10

Mary Magdalene, however, did not leave with the others; rather, in her grief 'she stood weeping outside the tomb'. She then saw two angels inside the tomb, who asked, 'Woman, why are you weeping?' Then the risen Christ, whom she mistook to be the gardener, approached her. In her grief she continues seeking answers to her questions, inquiring where they've laid the body of her beloved Jesus. Jesus then responds, addressing her by name, 'Mary!' Astounded, she recognizes his voice and turns to him, and addresses him as she had done before, 'Rabbouni', the Hebrew word for 'Teacher'. Now filled with joy, 'Mary Magdalene went and announced to the disciples, "I have seen the Lord"'. And indeed she had. Jesus was truly risen from the dead. (Read John 20:11–18.)

OVER TO YOU

◉ Think about Mary Magdalene and the other women as they approach the tomb 'in the early morning of the first day of the week', which Christians name Easter Sunday. They have vivid memories of Jesus' execution by crucifixion before a hostile crowd. How do you think they feel as they are walking toward the tomb? Perhaps their grief was deepened because the hope that they placed in Jesus and in his vision of a Kingdom of justice, love and peace had faded away, as it had for the two disciples traveling the road to Emmaus. As they arrive they see that the entrance to the tomb is open, the stone has been rolled back, and to their surprise they find the tomb empty and the body of Jesus gone. How do you think they felt then? Might their grief have been overcome by fear?

THE RESURRECTION | MATTHIAS GRÜNEWALD

- After Peter and the other disciples leave, Mary Magdalene, who has remained behind, hears the message from the angel that Jesus has risen . . . and then she sees the risen Christ. How do you think she felt now?
- Put yourself in their place during the various stages of their journey to the tomb. What are you feeling?
- What are you coming to see for yourself about the Resurrection of Jesus Christ?

The Good News—the astounding news—spread; first from the women; and then from the closest disciples (Peter, James and John) and the others. Jesus had been raised and was alive, a fact that the risen Jesus confirmed by his appearances to the disciples after his Resurrection, and to which Paul gave witness in his First Letter to the Corinthians, one of the earliest New Testament texts: the risen Christ 'appeared to more than five hundred brothers and sisters at one time, most of whom are still alive' (1 Corinthians 15:6).

We read of one such post-Resurrection appearance in John's Gospel:

When it was evening on that day, the first day of the week, and the doors of the house where the disciples had met were locked for fear of the Jews, Jesus came and stood among them and said, 'Peace be with you.' After he said this, he showed them his hands and his side. Then the disciples rejoiced when they saw the Lord. Jesus said to them again, 'Peace be with you. As the Father has sent me, so I send you.' When he had said this, he breathed on them and said to them, 'Receive the Holy Spirit. If you forgive the sins of any, they are forgiven them; if you retain the sins of any, they are retained.'

—John 20:19–23

OVER TO YOU

- Catholics of the Eastern Churches use this traditional Easter greeting: 'Christ is risen: he is risen indeed.' Would you use this greeting outside of the celebration of the Liturgy? Why or why not? Explain.
- If you did use this greeting, what difference should it make to your daily life—now?

What are you coming to see for yourself about the Resurrection of Jesus Christ?

Jesus' Resurrection: What really happened?

OPENING CONVERSATION

⊙ How would you explain Jesus' Resurrection to someone who had never heard about it?

⊙ What do you believe really happened and what does this mean for your faith?

WHAT IS THE RESURRECTION?

The mystery of Jesus' Resurrection is a real event and central to the faith of the Church. Recall Paul's statement to the Church in Corinth: 'Christ died for our sins . . . he was buried . . . and . . . was raised on the third day in accordance with the scriptures' (1 Corinthians 15:3–4). The mystery of the reality of Christ's Resurrection is so central to the faith of the Church that Paul also wrote, 'If Christ has not been raised, then our proclamation has been in vain and your faith has been in vain' (1 Corinthians 15:14). With so much riding on Jesus' Resurrection, it is only reasonable to ask, 'What really happened?'

There have been two extreme responses to that question, neither one of which is true. First, Jesus' Resurrection was a bodily resuscitation—he was brought back to the same life he had before his Death; second, Jesus' rising was only in the hearts of his heartbroken disciples.

First, Jesus' Resurrection does not mean that he was brought back to the same life he knew before his Death. The Resurrection was not the same kind of raising to life as when Jesus raised Lazarus from the dead (John 11:1–44), or the daughter of Jairus (Mark 5:21–43), or the son of the widow of Nain (Luke 7:11–17). These people, after Jesus brought them back to life, would live a while longer and eventually die again. Their bodies remained mortal, or subject to death.

Jesus was raised to a radically new life, a 'glorious life'. His body was so transformed that it had properties that were not limited by space and time and 'his humanity can no longer be confined

DOUBTING THOMAS | 16TH-CENTURY RUSSIAN ICON

to earth, and belongs henceforth only to the Father's divine realm' (CCC, no. 645). Unlike a mortal body, the body of the risen Jesus could pass through walls (John 20:19). The risen Jesus could walk along with two disciples without their recognizing him. Only after eating with him did they recognize that it was Jesus, who then 'vanished' from their midst (Luke 24:31). Jesus could appear in the room to which the disciples had locked the doors, yet Thomas could touch the wounds in his side (John 20:19–25). By all accounts, 'he appeared in another form' (Mark 16:12).

Second, Jesus' Resurrection was not just wishful thinking on the part of his disciples which they turned into a reality. The Scriptures attest to the fact that the risen Jesus appeared not only to his closest disciples but also to numerous others. The disciples knew that Jesus' Resurrection was 'real' because the risen Jesus had shown them the wounds in his body—even inviting Thomas to touch them (John 20:24–29). He had asked them for food and ate it (Luke 24:36–43); why, he had even invited them to breakfast (John 21:12). The disciples were transformed by their experiences of the risen Lord and proclaimed throughout the world that God the Father had raised up Jesus—many giving their lives in witness to this truth; such commitment is impossible from a conspiracy of fond hopes.

What really happened? What is the Resurrection? The Resurrection of Jesus is both a real event and a mystery of faith. We cannot fully describe nor fully understand it.

Christ's Resurrection was not a return to earthly life, as was the case with the raisings from the dead that he had performed before Easter: Jairus' daughter, the young man of Naim, Lazarus. . . . In his risen body he passes from the state of death to another life beyond time and space. At Jesus' Resurrection his body is filled with the power of the Holy Spirit: he shares the divine life in his glorious state, so that St. Paul can say that Christ is 'the man of heaven' [1 Corinthians 15:35–50].
—CCC, no. 646

The Resurrection is the entry of Christ's humanity into the glory of God. Now we are invited to join in the disciples' rock-solid conviction that 'Jesus was raised on the third day' (1 Corinthians 15:4) and that this has transformed life and everything about it for all people.

JUDGE AND DECIDE

⊙ In light of these two wrong answers, how would you state the right one about 'what really happened' at Jesus' Resurrection?

⊙ What do you imagine are the day-to-day consequences of the Resurrection for you? For all people?

THE ASCENSION OF JESUS INTO HEAVEN

The final episode of the risen Jesus' life on earth took place forty days after the Resurrection. Jesus spoke to his disciples about their mission and promised that the Holy Spirit would help them always. Then, before their very eyes, the risen Christ was taken up to Heaven. Luke describes the Ascension of Jesus as follows:

Then he led them out as far as Bethany, and, lifting up his hands, he blessed them. While he was blessing them, he withdrew from them and was carried up into heaven. And they worshiped him, and returned to Jerusalem with great joy; and they were continually in the temple praising God.
—Luke 24:50–53

WHAT ABOUT YOU PERSONALLY?

⊙ After Jesus' Resurrection and Ascension, his disciples were no longer afraid or confused. Luke's Gospel tells us, 'They returned to Jerusalem with great joy; and they were continually in the temple praising God.' How do *you* feel? Does Jesus' Resurrection and Ascension fill *you* with joy?

⊙ How does the Resurrection and Ascension give direction to your life as a disciple of Jesus Christ?

WHAT HAPPENED FOR US?

The reality of Jesus' Resurrection was the bedrock on which the early Church founded their proclamation of the Gospel, which Peter and the other disciples began ten days after the Ascension, during the celebration of the Jewish feast of Pentecost. (Read Acts of the Apostles 2.)

On that Pentecost, the first disciples, about 120 of them, including Mary the mother of Jesus, the Apostles and other disciples, men and women, were gathered in a room in Jerusalem when they experienced an outpouring of the Holy Spirit 'on each of them' (Acts of the Apostles 1:14; 2:3). This experience of the Spirit transformed them from a quiet band waiting for the fulfillment of Jesus' promise, into a courageous band boldly proclaiming Jesus in a marketplace filled with pilgrims, whom they admonished for rejecting Jesus. They were no longer 'deserters' but fearless and bold witnesses, enthusiastic to carry out their commission to bring Jesus' mission to the ends of the earth. Fully convinced of the Resurrection and empowered by the Holy Spirit, those first disciples began to proclaim their Jesus as 'Lord and Messiah' (Acts of the Apostles 2:36), as the Anointed One of God—the Christ. The mission of the Church on earth had begun.

After the outpouring of the Holy Spirit, the Advocate and Teacher, the disciples began to piece together the details and meaning of Jesus' Death, Resurrection and Ascension—the Paschal Mystery—and they came to believe that it was, indeed, the decisive catalyst in God's 'work of salvation', as the Scriptures had foretold. The early Church came to understand and believe more and more deeply that in Jesus Christ God had entered into a new and final Covenant with humankind (Luke 22:20), and that the Paschal Mystery was *the* turning point in human history.

But how should the Church teach about the *change* brought about through the Paschal Mystery of Jesus' dying and rising? The Evangelists and the other writers of the New Testament and, eventually, the early theologians of the Church began to search for and adopt language to teach about the 'difference' that the divine plan of Salvation accomplished for all creation.

The Four Evangelists and St. Paul, whose writings date from the early AD 50s, provide a treasure of teachings that help us understand the meaning of what the saving work of God the Holy Trinity has brought about through the dying and rising of Jesus, the Incarnate Son of God. Paul, the Apostle to the Gentiles, wrote of salvation (Romans 1:16), liberation (Galatians 5:1), justification (Galatians 2:16–21), reconciliation (2 Corinthians 3:16–18), sanctification (1 Corinthians 1:30), forgiveness (Romans 3:25), expiation (Romans 3:25), ransom (Galatians 4:5), new creation (Galatians 6:15), new life (1 Corinthians 15:45), divine adoption to be God's children (Galatians 4:4–6) . . . and the list goes on. In all these ways Paul was expressing and passing on the apostolic faith of the early Church—the mystery of faith of the saving work of the Trinity that eventually would be stated in the Apostles' Creed and the other Creeds of the Church.

ST. PAUL | EL GRECO

- How would you describe the 'difference' Jesus Christ has made and continues to make in human history? To your own life?
- How might human history and salvation history be the same?
- What might be a compelling way to express 'the Jesus difference' to your peers?

The quest has continued since Paul, as the Church found herself having to name the meaning of Jesus' Death and Resurrection in different times and places. Three classic ways of talking about the transformation effected by the Paschal Mystery of Jesus Christ are the titles or names '**Savior**', '**Redeemer**' and '**Lord**', by which the identity and mission of Jesus has been identified.

Savior: Christ *saves* us from all the powers of evil that threaten to destroy our lives.

Redeemer: Christ *redeems* us by paying the price (*redemio*) to buy us back from the bondage of sin, canceling whatever debt we owe to God.

Lord: This name for Jesus expresses the faith of the Apostolic Church that Jesus is truly God. The New Testament uses 'Lord' for both Jesus and God the Father. The Church from her very beginning has affirmed that the power, honor and glory given to God the Father are equally due to Jesus. Through Baptism a person is joined to Christ, becomes an adopted son or daughter of God the Father and a temple of the Holy Spirit. The Most Holy Trinity gives the baptized the gift of sanctifying grace (the word 'sanctifying' means 'making holy') and the person is made a sharer in the very life of God. Through Baptism one enters 'into communion with Christ's death, . . . and rises with him. . . .' (CCC, no. 1227).

A contemporary metaphor for Jesus is Liberator, the One who frees us from the slavery of sin and the death it brings upon humanity. This image calls to mind the work of God freeing, or liberating, his people from the sin of slavery and death in Egypt, which prefigured Jesus' life, Death and Resurrection. It is only by joining with God's work of freeing people *from* all that enslaves— personal and social—that his will 'will be done on earth as it is in heaven' and his Kingdom 'will come'. And we can be sure that new metaphors will emerge out of different cultures and as history unfolds. Human language can never exhaust the meaning for us of the Paschal Mystery.

PLEDGE OF THE JOY OF LIFE EVERLASTING

The Resurrection of Jesus is the foundation of our hope—our desire and expectation—that all the faithful who join with Christ and work to bring about the coming of the Kingdom, or reign, of

---

FAITH WORD

Paschal Mystery

In speaking of the Paschal Mystery we present Christ's death and Resurrection as one, inseparable event. It is *paschal* because it is Christ's passing into death and passing over it into new life. It is a *mystery* because it is a visible sign of an invisible act of God.

—*United States Catholic Catechism for Adults*, 522

11TH-CENTURY ITALIAN MOSAIC OF JESUS

God will rise to new life and be welcomed into that Kingdom. As a consequence of Original Sin, we now must suffer physical death. But because of the Paschal Mystery of Christ, death for the faithful is a new beginning. At the moment of the death of our body, our life is changed and not ended. In writing to the Church in Philippi (a city in Macedonia), Paul proclaimed, 'For to me, living is Christ and dying is gain' (Philippians 1:21). Jesus suffered death for us, and by his Death he conquered death and opened the possibility of **life everlasting** with the Trinity. The promise made to the first humans in Genesis 3:15 is fulfilled in Christ, who has crushed the head of the serpent. All who die in Christ's grace are the People of God beyond their physical death.

While the Paschal Mystery opens up the door to Heaven—life everlasting with the Trinity—responding to Christ and God's grace is still our choice. As Adam and Eve chose to turn a deaf ear to God and his plan of goodness, every person still has the radical option to turn a deaf ear to God and his plan of Salvation. One can still choose to live a self-centered life as our first parents did. One can still choose to follow one's own 'wisdom' and ignore and disobey the wisdom of God revealed in Jesus. One can choose to turn one's self away from God's love and separate one's self from God forever. During our life on earth, we can choose to live life everlasting in Hell—in a state of eternal separation from God.

But God is Love and steadfast in his loyalty to people. It is never God's desire and choice that anyone live separated from him eternally. It is always God's desire that the deepest longing of our heart be fulfilled. The Father, Son and Holy Spirit always desires that everyone be saved from sin and death (see 1 Timothy 2:4). God always desires and awaits everyone to be welcomed by Christ's words, 'Come, you that are blessed by my Father, inherit the kingdom prepared for you from the foundation of the world' (Matthew 25:34).

OVER TO YOU

⦿ Express in your own words or images what the Paschal Mystery—Jesus' Death, Resurrection and Ascension—means for people today? For you personally?
⦿ How will you respond?

JUDGE AND ACT

REFLECT ON WHAT YOU HAVE LEARNED

- ⊙ Review your opening reflections at the beginning of this chapter. What hope does the Death, Resurrection and Ascension of Jesus—the Paschal Mystery—bring to you?
- ⊙ What difference might it make in their everyday lives if Christians 'really' believed in the Resurrection of Jesus Christ?

- ⊙ How can you be an 'agent of hope' in your family? Among your friends? In your school?
- ⊙ Imagine you want to explain to someone how faith in Jesus is the source of boundless hope throughout life. What would you be sure to say?

LEARN BY EXAMPLE

The story of Mary Magdalene

Mary Magdalene knew well how faith in Jesus could transform a life and be the true source of boundless hope. We first encounter Mary Magdalene early in Luke's Gospel. Luke clearly identifies Mary as a constant disciple of Jesus, who traveled with Jesus and his closest disciples and who supported him during his public ministry. The Evangelist also identifies Mary as someone from whom Jesus had cast out 'seven demons' (Luke 8:2). In his healings and casting out of demons, or exorcisms, Jesus was fulfilling his work of inaugurating the reign, or Kingdom, of God. These wondrous works pointed to the power of God at work in the world and anticipated Jesus' victory over the 'ruler of the world' (John 12:31) through his Death on the Cross.

Mary Magdalene also played a key role in the accounts of Jesus' Passion and Resurrection. Matthew, Mark and John all place her at Calvary—making this a very reliable tradition. Matthew again explicitly states that Mary Magdalene, standing at Calvary, was one of the women who had 'followed Jesus from Galilee and had provided for him' (Matthew 27:55).

In all four Gospel accounts of the Resurrection, Mary Magdalene is the first disciple to receive the Good News. Mark,

MARY MAGDALENE | PAUL KLEE

the earliest Gospel, states it boldly and as if Jesus' first appearance was to her alone: 'He appeared first to Mary Magdalene, frww om whom he had cast out seven demons. She went out and told those who had been with him' (Mark 16:9–10). All four Gospel accounts make Mary Magdalene the first one to bring the Good News of the Resurrection to the other disciples.

The risen Christ made Mary and other women disciples the first messengers to announce his Resurrection to Peter and the other Apostles to whom the risen Jesus next appeared. This is all the more significant because, according to Jewish law, the testimony of women was not granted credibility and could not be accepted in important matters. It is on Peter's testimony and witness that the Church proclaims, 'The Lord has risen, indeed!'

In the Apostolic Church, a core requirement for being an 'Apostle' was to be a witness to the Resurrection of Jesus. (See Acts of the Apostles 1:22.) No wonder, then, that St. Augustine gave Mary Magdalene the title 'the apostle to the Apostles'—an accolade repeated in our time by Pope Benedict XVI. May the example of Jesus in choosing her as 'apostle to the Apostles', and her example as a faithful and hope-filled disciple, inspire us in our time.

TALK IT OVER

- ⊙ Judging from Mary Magdalene's actions, especially in view of the attitudes of the society in which she lived, what kind of person do you think she was? What qualities would you say she had?
- ⊙ What can you learn for your own faith life from Mary Magdalene?
- ⊙ Who are some people whom you think proclaim the Good News of the Resurrection in their lives? Some may be well known, some less so. Talk about the difference these people make to the world in which we live.

WHAT ABOUT YOU PERSONALLY?

- ⊙ Mary Magdalene was called to bring the Good News of the Resurrection to the disciples. Today all the baptized are called to proclaim the presence of the risen Jesus in their lives. How can you renew your own commitment to living boldly as a 'resurrection Christian'—one who really believes it?

RESPOND WITH YOUR FAMILY AND FRIENDS

- ⊙ Take some time with your family and/or friends to read and discuss some of the Resurrection stories from the Gospels. Talk about how these stories give meaning to your faith, as they did for the first disciples of Jesus.

WHAT WILL YOU DO NOW?

- ⊙ What commitment will you make to witness to the risen Jesus in your day-to-day life in your interactions with members of your family? Of your school? Of your local community?
- ⊙ Will you ask the risen Christ to grant you the grace and the courage you need to do this?

LEARN BY HEART

Come, you that are blessed by my Father, inherit the kingdom prepared for you from the foundation of the world.

MATTHEW 25:34

The Stations of the Cross

Pray the Sign of the Cross together.

LEADER
Looking at the pictures on this page, let us imagine ourselves moving from Station to Station together, praying as we go.

The first Station: Jesus is condemned to death. *(Pause)*
The second Station: Jesus is made to carry his Cross. *(Pause)*
The third Station: Jesus falls the first time. *(Pause)*
The fourth Station: Jesus meets his mother. *(Pause)*
The fifth Station: Simon helps Jesus to carry his Cross. *(Pause)*
The sixth Station: Veronica wipes the face of Jesus. *(Pause)*
The seventh Station: Jesus falls the second time. *(Pause)*
The eighth Station: Jesus meets the women of Jerusalem.
    (Pause)
The ninth Station: Jesus falls the third time. *(Pause)*
The tenth Station: Jesus is stripped of his garments. *(Pause)*
The eleventh Station: Jesus is nailed to the Cross. *(Pause)*
The twelfth Station: Jesus dies on the Cross. *(Pause)*
The thirteenth Station: Jesus is taken down from the Cross.
    (Pause)
The fourteenth Station: Jesus is laid in the tomb. *(Pause)*

ALL
We adore you, O Christ, and we praise you,
because by your holy Cross you have redeemed the world.

Pray the Sign of the Cross together.

CATHOLIC PRAYERS, DEVOTIONS AND PRACTICES

SIGN OF THE CROSS
In the name of the Father,
and of the Son,
and of the Holy Spirit. Amen.

OUR FATHER (LORD'S PRAYER)
Our Father who art in heaven,
hallowed be thy name;
thy kingdom come,
thy will be done
on earth as it is in heaven.
Give us this day our daily bread,
and forgive us our trespasses,
as we forgive those who trespass against us;
and lead us not into temptation,
but deliver us from evil. Amen.

GLORY PRAYER (DOXOLOGY)
Glory be to the Father,
and to the Son,
and to the Holy Spirit;
as it was in the beginning
is now, and ever shall be,
world without end. Amen.

PRAYER TO THE HOLY SPIRIT
Come, Holy Spirit, fill the hearts of your faithful.
And kindle in them the fire of your love.
Send forth your Spirit and they shall be created.
And you shall renew the face of the earth.

O God, by the light of the Holy Spirit you have
    taught the hearts of your faithful.
In the same Spirit, help us to know what is truly
    right and always to rejoice in your consolation.
We ask this through Christ, our Lord. Amen.

HAIL MARY
Hail Mary, full of grace,
the Lord is with thee.
Blessed art thou among women
and blessed is the fruit of thy womb, Jesus.
Holy Mary, Mother of God,
pray for us sinners,
now and at the hour of our death. Amen.

APOSTLES' CREED
I believe in God,
the Father almighty,
Creator of heaven and earth,
and in Jesus Christ, his only Son, our Lord,
who was conceived by the Holy Spirit,
born of the Virgin Mary,
suffered under Pontius Pilate,
was crucified, died, and was buried;
he descended into hell;
on the third day he rose again from the dead;
he ascended into heaven,
and is seated at the right hand of God the Father
    almighty,
from there he will come to judge the living and
    the dead.

I believe in the Holy Spirit,
the holy catholic Church,
the communion of saints,
the forgiveness of sins,
the resurrection of the body,
and life everlasting. Amen.

NICENE CREED
I believe in one God,
the Father almighty,
maker of heaven and earth,
of all things visible and invisible.

I believe in one Lord Jesus Christ,
the Only Begotten Son of God,
born of the Father before all ages.
God from God, Light from Light,
true God from true God,
begotten, not made, consubstantial with the
    Father;
through him all things were made.
For us men and for our salvation
he came down from heaven,

and by the Holy Spirit was incarnate of the Virgin Mary,
and became man.

For our sake he was crucified under Pontius Pilate,
he suffered death and was buried,
and rose again on the third day
in accordance with the Scriptures.
He ascended into heaven
and is seated at the right hand of the Father.
He will come again in glory
to judge the living and the dead,
and his kingdom will have no end.

I believe in the Holy Spirit, the Lord, the giver of life,
who proceeds from the Father and the Son,
who with the Father and the Son is adored and
    glorified,
who has spoken through the prophets.

I believe in one, holy, catholic and apostolic
    Church.
I confess one Baptism for the forgiveness of sins
and I look forward to the resurrection of the dead
and the life of the world to come. Amen.

JESUS PRAYER
Lord Jesus Christ, Son of God, have mercy on me,
    a sinner. Amen.

ACT OF FAITH
O my God, I firmly believe that you are one God
in three divine Persons, Father, Son, and Holy
Spirit. I believe that your divine Son became man
and died for our sins and that he will come to
judge the living and the dead. I believe these and
all the truths which the Holy Catholic Church
teaches because you have revealed them, who
are eternal truth and wisdom, who can neither
deceive nor be deceived. In this faith I intend to
live and die. Amen.

ACT OF HOPE
O Lord God, I hope by your grace for the pardon
of all my sins and after life here to gain eternal
happiness because you have promised it, who are
infinitely powerful, faithful, kind, and merciful. In
this hope I intend to live and die. Amen.

ACT OF LOVE
O Lord God, I love you above all things and I love
my neighbor for your sake because you are the
highest, infinite and perfect good, worthy of all
my love. In this love I intend to live and die. Amen.

PRAYER FOR VOCATIONS
Loving Mother, Our Lady of Guadalupe,
you asked Juan Diego to help build a Church that
    would serve a new people in a new land.
You left your image upon his cloak as a visible
    sign of your love for us,
so that we may come to believe in your Son, Jesus
    the Christ.
Our Lady of Guadalupe and St. Juan Diego,
help us respond to God's call to build your Son's
    Church today.
Help us recognize our personal vocation to serve
    God as married or single persons or priests,
    brothers or sisters as our way to help extend
    the Reign of God here on earth.
Help us pay attention to the promptings of the
    Holy Spirit.
May all of us have the courage of Juan Diego to
    say 'Yes' to our personal call!
May we encourage one another to follow Jesus,
    no matter where that path takes us. Amen.

Daily Prayers

Morning Prayer
CANTICLE OF ZECHARIAH (THE BENEDICTUS)
(based on Luke 1:67–79)
Blessed be the Lord, the God of Israel;
for he has come to his people and set them free.
He has raised up for us a mighty Savior,
born of the House of his servant David.
Through his prophets he promised of old
    that he would save us from our enemies,
    from the hands of all who hate us.
He promised to show mercy to our fathers
and to remember his holy covenant.
This was the oath he swore to our father Abraham:
to set us free from the hand of our enemies,
free to worship him without fear,
holy and righteous in his sight
    all the days of our life.

You, my child, shall be called the prophet of the
Most High,
for you will go before the Lord to prepare his way,
to give his people knowledge of salvation
by the forgiveness of their sins.
In the tender compassion of our God
the dawn from on high shall break upon us,
to shine on those who dwell in darkness and the
shadow of death,
and to guide our feet into the way of peace.
Amen.

MORNING OFFERING
O Jesus, through the Immaculate Heart of Mary,
I offer you my prayers, works, joys and sufferings
of this day
for all the intentions of your Sacred Heart,
in union with the Holy Sacrifice of the Mass
throughout the world,
for the salvation of souls, the reparation for sins,
the reunion of all Christians,
and in particular for the intentions of the Holy
Father this month. Amen.

Evening Prayer
CANTICLE OF MARY (THE *MAGNIFICAT*)
My soul proclaims the greatness of the Lord;
my spirit rejoices in God my savior
for he has looked with favor on his lowly servant.
From this day all generations will call me blessed:
the Almighty has done great things for me
and holy is his name.
He has mercy on those who fear him
in every generation.
He has shown the strength of his arm,
and has scattered the proud in their conceit.
He has cast down the mighty from their thrones,
and has lifted up the lowly.
He has filled the hungry with good things,
and the rich he has sent away empty.
He has come to the help of his servant Israel
for he has remembered his promise of mercy,
the promise he made to our fathers,
to Abraham and his children forever. Amen.

GRACE BEFORE MEALS
Bless us, O Lord, and these your gifts,
which we are about to receive from your bounty,
through Christ our Lord. Amen.

GRACE AFTER MEALS
We give you thanks for all your benefits, almighty
God, who lives and reigns forever.
And may the souls of the faithful departed,
through the mercy of God, rest in peace.
Amen.

PRAYER OF ST. FRANCIS (PEACE PRAYER)
Lord, make me an instrument of your peace:
where there is hatred, let me sow love;
where there is injury, pardon;
where there is doubt, faith;
where there is despair, hope;
where there is darkness, light;
where there is sadness, joy.

O divine Master, grant that I may not so much seek
to be consoled as to console,
to be understood, as to understand,
to be loved as to love.

For it is in giving that we receive,
it is in pardoning that we are pardoned,
it is in dying that we are born to eternal life.
Amen.

Contrition and Sorrow
CONFITEOR
I confess to almighty God
and to you, my brothers and sisters,
that I have greatly sinned,
in my thoughts and in my words,
in what I have done and in what I have failed to
do,
through my fault, through my fault,
through my most grievous fault;
therefore I ask blessed Mary ever-Virgin,
all the Angels and Saints,
and you, my brothers and sisters,
to pray for me to the Lord our God. Amen.

ACT OF CONTRITION
O my God, I am heartily sorry for having offended
you, and I detest all my sins because of your
just punishments, but most of all because
they offend you, my God, who are all good and
deserving of all my love. I firmly resolve with the
help of your grace to sin no more and to avoid
the near occasion of sin. Amen.

Prayers before the Holy Eucharist

THE DIVINE PRAISES

Blessed be God.

Blessed be his holy name.

Blessed be Jesus Christ, true God and true man.

Blessed be the name of Jesus.

Blessed be his most Sacred Heart.

Blessed be his most precious Blood.

Blessed be Jesus in the most holy Sacrament of
the altar.

Blessed be the Holy Spirit, the Paraclete.

Blessed be the great Mother of God, Mary most
holy.

Blessed be her holy and Immaculate Conception.

Blessed be her glorious Assumption.

Blessed be the name of Mary, Virgin and Mother.

Blessed be St. Joseph, her most chaste spouse.

Blessed be God in his angels and in his saints.

ANIMA CHRISTI (SOUL OF CHRIST)

Soul of Christ, sanctify me.

Body of Christ, save me.

Blood of Christ, inebriate me.

Water from the side of Christ, wash me.

Passion of Christ, strengthen me.

O good Jesus, hear me.

Within your wounds hide me.

Permit me not to be separated from you.

From the malicious enemy defend me.

In the hour of my death call me.

And bid me come to you,

that with your saints I may praise you

forever and ever. Amen.

AN ACT OF SPIRITUAL COMMUNION

My Jesus, I believe that you are present in the
Most Blessed Sacrament.

I love you above all things, and I desire to receive
you into my soul.

Since I cannot at this moment receive you
sacramentally, come at least spiritually into
my heart.

I embrace you as if you were already there and
unite myself wholly to you.

Never permit me to be separated from you. Amen.

Prayers to Mary, Mother of God

ANGELUS

Verse:	The Angel of the Lord declared unto Mary.
Response:	And she conceived of the Holy Spirit. Hail Mary, full of grace, the Lord is with thee. Blessed art thou among women and blessed is the fruit of thy womb, Jesus. Holy Mary, Mother of God, pray for us sinners, now and at the hour of our death. Amen.
Verse:	Behold the handmaid of the Lord.
Response:	Be it done unto me according to your Word. Hail Mary. . . .
Verse:	And the Word was made flesh,
Response:	And dwelt among us. Hail Mary. . . .
Verse:	Pray for us, O holy Mother of God,
Response:	That we may be made worthy of the promises of Christ.

Let us pray. Pour forth, we beseech you, O Lord,
your grace into our hearts: that we, to whom the
Incarnation of Christ your Son was made known by
the message of an Angel, may by his Passion and
Cross be brought to the glory of his Resurrection.
Through the same Christ our Lord. Amen.

MEMORARE

Remember, O most gracious Virgin Mary, that
never was it known that anyone who fled to your
protection, implored your help, or sought your
intercession, was left unaided. Inspired by this
confidence, I fly unto you, O Virgin of virgins, my
mother; to you do I come, before you I stand,
sinful and sorrowful. O Mother of the Word
Incarnate, despise not my petitions, but in your
mercy hear and answer me. Amen.

REGINA CAELI (QUEEN OF HEAVEN)

Queen of Heaven, rejoice, alleluia:
for the Son you were privileged to bear, alleluia,
is risen as he said, alleluia.
Pray for us to God, alleluia.

Verse: Rejoice and be glad, O Virgin Mary, Alleluia!

Response: For the Lord is truly risen, Alleluia.

Let us pray. O God, who gave joy to the world through the resurrection of your Son, our Lord Jesus Christ, grant, we beseech you, that through the intercession of the Virgin Mary, his Mother, we may obtain the joys of everlasting life. Through the same Christ our Lord. Amen.

SALVE, REGINA (HAIL, HOLY QUEEN)

Hail, holy Queen, Mother of mercy: Hail, our life, our sweetness and our hope. To you do we cry, poor banished children of Eve. To you do we send up our sighs, mourning and weeping in this valley of tears. Turn then, most gracious advocate, your eyes of mercy toward us; and after this our exile show unto us the blessed fruit of your womb, Jesus. O clement, O loving, O sweet Virgin Mary. Amen.

PRAYER TO OUR LADY OF GUADALUPE

God of power and mercy,
you blessed the Americas at Tepeyac
with the presence of the Virgin Mary of
    Guadalupe.
May her prayers help all men and women
to accept each other as brothers and sisters.
Through your justice present in our hearts
may your peace reign in the world. Amen.

THE ROSARY

THE JOYFUL MYSTERIES: Traditionally prayed on Mondays and Saturdays and on Sundays of the Christmas Season.

1. The Annunciation
2. The Visitation
3. The Nativity
4. The Presentation in the Temple
5. The Finding of Jesus after Three Days in the Temple

THE LUMINOUS MYSTERIES: Traditionally prayed on Thursdays.

1. The Baptism at the Jordan
2. The Miracle at Cana
3. The Proclamation of the Kingdom and the Call to Conversion
4. The Transfiguration
5. The Institution of the Eucharist

THE SORROWFUL MYSTERIES: Traditionally prayed on Tuesdays and Fridays and on the Sundays of Lent.

1. The Agony in the Garden
2. The Scourging at the Pillar
3. The Crowning with Thorns
4. The Carrying of the Cross
5. The Crucifixion and Death

THE GLORIOUS MYSTERIES: Traditionally prayed on Wednesdays and Sundays, except on the Sundays of Christmas and Lent.

1. The Resurrection
2. The Ascension
3. The Descent of the Holy Spirit at Pentecost
4. The Assumption of Mary
5. The Crowning of the Blessed Virgin as Queen of Heaven and Earth

How to pray the Rosary

1. Pray the *Sign of the Cross* and pray the *Apostles' Creed* while holding the Crucifix.
2. Touch the first bead after the Crucifix and pray the *Our Father*, pray the *Hail Mary* on each of the next three beads, and pray the *Glory Prayer* on the next bead.
3. Go to the main part of your rosary. Say the name of the Mystery and quietly reflect on the meaning of the events of that Mystery. Pray the *Our Father*, and then, fingering each of the ten beads, pray ten *Hail Marys*. Then touch the next bead and pray the *Glory Prayer*. (Repeat the process for the next four decades.)
4. Pray the *Salve Regina (Hail, Holy Queen)* and conclude by praying:

    Verse: Pray for us, O holy Mother of God.

    Response: That we may be made worthy of the promises of Christ.

    Let us pray. O God, whose only-begotten Son, by his life, death and Resurrection, has purchased for us the rewards of eternal life, grant, we beseech you, that meditating on these mysteries of the most holy rosary of the Blessed Virgin Mary, we may imitate what they contain and obtain what they promise, through the same Christ our Lord. Amen.

5. Conclude by praying the *Sign of the Cross*.

STATIONS, OR WAY, OF THE CROSS

The tradition of praying the Stations, or Way, of the Cross dates from the fourteenth century. The tradition, which is attributed to the Franciscans, came about to satisfy the desire of Christians who were unable to make a pilgrimage to Jerusalem. The traditional Stations of the Cross are:

FIRST STATION: Jesus is condemned to death
SECOND STATION: Jesus is made to carry his Cross
THIRD STATION: Jesus falls the first time
FOURTH STATION: Jesus meets his mother
FIFTH STATION: Simon helps Jesus to carry his Cross
SIXTH STATION: Veronica wipes the face of Jesus
SEVENTH STATION: Jesus falls the second time
EIGHTH STATION: Jesus meets the women of Jerusalem
NINTH STATION: Jesus falls the third time
TENTH STATION: Jesus is stripped of his garments
ELEVENTH STATION: Jesus is nailed to the Cross
TWELFTH STATION: Jesus dies on the Cross
THIRTEENTH STATION: Jesus is taken down from the Cross
FOURTEENTH STATION: Jesus is laid in the tomb.

In 1991 Blessed Pope John Paul gave the Church a scriptural version of the Stations. The individual names given to these stations are:

FIRST STATION: Jesus in the Garden of Gethsemane—Matthew 25:36–41
SECOND STATION: Jesus, Betrayed by Judas, Is Arrested—Mark 14:43–46
THIRD STATION: Jesus Is Condemned by the Sanhedrin—Luke 22:66–71
FOURTH STATION: Jesus Is Denied by Peter—Matthew 26:69–75
FIFTH STATION: Jesus Is Judged by Pilate—Mark 15:1–5, 15
SIXTH STATION: Jesus Is Scourged and Crowned with Thorns—John 19:1–3
SEVENTH STATION: Jesus Bears the Cross—John 19:6, 15–17

EIGHTH STATION: Jesus Is Helped by Simon the Cyrenian to Carry the Cross—Mark 15:21
NINTH STATION: Jesus Meets the Women of Jerusalem—Luke 23:27–31
TENTH STATION: Jesus Is Crucified—Luke 23:33–34
ELEVENTH STATION: Jesus Promises His Kingdom to the Good Thief—Luke 23:39–43
TWELFTH STATION: Jesus Speaks to His Mother and the Disciple—John 19:25–27
THIRTEENTH STATION: Jesus Dies on the Cross—Luke 23:44–46
FOURTEENTH STATION: Jesus Is Placed in the Tomb—Matthew 27:57–60

Some parishes conclude with a prayerful meditation on the Resurrection.

The Way of Jesus: Catholic Practices

THE SEVEN SACRAMENTS

Sacraments of Christian Initiation

BAPTISM: The Sacrament by which we are freed from all sin and are endowed with the gift of divine life, are made members of the Church, and are called to holiness and mission.

CONFIRMATION: The Sacrament that completes the grace of Baptism by a special outpouring of the Gifts of the Holy Spirit, which seals and confirms the baptized in union with Christ and calls them to a greater participation in the worship and apostolic life of the Church.

EUCHARIST: The ritual, sacramental action of thanksgiving to God which constitutes the principal Christian liturgical celebration of and communion in the Paschal Mystery of Christ. This liturgical action is also traditionally known as the Holy Sacrifice of the Mass.

Sacraments of Healing

PENANCE AND RECONCILIATION: The Sacrament in which sins committed after Baptism are forgiven, which results in reconciliation with God and the Church. This Sacrament is also called the Sacrament of Confession.

ANOINTING OF THE SICK: This Sacrament is given to a person who is seriously ill or in danger of death or old age which strengthens the person with the special graces of healing and comfort and courage.

Sacraments at the Service of Communion

MARRIAGE (MATRIMONY): The Sacrament in which a baptized man and a baptized woman enter the covenant partnership of the whole of life that by its nature is ordered toward the good of the spouses and the procreation and education of offspring.

HOLY ORDERS: The Sacrament in which a bishop ordains a baptized man to be conformed to Jesus Christ by grace, to service and leadership in the Church as a bishop, priest, or deacon.

GIFTS OF THE HOLY SPIRIT

The Seven Gifts of the Holy Spirit are permanent dispositions which move us to respond to the guidance of the Spirit. The traditional list of these Gifts is derived from Isaiah 11:1–3.

WISDOM: A spiritual gift which enables one to know the purpose and plan of God.

UNDERSTANDING: This Gift stimulates us to work on knowing ourselves as part of our growth in knowing God.

COUNSEL (RIGHT JUDGMENT): This Gift guides us to follow the teaching the Holy Spirit gives us about our moral life and the training of our conscience.

FORTITUDE (COURAGE): This Gift strengthens us to choose courageously and firmly the good, despite difficulty, and also to persevere in doing what is right, despite temptation, fear or persecution.

KNOWLEDGE: This Gift directs us to a contemplation, or thoughtful reflection, on the mystery of God and the mysteries of the Catholic faith.

PIETY (REVERENCE): This Gift strengthens us to grow in respect for the Holy Trinity, for the Father who created us, for Jesus who saved us, and for the Holy Spirit who is sanctifying us.

FEAR OF THE LORD (WONDER AND AWE): This Gift infuses honesty in our relationship with God.

FRUITS OF THE HOLY SPIRIT

The Fruits of the Holy Spirit are the perfections that the Holy Spirit forms in us as the 'first fruits' of eternal glory. The Tradition of the Church lists twelve Fruits of the Holy Spirit. They are: love, joy, peace, patience, kindness, goodness, generosity, gentleness, faithfulness, modesty, self-control and chastity.

VIRTUES

The Theological Virtues

Gifts from God that enable us to choose to and to live in right relationship with the Holy Trinity.

FAITH: The virtue by which the believer gives personal adherence to God (who invites his or her response) and freely assents to the whole truth that God revealed.

HOPE: The virtue through which a person both desires and expects the fulfillment of God's promises of things to come.

CHARITY (LOVE): The virtue by which we give love to God for his own sake and love to our neighbor on account of God.

The Cardinal Moral Virtues

The four moral virtues on which all other human virtues hinge.

FORTITUDE: The virtue by which one courageously and firmly chooses the good despite difficulty and also perseveres in doing what is right despite temptation.

JUSTICE: The virtue by which one is able to give God and neighbor what is due to them.

PRUDENCE: The virtue by which one knows the true good in every circumstance and chooses the right means to reach that end.

TEMPERANCE: The virtue by which one moderates the desire for the attainment of and pleasure in earthly goods.

THE NEW LAW

The Great, or Greatest, Commandment

'You shall love the Lord your God with all your heart, and with all your soul, and with all your mind. . . . You shall love your neighbor as yourself.'
—Matthew 22:37, 39, based on Deuteronomy 6:5 and Leviticus 19:18

THE NEW COMMANDMENT OF JESUS

'Love one another. Just as I have loved you, you also should love one another.' John 13:34

THE BEATITUDES

Blessed are the poor in spirit, for theirs is the kingdom of heaven.

Blessed are those who mourn, for they will be comforted.

Blessed are the meek, for they will inherit the earth.

Blessed are those who hunger and thirst for righteousness, for they will be filled.

Blessed are the merciful, for they will receive mercy.

Blessed are the pure in heart, for they will see God.

Blessed are the peacemakers, for they shall be called children of God.

Blessed are those who are persecuted for righteousness' sake, for theirs is the kingdom of heaven.

Blessed are you when people revile you and persecute you and utter all kinds of evil against you falsely on my account. Rejoice and be glad, for your reward is great in heaven, for in the same way they persecuted the prophets who were before you.

—Matthew 5:3–11

SPIRITUAL WORKS OF MERCY

Admonish and help those who sin.
Teach those who are ignorant.
Advise those who have doubts.
Comfort those who suffer.
Be patient with all people.
Forgive those who trespass against you.
Pray for the living and the dead.

CORPORAL WORKS OF MERCY

Feed the hungry.
Give drink to the thirsty.
Shelter the homeless.
Clothe the naked.
Visit the sick and those in prison.
Bury the dead.
Give alms to the poor.

THE TEN COMMANDMENTS, OR THE DECALOGUE

Traditional Catechetical Formula

FIRST: I am the LORD your God: you shall not have strange gods before me.

SECOND: You shall not take the name of the LORD your God in vain.

THIRD: Remember to keep holy the LORD'S Day.

FOURTH: Honor your father and mother.

FIFTH: You shall not kill.

SIXTH: You shall not commit adultery.

SEVENTH: You shall not steal.

EIGHTH: You shall not bear false witness against your neighbor.

NINTH: You shall not covet your neighbor's wife.

TENTH: You shall not covet your neighbor's goods.

Scriptural Formula

FIRST: I am the LORD your God, who brought you out of the land of Egypt, out of the house of slavery; you shall have no other gods before me.

SECOND: You shall not make wrongful use of the name of the LORD your God, for the LORD will not acquit anyone who misuses his name.

THIRD: Observe the sabbath day to keep it holy. . . .

FOURTH: Honor your father and your mother. . . .

FIFTH: You shall not murder.

SIXTH: Neither shall you commit adultery.

SEVENTH: Neither shall you steal.

EIGHTH: Neither shall you bear false witness against your neighbour.

NINTH: Neither shall you covet your neighbor's wife.

TENTH: Neither shall you desire . . . anything that belongs to your neighbor.

—From Deuteronomy 5:6–21

PRECEPTS OF THE CHURCH

The Precepts are positive laws made by the Church that name the minimum in prayer and moral effort for the growth of the faithful in their love of God and neighbor.

FIRST PRECEPT: Participate in Mass on Sundays and on holy days of obligation and rest from work that impedes keeping these days holy.

SECOND PRECEPT: Confess sins at least once a year.

THIRD PRECEPT: Receive the Sacrament of the Eucharist at least during the Easter Season.

FOURTH PRECEPT: Fast and abstain on the days established by the Church.

FIFTH PRECEPT: Provide for the materials of the Church according to one's ability.

SOCIAL DOCTRINE OF THE CHURCH

These seven key principles are at the foundation of the Social Doctrine, or Social Teachings, of the Catholic Church:

1. *Life and dignity of the human person.* Human life is sacred and the dignity of the human person is the foundation of the moral life of individuals and of society.

2. *Call to family, community and participation.* The human person is social by nature and has the right to participate in family life and in the life of society.

3. *Rights and responsibilities.* The human person has the fundamental right to life and to the basic necessities that support life and human decency.

4. *Option for the poor and the vulnerable.* The Gospel commands us 'to put the needs of the poor and the vulnerable first'.

5. *Dignity of work and workers.* Work is a form of participating in God's work of Creation. 'The economy must serve people and not the other way around.'

6. *Solidarity.* God is the Creator of all people. 'We are one human family whatever our national, racial, ethnic, economic and ideological differences.'

7. *Care for God's creation.* Care of the environment is a divine command and a requirement of our faith.

FAITH GLOSSARY

Abbreviations: CCC = *Catechism of the Catholic Church*; USCCA = *United States Catholic Catechism for Adults*

A–B

Advocate: *see* **Paraclete**.

apocrypha: Writings about Jesus and God's Revelation that the Church has judged not to be inspired by the Holy Spirit. There were numerous apocryphal gospels being written and circulating during the first four centuries which were not included in the canon of Scripture. The judgment of the Church was that these erred in passing on the Apostolic Tradition and the teaching of the early Church. *See also* **canon of Scripture**.

Apostle(s): 'The title traditionally given to those specially chosen by Jesus to preach the Gospel and to whom he entrusted responsibility for guiding the early Church' (USCCA, 504). The names of the first Apostles, also called the Twelve, are Peter, Andrew, James, John, Thomas, James, Philip, Bartholomew (also known as Nathaniel), Matthew, Judas, Simon, and Jude (also known as Thaddeus). After the Ascension of Jesus, Matthias, who replaced Judas Isacariot, and Paul were also called to be Apostles.

Apostolic Tradition: Jesus entrusted his revelation and teachings to his Apostles. They passed it on by their preaching and witness. Along with others, they began writing the message down in what became the New Testament. (USCCA, 504)

Ascension: 'The entry of Jesus' humanity into divine glory to be at the right hand of the Father; traditionally, this occurred forty days after Jesus' Resurrection' (USCCA, 504). 'Christ's ascension marks the definitive entrance of Jesus' humanity into God's heavenly domain, whence he will come again [see Acts of the Apostles 1:11]; this humanity in the meantime hides him from the eyes of men [see Colossians 3:3]' (CCC, no. 665).

Baptism, Sacrament of: The first Sacrament of Initiation by which we are freed from all sin and are endowed with the gift of divine life, are made members of the Church, and are called to holiness and mission. (USCCA, 505)

baptism of Jesus: In presenting himself for baptism, Jesus was affirming John the Baptist's call to the people to repentance. Obviously Jesus did not need to be baptized in order to have his sins forgiven, but, as the *Catechism of the Catholic Church* states, 'he allows himself to be numbered among sinners' (CCC, no. 536).

Beatitudes: The eight Beatitudes form part of the teaching given by Jesus during the Sermon on the Mount, which set forth fundamental attitudes and virtues for living as a faithful disciple. (USCCA, 505)

Bible: The books that contain the truth of God's Revelation and that were composed by human authors inspired by the Holy Spirit. The Bible contains both the forty-six books of the Old Testament and the twenty-seven books of the New Testament. (CCC, Glossary) *See also* **canon of Scripture**; **Old Testament**; **New Testament**; **Sacred Scripture**.

blasphemy: Speech, thought, or action involving contempt for God or the Church, or persons or things dedicated to God. Blasphemy is directly opposed to the second commandment. (CCC, Glossary)

C

canon of Scripture: The canon of Scripture refers to the list of Old Testament and New Testament books that are accepted by the Catholic Church as the inspired Word of God. The Catholic canon lists seventy-three books—forty-six in the Old Testament and twenty-seven in the New Testament. The Catholic canon of Scripture differs from the Protestant canon, which also includes writings that the Catholic Church has judged to be apocryphal. *See also* **apocrypha.**

charity (love): One of the three Theological Virtues by which we give our love to God for his own sake and our love to our neighbor on account of our love of God. (Based on USCCA, 506).

chesed: *Chesed* is the Hebrew word for 'commitment'. The sacred authors of the Old Testament often described God's steadfast loyalty and love by using the word *chesed. Chesed* is committed love. *Chesed* is a key attribute of God as well as a quality that describes the relationship between God and the human family. *Chesed* is often translated as 'covenant love', a term that describes the nature and depth of the relationship that binds God with people and, in turn, people with God.

Christ: The title given to Jesus, meaning 'The Anointed One'; it comes from the Latin word *Christus*, which in its Greek root is the word for *Messiah*. (USCCA, 507)

Church: This term refers to the whole Catholic community of believers throughout the world. The term can also be used in the sense of a diocese or a particular parish. (USCCA, 507)

compassion: In the Bible, the English word 'compassion' is a translation of a Greek word meaning 'womb' and of a Hebrew word that is also translated as 'mercy'. Compassion is the quality of a person who so closely identifies with the suffering and condition of another person that the suffering of the other becomes their own, or 'enters their womb'. The Latin roots of the English word 'compassion' are *cum* and *passio*, which mean 'suffering with'.

conversion: Conversion means turning around one's life toward God and trying 'to live holier lives according to the Gospel' (Vatican II, *Decree on Ecumenism*, quoted in CCC, no. 821).

covenant: A covenant is a solemn agreement made between human beings or between God and a human being involving mutual commitments or guarantees. The Bible speaks of covenants that God made with Noah and, through him, 'with every living creature' (Genesis 9:10). Then God made the special Covenant with Abraham and renewed it with Moses. The prophets constantly pointed to the New Covenant that God would establish with all humankind through the promised Messiah—Jesus Christ.

Covenant (The): *see* **covenant**.

Creation: The act by which the eternal God gave a beginning to all that exists outside of himself. Creation also refers to the created universe or totality of what exists, as often expressed by the formula 'the heavens and the earth'. (CCC, Glossary)

Creator: God alone is the 'Creator'. God—Father, Son and Holy Spirit—out of love for us created the world out of nothing, wanting to share divine life and love with us.

Crucifixion: The nailing of Jesus to the Cross which resulted in his *real* death; Jesus freely offered his life on the Cross for our salvation.

D–E

Deposit of Faith: The heritage of faith contained in Sacred Scripture and Tradition, handed on in the Church from the time of the Apostles, from which the Magisterium draws all that it proposes for belief as divinely revealed. (USCCA, 509)

Divine Inspiration: 'Divine Inspiration' is the term the Catholic Church uses to describe the Gift of the Holy Spirit given to the human writers of the Bible, so that, using their talents and abilities, they wrote the truth that God wanted people to know for their salvation.

Divine Revelation: God's communication of himself and his loving plan to save us. This is a gift of self-communication, which is realized by deeds and words over time and most fully by his sending us his own divine Son, Jesus Christ. (USCCA, 526)

doctrine/dogma: The name given to divinely revealed truths proclaimed or taught by the Church's Magisterium; the faithful are obliged to believe these truths. (USCCA, 510)

eternal life: Eternal life is living for ever with God in the happiness of Heaven, entered after death by the souls of those who die in the grace and friendship of God.

Evangelist(s): The word 'evangelist' means 'one who announces good news'; the title 'Evangelist' is given to the writers of the four accounts of the Gospel (the Good News of Jesus Christ) in the New Testament. The four Evangelists are St. Matthew the Apostle, St. Mark, St. Luke and St. John the Apostle. 'The term "evangelist" is also used for one who works actively to spread and promote the Christian faith' (CCC, Glossary).

evil: The opposite or absence of good. One form of evil, physical evil, is a result of the 'state of journeying' toward its ultimate perfection in which God created the world, involving the existence of the less perfect alongside the more perfect, the constructive and the destructive forces of nature, the appearance and disappearance of certain beings. Moral evil, however, results from the free choice to sin which angels and men have; it is permitted by God, who knows how to derive good from it, in order to respect the freedom of his creatures. The entire revelation of God's goodness in Christ is a response to the existence of evil. The devil is called the Evil One. (CCC, Glossary)

exegesis: Exegesis is the process used by Scripture scholars to determine the literal and spiritual meanings of the biblical text. (USCCA, 512)

Exile (The): A word meaning 'removal from one's own country. In the context of the Old Testament,

the Exile refers to the period between 586 and 539 BC when the upper classes of Judah were exiles in Babylon. A previous exile, from the northern kingdom of Israel, had been enforced in 722–721. (The Catholic Study Bible, Second Edition, *New American Bible,* Glossary)

Exodus (The): God's saving intervention in history by which he liberated the Hebrew people from slavery in Egypt, made a covenant with them, and brought them into the Promised Land. The Book of Exodus, the second of the Old Testament, narrates this saving history. The Exodus is commemorated by the Jewish people at Passover, which for Christians is a foreshadowing of the 'passover' of Jesus Christ from death to life and is celebrated in the memorial of the Eucharist. (CCC, Glossary)

F–G–H

faith: Faith 'is both a gift of God and a human act by which the believer gives personal adherence to God (who invites his or her response) and freely assents to the whole truth that God has revealed' (USCCA, 512).

faithfulness/fidelity (divine): *see* **chesed**.

Fall (the): (1) Biblical revelation about the reality of sin in human history. The Biblical story begins with the original sin freely committed by the first human beings. This primeval event is narrated in figurative language in the Book of Genesis, which describes this sin as a 'fall' from God's friendship and grace, which they had received from God not only for themselves but for the whole human race. (2) In the 'fall' of angels, Scripture and Church Tradition see the emergence of Satan and the 'devil'; the 'fall' of these angelic spirits was due to their freely chosen rejection of God and His reign. (CCC, Glossary)

Fourth Gospel: Another name for the Gospel according the John.

free will/freedom: Our God-given power and ability to choose what we have come to know and understand to be good and true, and to love

God, others and ourselves because of our love for God. Our free will and our intellect are the bases of our responsibility and accountability for our moral choices. *See also* **intellect/reason**.

fundamentalism: Biblical fundamentalism tends to interpret the Bible as being always without error or as literally true in a way quite different from the Catholic Church's teaching on the inerrancy of the Bible. For some biblical fundamentalists, inerrancy extends even to scientific and historical matters. The Bible is presented without regard for its historical context and development. *See also* **inerrancy**; **senses of Scripture.**

Gentile: A non-Jew.

Gnostics/Gnosticism: Gnosticism refers to a variety of Christian 'sects' that arose in the first century AD. Gnostics traced their origins back to Simon Magus (see Acts of the Apostles 8:4–25) and existed into the fifth century AD. Gnostics, who considered themselves 'elitist', falsely claimed to have a special and secret spiritual knowledge; for example, secret teachings that the risen Jesus gave to one or the other of the Apostles. In their teaching, Gnostics also often used a mythology to teach erroneously that the physical world is evil, 'the product of the fall, and is thus to be rejected or left behind' (CCC, no. 285).

Gospel/Gospels: The term 'gospel' comes from an Old English word *godspel*, meaning 'good news'. *Godspel* was originally used to translate the Greek word *euangelion* (Latin *evangelium*), a term the early Church used for the Good News of Jesus. The Church uses the word 'Gospel' to refer to the four New Testament books that proclaim the life, teaching, Death and Resurrection of Jesus. More generally, however, the word 'Gospel' refers to the proclamation of the entire message of faith revealed in and through Jesus Christ, the Incarnate Son of God, the Second Person of the Blessed Trinity.

grace: The word 'grace' comes from the Latin word *gratia,* which means 'free'. Grace is the 'free and undeserved gift that God gives us to respond to our vocation to become his adopted children. As sanctifying grace, God shares his divine life and friendship with us in a habitual gift, a stable and supernatural disposition that enables the soul to live with God, to act by his love. As actual grace, God gives us the help to conform our lives to his will. Sacramental grace and special graces (charisms, the grace of one's state of life) are gifts of the Holy Spirit to help us live out our Christian vocation'. (CCC, Glossary)

Great Commandment: The commandment to love God with our whole heart, soul and mind and to love others as ourselves because of our love for God. In this commandment Jesus combined the Old Testament revelation of the Law of Love in Deuteronomy 6:5 and Leviticus 19:18 that is at the heart of God's will and plan for Creation and of the Covenant.

Hebrews: Another name for the ancient Israelites and the Jews.

Holy Spirit: The proper name for the Third Divine Person of the Holy Trinity; the Lord and giver of life, who proceeds from the Father and the Son, and who with the Father and the Son is adored and glorified.

Holy Trinity (Triune God): The one true God, eternal, infinite, unchangeable, incomprehensible and almighty, in three divine Persons: the Father, the Son and the Holy Spirit. (CCC, no. 202)

hope: One of the three Theological Virtues 'through which a person both desires and expects the fulfillment of God's promises of things to come' (USCCA, 515). Hope is the desire and expectation of the salvation God promised. It is based on God's unwavering fidelity to keeping and fulfilling his promises.

human person: The human individual, made in the image of God; not some thing but some one, a unity of spirit and matter, soul and body, capable of knowledge, self-possession, and freedom, who can enter into communion with other persons—and with God. The human person needs to live in society, which is a group of persons bound together organically by a principle of unity that goes beyond each one of them. (CCC, Glossary)

hypostatic union: The union of the divine and human natures in the one divine Person (Greek: *hypostasis*) of the Son of God, Jesus Christ. (CCC, Glossary)

I–J–K

'I AM' statements: A key and unique writing technique in John's Gospel is his use of seven 'I AM' sayings or statements to teach that Jesus is divine, truly God. These two words, 'I AM', have their roots in the Book of Exodus, when God reveals his identity, his name, to Moses. When Moses asks the voice in the burning bush, 'If I come to the Israelites and say to them, "The God of your ancestors has sent me to you", and they ask me, "What is his name?", what shall I say to them?', God says to Moses, 'I AM WHO I AM. . . . Thus you shall say to the Israelites, "I AM has sent me to you"' (Exodus 3:13–14).

imago Dei: This term means 'image of God'. We are all made in the image and likeness of God.

Incarnation: By the Incarnation, the Second Person of the Holy Trinity assumed our human nature, taking flesh in the womb of the Virgin Mary. There is one Person in Jesus and that is the divine Person of the Son of God. Jesus has two natures, a human one and a divine one. (USCCA, 515)

inerrancy (of the Bible): Because the authors of Sacred Scripture were inspired by God, the saving meaning or truth found in the Scriptures cannot be wrong. (USCCA, 516)

Infancy Narratives: The accounts of Jesus' birth and infancy in the Gospel according to Matthew (Matthew 1:1—4:22) and the Gospel according to Luke (Luke 1:5—2:52)

inspiration: see **Divine Inspiration**.

intellect/reason: Our God-given power and ability to know what is good and true. Our intellect enables us to come to know God through creation and to know and understand the order that God wills among things. Our intellect and free will are the bases of our responsibility and accountability for our moral choices. *See also* **free will/freedom.**

Jesus (name): Hebrew name that means 'God saves'.

Jesus Christ: The Incarnate Son of God who became one of us in all ways except sin without giving up his divinity. Jesus is true God and true man. He is fully divine and fully human. In the one divine Person, Jesus, the divine nature and a human nature are united. *See also* **Christ**.

Kingdom of God: The actualization of God's will for human beings proclaimed by Jesus Christ as a community of justice, peace, mercy, and love, the seed of which is the Church on earth, and the fulfillment of which is in eternity. (USCCA, 517)

L-M-N

Last Supper: The last meal, a Passover supper, which Jesus ate with his disciples the night before he died. Jesus' passing over to his Father by his death and Resurrection, the new Passover, is anticipated in the Last Supper and celebrated in the Eucharist, which fulfills the Jewish Passover and anticipates the final Passover of the Church in the glory of the kingdom. Hence the Eucharist is called 'the Lord's Supper'. (CCC, Glossary)

Last Supper discourse: The final words of Jesus to the Apostles that are found In John 13:1—17:26.

Law of Love: The heart of God's Law revealed in Leviticus 19:18 and Deuteronomy 6:4–5 that was fulfilled in Jesus Christ and expressed in his teaching on the New Commandment in John 13:34–35.

lectio divina: A manner of praying with Scripture; the person praying either reflectively reads a passage from Scripture or listens attentively to its being read, and then meditates on words or phrases that resonate. (USCCA, 518)

Lectionary: The official liturgical book of the Church containing Scripture passages for use in the Liturgy of the Word. (USCCA, 518)

life everlasting: Life after death. *See also* **eternal life**.

literary genres/literary forms: Forms of literary expression, such as history, hymns, psalms, letters, metaphor and simile, poetry, proverbs, parables and songs. The human authors whom God inspired to write Sacred Scripture used literary forms known to them and the people of their time to teach the truth that God wanted to reveal to us by their words.

liturgical year: The calendar that guides the liturgies and prayers of the Church. (USCCA, 518)

Liturgy: 'Liturgy refers especially to the public worship of the Church, including the Mass and the Liturgy of the Hours' (USCCA, 518). 'The word "liturgy" originally meant a "public work" or a "service in the name of/on behalf of the people". In Christian tradition it means the participation of the People of God in "the work of God"' (CCC, no. 1069). 'In the liturgy of the Church, God the Father is blessed and adored as the source of all the blessings of creation and salvation with which he has blessed us in his Son, in order to give us the Spirit of filial adoption' (CCC, no. 1110)

Liturgy of the Hours: The public daily prayer of the Church which extends the praise given to God in the Eucharistic celebration. (USCCA, 518)

Liturgy of the Word: The first main part of the Mass during which the Scriptures are proclaimed, their meaning is explained, and the people respond in faith. The Liturgy of the Word is an integral part of all sacramental celebrations. 'The meaning of the celebration is expressed by the Word of God which is proclaimed and by the response of faith to it' (CCC, no. 1190).

Lord: The name used in Scripture for the divine name revealed to Moses. The title 'Lord' indicated divine sovereignty. To confess or invoke Jesus as Lord is to profess that he is truly and fully God.

Lord's Day (The): Name used synonymously for Sunday, the day of the Lord Jesus' Resurrection. (USCCA, 518)

Lord's Prayer (The): Another name for the prayer more commonly known as the Our Father. This prayer is sometimes called the Lord's Prayer because it is a prayer taught by Jesus to his Apostles and disciples. (USCCA, 518)

love, or charity: One of the three Theological Virtues by which we give our love to God for his own sake and our love to our neighbor on account of our love of God. (Based on USCCA, 506)

Magisterium: The living teaching office, or teaching authority, of the Catholic Church, made up of the Pope and bishops, guided by the Holy Spirit, whose responsibility and task is to give authentic interpretation to the Word of God contained in both Sacred Scripture and Sacred Tradition. 'The Magisterium ensures the Church's fidelity to the teaching of the Apostles in matters of faith and morals' (CCC, Glossary).

Mass: The Eucharist or principal sacramental celebration of the Church, established by Jesus at the Last Supper, in which the mystery of our salvation through participation in the sacrificial death and glorious resurrection of Christ is renewed and accomplished. The Mass renews the paschal sacrifice of Christ as the sacrifice offered by the Church. It is called 'Mass' (from the Latin *missa*) because of the 'mission' or 'sending' with which the liturgical celebration concludes [Latin: '*Ite, Missa est.*']. (CCC, Glossary)

Messiah: A Hebrew word meaning 'anointed'. The Messiah is the one whom God would send to inaugurate his Kingdom definitively. 'The word "Christ" comes from the Greek translation of the Hebrew *Messiah*, which means 'anointed'. [Christ] became the proper name to Jesus only because he accomplished perfectly the divine mission that "Christ" signifies. . . It was necessary that the Messiah be anointed by the Spirit of the Lord at once as king and priest, and also as prophet. Jesus fulfilled the messianic hope of Israel in his threefold office of priest, prophet, and king' (CCC, no. 436).

miracle(s): Miracles are signs of the presence of God at work among us. 'The miracles and other deeds of Jesus are acts of compassion and signs of the Kingdom and salvation' (USCCA, 80).

morality/moral law: Morality refers to the goodness or evil of human acts. For a Catholic, morality 'refers to the manner of life and action formed according to the teaching laid down by Christ Jesus and authoritatively interpreted by the Church' (USCCA, 520).

Mystery (of God): The term has several complementary meanings. First, it reminds us that we can never exhaust God's divine and infinite meaning. Second, mystery tells us that God is 'wholly other' (not us) and yet so near that in him we live and move and have our being. Third, the union of the divine and human in Christ is so unique that we revere it as holy mystery. Fourth, mystery also applies to the celebration of the Sacraments in which God, Father, Son, and Spirit, are present and active for our salvation. (USCCA, 520)

natural reason: *see* **intellect/reason**.

New Commandment: The commandment Jesus gave to his disciples at the Last Supper (in John 13:34–35). The New Commandment summarizes the manner of living and acting that Jesus taught. When we live by the New Commandment we are following the New Law that Jesus revealed.

New Covenant: The new 'dispensation', order or Covenant, established by God in Jesus Christ, to succeed and perfect the Old Covenant. The New Law or Law of the Gospel is the perfection here on earth of the divine law, natural and revealed; this law of the New Covenant is called a law of love, grace, and freedom. (CCC, Glossary) *See also* **Covenant (The)**.

New Testament: 'The designation for the second part of the Bible, which contains the four accounts of the Gospel, the Acts of the Apostles, Letters or Epistles, and the Book of Revelation' (USCCA, 521). 'The twenty-seven books of the Bible written by the sacred authors in apostolic times, which have Jesus Christ, the Incarnate Son of God—his life, teachings, Passion and glorification, and the beginnings of his Church—as their central theme. The promises and mighty deeds of God in the old alliance or covenant, reported in the Old Testament, prefigure and are fulfilled in the New Covenant established by Jesus Christ, reported in the sacred writings of the New Testament' (CCC, Glossary). See also **Bible**; **canon of Scripture**; **Sacred Scripture**.

O–P–Q–R

Old Testament: The first part of Sacred Scripture that contains the Pentateuch (the first five books), the Historical Books, the Wisdom Literature and the Prophetic Books. These come to us from the people of ancient Israel before the coming of Christ. The Books of the Old Testament were inspired by God. *See also* **Bible**; **canon of Scripture**; **Sacred Scripture**.

oral tradition: The passing on of Revelation by word of mouth before it was committed to writing by the inspired human authors of Sacred Scripture.

Original Sin: The personal sin of disobedience committed by the first human beings, resulting in the deprivation of original holiness and justice and the experience of suffering and death. (USCCA, 522)

paganism: 'Paganism' was a term used in the early Church to designate a religion other than Christianity or Judaism whose values were contrary to the teachings of Sacred Scripture. Pagan religions practiced polytheism, or the belief in many gods.

parable: A characteristic feature of the teaching of Jesus. Parables are simple images or comparisons which confront the hearer or reader with a radical choice about his invitation to enter the Kingdom of God. (CCC, Glossary)

Paraclete: A name for the Holy Spirit. The term was used by Jesus in the New Testament (see John 14:16) to indicate the promised gift of the Spirit as another consoler and advocate, who would continue his own mission among the disciples. (CCC, Glossary)

Paschal Mystery: In speaking of the Paschal Mystery we present Christ's Death and Resurrection as one, inseparable event. It is *paschal* because it is Christ's passing into death and passing over it into new life. It is a *mystery* because it is a visible sign of an invisible act of God. (USCCA, 522–523)

Passion (of Jesus): The suffering and death of Jesus. Passion or Palm Sunday begins Holy Week, during which the annual liturgical celebration of the Paschal Mystery of Christ takes place. (CCC, Glossary)

Passion Narratives: All four accounts of the Gospel pass on a narrative of Jesus' arrest, trial and Crucifixion on Calvary. These narratives are often referred to as the Passion Narratives. You will hear the account of the Passion proclaimed many times at the Liturgy celebrated during Holy Week.

Passover: The name of the Jewish feast that celebrates the deliverance of Israel from Egypt and from the Angel of Death who passed over their doors marked by the blood of sacrificed lamb. Jesus Christ inaugurated the new Passover by delivering all people from death and sin through his blood shed on the Cross. The celebration of the Eucharist is the Passover feast of the New Covenant. (USCCA, 523)

Pentecost: The 'fiftieth day' at the end of the seven weeks following Passover (Easter in the Christian dispensation). At the first Pentecost after the Resurrection and Ascension of Jesus, the Holy Spirit was manifested, given and communicated as a divine Person to the Church, fulfilling the paschal mystery of Christ according to his promise. (CCC, Glossary)

People of God: The biblical name given to those called by God to announce and bring about the divine plan of Salvation; first given to the people of ancient Israel and then to the Church. The Church is the new People of God whom God calls into existence 'as his people centered in Christ and sustained by the Holy Spirit'. The visible structures of the Church are the means intended by God 'to help guarantee the life of grace' for the whole People of God. (Quoted material from USCCA, 523)

person: *see* **human person.**

Petrine ministry (office): The supreme jurisdiction and ministry of the Pope as shepherd of the whole Church. As successor of St. Peter, and therefore Bishop of Rome and Vicar of Christ, the Pope is the perpetual and visible principle of unity in faith and communion in the Church. (CCC, Glossary)

polytheism: The belief in many 'gods'.

prayer: The raising of one's mind and heart to God in thanksgiving and in praise of his glory. It can also include the requesting of good things from God. It is an act by which one enters into an awareness of a loving communion with God. (USCCA, 523–524) Prayer is the response of faith to the free promise of salvation and also a response of love to the thirst of the only Son of God. (CCC, no. 2561)

prophet: One sent by God to form the people of the Old Covenant in the hope of salvation. The prophets are often authors of books of the Old Testament. The prophetic books constitute a major section of the Old Testament. John the Baptist concludes the work of the prophets of the Old Covenant. (CCC, Glossary)

proverb: A proverb is a succinct statement that is used to make a point or state a well-accepted truth. Their power lies in the use of various figures of sound and sense. The Book of Proverbs is one of the writings in the Wisdom Literature of the Old Testament. Wisdom is not just knowledge reserved for a few highly intelligent people; wisdom can be sought by all. It is found through the difficult process of making well-informed choices in life. The Old Testament Book of Proverbs sought to guide the People of God in making 'wise' choices to live the Covenant. (*The New Jerome Biblical Commentary*, 28:8B and 11A)

Psalms: Prayers in the Book of Psalms of the Old Testament, assembled over several centuries; a collection of prayers in the form of hymns or poetry. The psalms have been used since Jesus' time as the public prayer of the Church. (CCC, Glossary)

public ministry of Jesus: The public life and ministry of Jesus began at his baptism and concluded with his entry into Jerusalem as the King-Messiah. It includes the 'mysteries' of his life that reveal him to be the 'Servant' wholly consecrated to the redemptive work that he would accomplish by his Passion.

reason: *See* **intellect/reason.**

Redeemer: Jesus Christ, redeemer of mankind. Christ paid the price of his own sacrificial death on the Cross to ransom us, to set us free from the slavery of sin, thus achieving our redemption. (CCC, Glossary)

redemption: Redemption is the salvation won for us by Jesus by his paying the price of his own sacrificial death on the Cross to ransom us, to set us free from the slavery of sin.

Resurrection (of Christ): 'The triumph of Jesus over death on the third day after his crucifixion. Christ's [risen] body is real, but glorified, not restrained by space or time' (USCCA, 525). The Resurrection confirms the 'saving', 'redeeming' and 'liberating' power of Jesus and the truth of his divinity.

Resurrection Narratives: The Gospel accounts of the appearances of the risen Christ to his disciples.

Revelation: *see* **Divine Revelation.**

S

Sabbath: In Scripture, the Sabbath was the seventh day of the week that the people of Ancient Israel were to keep holy by praising God for the creation and the covenant and by resting from their ordinary work. For Christians, the observance of the Sabbath has been transferred to Sunday, the day of the Lord's Resurrection. (USCCA, 526)

Sacrament(s): The seven 'efficacious sign(s) of grace, instituted by Christ and entrusted to the Church, by which divine life is dispensed to us by the work of the Holy Spirit' (USCCA, 526). The Seven Sacraments are the three Sacraments of Christian Initiation (Baptism, Confirmation, and Eucharist), the two Sacraments of Healing (Penance and Reconciliation, and Anointing of the Sick), and the two Sacraments at the Service of Communion (Marriage and Holy Orders).

Sacred Scripture (Bible): The inspired written Word of God. 'The books that contain the truth of God's revelation and that were composed by human authors, inspired by the Holy Spirit, and recognized by the Church' (USCCA, 527). *See also* **Bible.**

Sacred Tradition: The Tradition of the Catholic Church refers to the body of teaching of the Church, expressed in her beliefs, doctrines, rituals and Scripture, that has been handed down from the Apostles to their successors, the Pope and the bishops, through the ages, in an unbroken line of succession.

sacrifice: Sacrifice is a free offering, a gift, made by a person for the welfare of others. The word comes from two Latin words meaning 'to make sacred'. Such a gift is deemed to be sacred—a special and a sincere sign of love and life. The greatest sacrifice of all is to give one's life for another. In a religious context a sacrifice is 'a ritual offering made to God by a priest on behalf of the people as a sign of adoration, gratitude, supplication, penance, and/or communion' (USCCA, 527).

Sacrifice of the Cross: The perfect sacrifice was Christ's death on the cross; by this sacrifice, Christ accomplished our redemption as high priest of the new and eternal covenant. The sacrifice of Christ on the cross is commemorated and mysteriously made present in the Eucharistic sacrifice of the Church. (CCC, Glossary)

salvation: Salvation is the forgiveness of sins and restoration of friendship with God, which can be done by God alone. (CCC, Glossary)

sanctification: The term comes from Latin words meaning 'to make holy'. Sanctification is the work of the Holy Trinity attributed to the Holy Spirit. It is the 'healing of our human nature wounded by sin by giving us a share in the divine life of the Trinity; . . . the work of making us 'perfect', holy, and Christlike. (CCC, Glossary)

Satan: A fallen angel or the devil; the Evil One. (CCC, Glossary)

Savior: Title for Jesus Christ. The Hebrew name 'Jesus' means 'God saves'. The Son of God became man to achieve our salvation; he is the unique Savior of humanity. (CCC, Glossary)

Second Coming (of Christ): The glorious return and appearance of our Lord and Savior Jesus Christ at the end of time to judge the living and the dead, when history and all creation will achieve their fulfillment.

senses of Scripture: Tradition notes that there are two senses or aspects of Scripture—the literal and the spiritual. The literal meaning is that meaning conveyed by the words of Scripture and discovered by exegesis following rules of sound interpretation. The spiritual meaning points to realities beyond the words themselves. (USCCA, 527–528)

Septuagint: A pre-Christian Greek translation of the Hebrew Scriptures made by Jewish scholars, and later adopted by Greek-speaking Christians. (CCC, Glossary)

Sermon on the Mount: The summary of Jesus' teaching on discipleship found in Matthew 5:1—7:29; it is a blueprint on how to live as his Church, the new People of God.

sin: 'Sin is an offense against God as well as against reason, truth, and right conscience' (USCCA, 528), in which a person freely and knowingly chooses evil over good. Sin involves a serious lack of effort in meeting duties and responsibilities to God, to others and to oneself. Sins are mortal or venial. **Mortal sin** is 'when we consciously and freely choose to do something grave against the divine law and contrary to our final destiny' (USCCA, 520). **Venial sin** is a less serious offense. *See also* **social sin**.

Son of God: The Second Divine Person of the Holy Trinity. 'The title "Son of God" signifies the unique and eternal relationship of Jesus Christ to God his Father; he is the only Son of the Father; he is God himself. To be a Christian, one must believe that Jesus Christ is the Son of God' (CCC, no. 454).

soul: 'The soul is the subject of human consciousness and freedom; soul and body together form one unique human nature. Each human soul is individual and immortal, immediately created by God' (CCC, Glossary). 'The immortal spiritual part of a person; the soul does not die with the body at death, and it is reunited with the body in the final resurrection' (USCCA, 529).

Stations of the Cross/Way of the Cross: A devotional exercise which follows the 'way of the cross' in the Savior's steps, observing stops or 'stations' to meditate on the path Jesus took from the Praetorium in Jerusalem to Golgotha and the tomb. (CCC, Glossary)

symbols/symbolic language: Symbols can communicate the meaning of realities, both seen and unseen, when the literal meaning of words is not enough. Symbols point to deeper realities and convey meaning when an experience is so profound that it is difficult to find the words to communicate its meaning. For example, the inspired sacred writers of Scripture used several symbols for the Holy Spirit to reveal God's presence and work among his people. These included 'water', 'anointing', 'fire', 'cloud and light' and 'the dove' (CCC, nos. 694–697, 701).

Synoptics /Synoptic Gospels: The word 'synoptic' comes from two Greek words that mean 'to see together'. The Synoptics, or Synoptic Gospels, are the accounts of the Gospel written by St. Matthew, St. Mark and St. Luke. These three accounts of the Gospel are called the Synoptics because there are many similarities between them in terms of their content and the order in which the content is presented.

T–U-V-W

temptation: Temptation is 'an attraction either from outside or inside oneself' to choose to sin, or to act in ways that are contrary to the will of God.

Tradition: *see* **Sacred Tradition**.

transcendence: Transcendence refers to the idea that God is so 'beyond' the universe, and so different from anything else that exists, that God cannot be directly experienced by human beings. A shorthand way of saying that God is transcendent is: 'God is the absolute Other.'

typology: The discernment of persons, events, or things in the Old Testament which prefigured, and thus served as a 'type' (or prototype) of, the fulfillment of God's plan in the Person of Christ. The typology of the Old Testament which is made clear in the New Testament demonstrates the dynamic unity of the divine plan of salvation. (CCC, Glossary)

Way of the Cross: *see* **Stations of the Cross.**

wisdom: A spiritual gift that enables one to know the purpose and plan of God; one of the seven gifts of the Holy Spirit. Wisdom is also the name of one of the books of the Old Testament. (CCC, Glossary)

Word of God: The entire content of Revelation as contained in the Holy Bible and proclaimed in the Church. In John's Gospel, God's 'Word' means his only-begotten Son, who is the fullness of God's Revelation and who took flesh (the Word incarnate) and became man for the sake of our salvation. (CCC, Glossary)

Works of Mercy: Charitable actions by which we come to the aid of our neighbors in their bodily and spiritual needs. The *spiritual works of mercy* include instructing, advising, consoling, comforting, forgiving, and patiently forbearing. *Corporal works of mercy* include feeding the hungry, clothing the naked, visiting the sick and imprisoned, sheltering the homeless, and burying the dead. (CCC, Glossary)

worship: Adoration and honor given to God, which is the first act of the virtue of religion. Public worship is given to God in the Church by the celebration of the Paschal Mystery of Christ in the liturgy. (CCC, Glossary)

YHWH: The divine name God revealed to Moses in Exodus 3:13–15; the Hebrew letters YHWH are the first letters of the words meaning 'I AM WHO I AM', or 'I AM HE WHO IS', or 'I AM WHO AM'. The divine name is so sacred that the people of ancient Israel did not speak it, nor do Jews today. In its place they use the Hebrew word ADONAI, or LORD.

Acknowledgments

Scripture quotations taken from or adapted from the New Revised Standard Version Bible: Catholic Edition, copyright © 1989, 1993, Division of Christian Education of the National Council of Churches of Christ in the United States of America; used by permission; all rights reserved.

Excerpts from the English translation of the *Catechism of the Catholic Church* for use in the United States, second edition, copyright © 1997, United States Catholic Conference, Inc., Libreria Editrice Vaticana; all rights reserved.

Excerpts from the *United States Catholic Catechism for Adults*, copyright © 2006 United States Conference of Catholic Bishops, Washington D.C.; all rights reserved.

Excerpts from the English translation of *The Roman Missal* © 2010 International Committee on English in the Liturgy (ICEL); used with permission; all rights reserved.

Excerpts from documents of Vatican II from A. Flannery (ed.), *Vatican Council II: Constitutions, Decrees, Declarations* (New York/Dublin: Costello Publishing/ Dominican Publications, 1996).

Excerpt from *Pastoral Statement for Catholics on Biblical Fundamentalism*, National Conference of Catholic Bishops Ad Hoc Committee on Biblical Fundamentalism, Archbishop John Whealon of Hartford, Connecticut, March 26, 1987.

Prayers from *Catholic Household Blessings & Prayers, Revised Edition*, copyright © 2007, Bishops Committee on the Liturgy, United States Conference of Catholic Bishops, Washington, D.C.

Excerpts and adaptations from 'Themes of Catholic Social Teaching' from United States Conference of Catholic Bishops Justice, Peace and Human Development Department on the online resource: usccb.org/sdwp/projects/socialteaching/excerpt.shtml

'Loving God, may your love play upon my voice', p. 12, and 'Conflicting Desires', p. 23, by Fr. Donal Neary S.J., from *The Calm Beneath the Storm: Reflections and Prayers for Young People* (Dublin, Ireland: Veritas, 1983; reprinted 1997), copyright © Donal Neary, 1983.

Excerpts from *Mother Teresa: Come Be My Light—The Private Writings of the 'Saint of Calcutta'*, p. 34, by Brian Kolodiejchuk (ed.), (New York: Doubleday, 2007), copyright © 2007 The Mother Teresa Center.

Excerpt from 'The Great Hunger', p. 35, by Patrick Kavanagh is reprinted from *Collected Poems*, edited by Antoinette Quinn (London: Allen Lane, 2004), by kind permission of the Trustees of the Estate of the late Katherine B. Kavanagh, through the Jonathan Williams Literary Agency.

Excerpt from *Playing Poker with Nana*, p. 42, by Megan McKenna (Dublin, Ireland: Veritas, 2008), copyright © Megan McKenna, 2008.

Excerpt from *Psalms 2000*, p. 64, by Mark Link SJ (Chicago: Thomas More Association, 1951), copyright © Mark Link, 1951.

'Interesting facts about the Bible', p. 73, from *God Is Back* by John Micklethwait and Adrian Wooldridge (New York: The Penguin Press), © John Micklethwait and Adrian Wooldridge, 2009.

Excerpt from 'I Have a Dream' speech, p. 74, reprinted by arrangement with The Heirs to the Estate of Dr. Martin Luther King Jr., c/o Writers House as agent for the proprietor New York, NY.

Excerpts from *Tuesdays with Morrie: An Old Man, A Young Man, and Life's Greatest Lesson*, p. 103, by Mitch Albom (New York: Doubleday, 1997), copyright © Mitch Albom, 1997.

'One Solitary Life', p. 193, by Dr. James Allen Francis, 1926; http://jmm.aaa.net.au/articles/4252.htm.

'Prayer for Vocations', p. 264, from the National Coalition for Church Vocations, copyright © NCCV, *www.nccv-vocations.org*.

'Canticle of Zechariah (The Benedictus)', p. 264, and 'Canticle of Mary (The Magnificat)', p. 265, International Consultation on English Texts (ICET).

Image credits

Index